The Other Side of the Bonfire

ALSO BY MELINDA JOHNSON

Letters to Saint Lydia

The Other Side of the Bonfire

Melinda Johnson

LINGUA SACRA PUBLISHING
Roxbury, New Jersey

The Other Side of the Bonfire
Copyright © 2012 by Melinda Johnson

Published in the United States of America. For information, address Lingua Sacra Publishing.
www.linguasacrapublishing.com
ISBN 978-0-9843432-6-3

Cover design and photograph: Stephanie Platis
Jewelry created by Danielle Barber, Little Bird Jewelry

First Edition: August 2012

For my father, Kurt Simons.

Tho' much is taken, much abides; and tho'
We are not now that strength which in old days
Moved earth and heaven, that which we are, we are;
One equal temper of heroic hearts,
Made weak by time and fate, but strong in will
To strive, to seek, to find, and not to yield.
—From "Ulysses," by Alfred Tennyson

And for my mother, Kathleen Simons, and her slice of bread with apple butter on it, without which there might have been nothing else.

Chapter 1

"I can't believe this," Jewel said to the empty room. "What did I click? Is this right? I can't believe this."

But she could. Trevor was in the pictures. When she rolled the cursor over his face, his name popped up, a little black sign with white letters on it, hiding his eyes. The woman who had posted the pictures was beautiful, artfully so, and she radiated a raw, animal confidence that could be felt even through layers of electronic dissociation. Jewel touched the laptop screen with one finger. It was real. She went back to Trevor's Facebook page and clicked the link again to make sure this tiny motion of her finger would have the same cataclysmic effect a second time.

It did. There he was, the man she'd been living with for seven months, parading all over Seattle with "Selena Davis-Jones, Realtor." A realtor? Where on earth could he have met her? He wasn't house-hunting, was he? Maybe he was. Maybe he was about to cure cancer. Only Selena Davis-Jones would know. With fingers that were beginning to shake, Jewel scrolled down Trevor's page, reading every post, clicking every link. Most of it was about sports, or work, or going out for drinks with the guys on Friday night. None of it was about Jewel Marie Jordan, his unsuspecting girlfriend. Some of it might be about Selena Davis-Jones. "We saw you man—might have to sell my house now, baby!" "You coming tomorrow night? Don't come alone."

"What's new, Trev? Saw your pics—yowza!" "Nice LIPS, Big T."

Like a snake swayed by a charmer, Jewel went back again to Selena's page. She clicked the "Refresh" button, and a new photo album appeared, just posted. "City Kisses." With a shudder, Jewel let herself look. Trevor and Selena at Alki Beach, kissing on a red-and-orange beach towel. Trevor and Selena at a Thai restaurant downtown, feeding each other Crying Tiger with chopsticks. Trevor and Selena riding the elevator up the Space Needle, kissing again. Jewel clicked into another album. More kissing. They seemed to do a lot of kissing. They liked to document it, apparently. A kiss at the Museum of Flight, posing with John F. Kennedy's Air Force One jet. Oh, look, a picture of Selena with her back turned, blowing kisses to the geese at Green Lake. Apparently the geese shared Trevor's appreciation of her truly perfect derriere in its truly too-short skirt.

Jewel was still staring at the screen, spasmodically clicking her way through Selena's entire photo collection, when the telephone began to ring. Jewel reached for it with one hand, without turning her head or blinking her eyes.

"Hello?" She had a premonition, even as she said the word.

"Hey, there, let me talk to Trevor for a sec." The woman's voice was casual, deceptively friendly.

"He's not here. May I ask who's calling?"

"I'll try him back in a little while. Thanks, babe." The call ended.

Thanks, babe? Doesn't she want to know why a woman is answering Trevor's phone? Jewel slammed the phone onto the desk and pushed her chair back. She tried to envision herself as an invincible predator. How did it feel to be the woman who didn't see any other woman as competition? Something—rage, nausea, despair—heaved itself into Jewel's throat. For several seconds, she fought for air while blood thundered in her ears and her lungs seemed to collapse on themselves. Her hands clawed at her chest. She sank to her knees on the rug as her throat slowly reopened. As panic subsided, a horrible feeling of familiarity took its place. She had been through this before, twice in college, three times since. Trevor was number six. She knew, too well, what she needed to do. All that remained was finding the strength to do it.

Her eyes fell on the laptop, and she stood up, trying to rekindle her rage without driving herself into another panic attack. She began circling through the apartment, collecting her possessions and piling them in the middle of the living room floor. She glanced at the clock. If he came home tonight as promised, Trevor would arrive in one hour and forty-five minutes. She began to move faster, muttering to herself.

"What's mine here? Clothes, all my clothes. Books over there. My old laptop, under the bed. Some mugs. Shower stuff. Too bad I can't take the coffee table. If I had any spray paint...the pillows are all mine, except that stinky one he always sleeps on. Actually, I don't think I want these pillows anymore. What am I going to carry this stuff in? Suitcase, duffle bag, that other duffle is his...he owes me way more than a duffle bag, but I don't want his stupid duffle bag following me through life. Bags in the kitchen. Better than nothing. Thank you, Trader Joe's, for putting handles on them." The rattle of paper bags unfolding seemed to fill the room with chaos. She moved faster, grabbing things from the closet, from the dresser, from the shelves, pouring the trappings of her life into grocery bags, zipping her underwear and her jewelry into the small suitcase. "Why don't I have a bigger suitcase? I get dumped so often. I should be more prepared." A large plastic trash bag from the kitchen swallowed her toiletries and makeup, hats, mittens, socks, and a handful of pens and pencils from the jar on the desk. She fumbled through the desk drawers, pulling out her papers and stuffing everything she wasn't taking through the paper shredder. She resisted the temptation to shred all Trevor's personal papers, too. There wasn't time. Her duffle bag and four more trash bags fit all her clothes, her winter coat and umbrella, and her few personal treasures. She heaved her shoes into the rest of the paper grocery bags.

There.

Anything else?

The rocking chair that had been her mother's. Jewel stared at it helplessly. She could carry it downstairs, but then what? Well, she couldn't leave it here. Tearfully, she pushed it into the center of the room with her other belongings.

On the mantel, across from the bay window, stood a row of black-and-white photographs in red-painted frames. Jewel let go of the rocker and charged at them. One by one, she opened the frames and tore up the pictures. She left the open frames in a row on the mantel, the pile of shredded photographs beside them. She opened Trevor's laptop again, clicked to Selena's photo albums, and left Facebook to tell Trevor its own tale when he came home.

It was time to go. She filled her arms with grocery bags and opened the apartment door. She was on the second floor of the building. She would have to haul everything downstairs to the sidewalk and leave it there each time while she went back up for the next load. *Dear God, please don't let my stuff get stolen while I move out of here.*

The air outside was hot, the sun brilliant. Seattle was basking in its brief annual heat wave. Jewel began to sweat before the first load was on the sidewalk. Her long hair slithered around her as she moved, sticking to her neck and catching under her arms. Her bare feet flinched away from the hot pavement. She raced up the stairs and stepped into a pair of flip-flops before hoisting another load of bags into her arms. The flip-flops slapped loudly against the stairs. Slap, slap, slap down twelve steps to the hall. Slap, slap, slap out the main door to the sidewalk. Her first two bags were still there. She dumped the next two on top of them, squinting against the glare. Slap, slap, slap back up the steps. By the fourth trip, she felt that she had been traveling up and down this staircase for most of her life, one man after another, one gut-wrenching humiliation after another, one pile of bags after another, with no end in sight.

As she made the fifth trip up the stairs, the memories began to reel through her mind: Tony, her first college love, Wes, who picked her up when Tony dropped her, Chris, who rescued her from Wes, Albert, who was twice her age, Justin, who claimed to be rescuing her from Albert, Trevor, who stole her from Justin. She came down again slowly, dragging the rocking chair, wincing each time it banged into her ankles. She pushed it across the hall, backed herself through the door, and lifted the chair so its rockers would not be scratched by the pavement. With her teeth clenched, she carried it, a few steps at a time, to the pile of bags on the sidewalk.

It was at this moment that Jewel remembered that her car was at the dealer. Trevor was going to take her to pick it up tonight, in thirty-five minutes, when he came home. Jewel blew her hair out of her eyes and sat down on the rocking chair. She pulled her phone out of a paper bag full of shoes and clicked on Trevor's number. Options. Text message. Her thumbs jabbed out the words "Don't bother." She pressed "send."

The door at the top of the stairs was still open. She dug her purse out of one of the duffle bags, climbed the stairs, and locked the door. Then she slipped the key off her key ring and shoved it under the mat. There would be no going back. As she turned away from the door, she heard the phone ringing again inside.

Back on the sidewalk, Jewel looked at her watch. A bus lumbered around the corner and pulled up next to her. The doors opened, and she found herself staring up at the bus driver, a red-faced man in his fifties who frowned at the rocking chair and the pile of bags on the sidewalk.

"You're not taking that on the bus!"

Jewel stared at him. He pointed imperatively at a spot just above her right shoulder. "You're at the bus stop, but you can't bring all that on here."

"Oh! No, I wasn't—I forgot this was a stop. I just came out—" The doors closed and the bus pulled away. Embarrassed, Jewel kicked and shoved her possessions further down the sidewalk, clarifying her position to any other bus drivers who might pass before she figured out what to do next. It better be soon. Trevor would be home in twenty minutes.

Jewel shut her eyes and rubbed her temples with her fingertips, urging her brain to overcome the fog of heat and chagrin and solve her problem. A taxi passed as she opened her eyes. She waved frantically, but it did not stop. "Maybe another will come," she said aloud.

People walked past her, stepping around the overflowing bags. A woman running, three men arguing about football, a college student listening to music on an iPod, a family with three children and two dogs. Jewel's eyes were fixed unblinkingly on the street. Certainly another cab would appear. She remembered her cell phone. She could call a cab. Directory assistance. 411. It was made for moments like this. She dug the phone back out of her purse. Her hands felt clumsy. She spilled some things out of her purse onto the sidewalk and had to pick them up before she could make her call. Her smallest movement began to assume the frustrating complexity of a nightmare in which she could not lift her feet fast enough to escape what was pursuing her.

The dispatcher's voice crackled in her ear. Jewel squinted, concentrating on the fragments of sound. "I'm sorry, can you say that again? I have a bad signal, I think." The crackle repeated itself, sounding very far away, too far to arrive in time to rescue her from Trevor's return. She could not wait to understand the voice. She said her address as loudly and clearly as she could, and she thought she heard the words "on the way" before she hung up.

Fifteen minutes lumbered past. She paced around her pile of bags, chewing her thumbnail. She felt her skin burning in the sunlight, but she couldn't remember which bag held her sunscreen, and she was afraid of missing the taxi if she stopped staring at the street and rummaged through the bags to look for it.

A dusty orange taxi slid to a stop in front of her, and the driver hopped out. He came around the front of the car and stared at her pile of bags and her rocking chair. He made a slight movement, as if he planned to leave her there on the sidewalk.

"No, no, please!" Jewel stretched out her hand, begging. "I'll help you put everything in. The chair isn't so big; it could fit in the back if you'll let me sit up front. It was my mother's. Please, I need a cab very much. Don't leave."

The driver rolled his eyes and muttered something that sounded rude, but after a few suspenseful seconds, he shrugged and went to open the trunk of the cab. He started heaving her bags into it, careless of the contents. Jewel was too busy maneuvering the rocker awkwardly into the back seat to criticize his methods. It almost fit. She paused on the curb, with the door still open, waiting for the driver to finish so he could help her position it. When the last bag was in, she scanned the sidewalk. A book lay open on the grass, next to the place where her bags had been. She took a step toward it. *A Treasury of Love Poems*. She left it in the grass and turned back to the cab in time to see the driver slamming the back door, crushing her rocker inside. She climbed numbly into the front seat of the cab and looked back. The chair lay with its head rest against the far door and its rockers wedged against the near door. Every dowel in its back had been snapped and bowed inward awkwardly, like broken bones. Jewel sank down in her seat and stared at the windshield.

"Where to?" The driver's voice implied that he expected a request to drive her straight up the Rainier glacier.

Jewel opened her mouth and said the first thing that came into her head. "Go north. Out of the city. Just go up Highway 99 for a while. I'll tell you when to stop."

"I need a destination."

Jewel gasped, recalling for a second time that her car was waiting at the dealer. "The dealer! My car's at the dealer. Here, I'll give you the address. I'm sure I have the card in my purse." She clawed through its jangling contents. "Here." She handed the white card to him and watched while he typed the address into his GPS. He flicked the card back to her, and she zipped it into her purse.

The driver sighed heavily and pulled into traffic. When the cab reached the corner, Jewel shut her eyes tight so she couldn't look back.

Chapter 2

Jewel asked the cab driver to wait while she went into the dealership to pay what she owed and retrieve her keys. An attendant brought her car around to the front, and she opened all four doors and the trunk.

Turning back to the waiting cab, she knocked on the driver's window. "If you'll just pop the trunk, I'll take everything out myself."

The driver grunted at her and climbed out of the car, pushing past her to open the trunk. He heaved the bags out, two at a time, and dropped them on the pavement behind her car. Jewel felt the eyes of the dealership staring disapprovingly through the large plate-glass windows. Curious glances seemed to fall on her from all sides as she opened the back door of the cab and pulled the broken rocker carefully out, resting it on the pavement while she climbed inside to retrieve every piece of splintered wood. She had no clear plan for its remains, but she could not abandon any part of it.

Seeing that the cab's trunk was now empty, Jewel bundled the headrest and the broken pieces of doweling into the front seat of her car, heaved the rest of the chair across the curb, and returned to pay the driver with a credit card. She tipped him extravagantly and said thank you. He grunted one last time and climbed into his cab. He had no courtesy to spare on her, no matter how well she paid him.

Wearily, Jewel packed her bags into the trunk of her own car and lifted the broken rocking chair into the back seat. She closed the door carefully, although it was plain to see that in its broken form, the chair fit inside easily.

Jewel looked at her car, full of every single thing she possessed in the world except that cheap coffee table she had abandoned at Trevor's. This was it, her stake in the planet. Unfortunately, it had no bathroom. Locking the doors, she trudged inside to use the dealership's facilities.

Back in her car, Jewel pulled out of the parking lot and drove aimlessly down the street, listening to the sound of her own breathing, trying to make sense of the landscape she could see gliding by outside. After a while, she pulled into a gas station, parked next to the mini-mart, and turned off her car.

She sat still and closed her eyes. Her hand fumbled against the door, locking it. Safe. More or less. Now what?

Reluctantly, she opened her eyes and began to talk to herself. "I'm hungry. I want to go to sleep. Well, I can't sleep in the car. Or at least, I don't want to. How about a motel? A friend? Nobody Trevor knows. Who is my own friend?" She found she couldn't think through the problem. Her head felt heavy. The air inside the car was stifling. It was too hot to sit in the sun in a closed car. She should do something about this, but what?

Her cell phone rang inside her purse, startling her. She reached for the phone automatically and was about to answer the call when she saw who it was. Trevor. Should she tell him—no, no, no! Jewel turned off the telephone and dropped it back into her purse, yanking the zipper shut. Looking up, she encountered the eyes of a man who was standing just outside the door of the mini-mart, staring speculatively in her direction. Jewel was very familiar with this look and the message it was intended to convey. With a jerk, her hand came up to the ignition and she turned on the car, backed sloppily out of her parking space, and drove away quickly. In a few minutes, the air conditioner began to cool the air inside the car, and when she tried to think again, she found it was no longer impossible.

"I'll call Sara," she said out loud. This solution now seemed stupidly obvious, a plan any intelligent life form could have thought up. Sara would know what to do, and Sara would help her do it. Sara was her best friend in kindergarten, and nothing had happened in the twenty-three years since to change that. Too bad men weren't like Sara.

Looking for a place to park and make the call, Jewel's eye fell on her dashboard clock and she realized that by this time, Sara would be coming home from work. There was no need to call. She pulled off the road as soon as she could, turned her car in the other direction, and headed for the highway. Sara lived twenty minutes north of Seattle, in a little town called Edmonds. The highway was the quickest way there.

Sara Carlson was just getting out of her husband's red pickup, which was parked in front of her townhouse, when Jewel pulled in beside her. Sara was a short, sturdy brunette with friendly brown eyes, a square chin, and an air of cheerful practicality. She was a gym teacher at a Catholic elementary school, and she was still dressed in her work clothes, yoga pants and a short-sleeved polo shirt, her keys swinging from a strap around her neck, her hair bouncing in a ponytail behind her head. She slammed the door of the truck, swung a backpack over her shoulder, and turned at the sound of Jewel's car behind her. Her face lit and she waved enthusiastically.

Jewel climbed out of her car and stood beside it. "Clay let you drive his truck?" she asked, attempting light conversation.

"He's back home in Texas for the weekend, big old mama's boy that he is. Helping them remodel the bathroom, or some such thing." Sara frowned at her. "Babe, you look like you ran over your dog, and I see there's a rocking chair in your car. Why don't you come inside and tell me what happened?"

Jewel pointed her keychain at her car and pressed the button. The car beeped, flashed its lights, and locked itself. She felt shocked. It was the first thing she had done all afternoon that had gone as planned. Letting her hand fall to her side, she followed her friend into the house. As Sara shut the door behind them, Jewel moved toward the couch and dropped bonelessly into the deep leather cushions. Sara stood in front of her, planted her hands on her hips, and said, "Well?"

"Trevor left me. I mean, he has a new girlfriend. I found her on Facebook this afternoon. She's really h-hot..." Jewel gazed piteously up at Sara's face and burst into tears. Sara dropped her bag on the floor and leaped to the rescue, plopping herself down on the couch and wrapping her arms around Jewel, patting her back, reaching for tissues from a box on the coffee table and stuffing them into Jewel's curled fingers.

"Oh, Jewelie, I'm so sorry. What an animal he is. She can't be hotter than you are, it's just not possible. What a bad day you're having. Don't be sad, baby, you still have me. You deserve so much better than this. There are other fish in the sea, and they aren't all rotten like he is. Here's another tissue, just drop that one on the floor. There's no one here but us, and we can make a mess if we want to."

Her words ran over Jewel's head and down her back like a cascade of warm water. Jewel was crying too hard to hear them clearly, but the general effect was soothing, and after a while, she was too tired to cry so hard anyway. The tears slowed, she blew her nose one more time, and Sara helped her sit up, keeping an arm around her.

"Bed for you, sweetie pie," said Sara decisively. "Tomorrow's Saturday. We'll sleep late and talk things over. Let me put some dinner into you and then you can curl up in the guest bed and pass out. I can see that's all you want in the world."

"That and true love," squeaked Jewel, starting to cry again. Sara handed her the tissue box and went into the kitchen. Jewel lay in the sofa corner, pressing tissues to her eyes, one after another, and dropping them on the floor. She felt too tired to do anything at all, too tired even to continue existing as a limp body entirely supported by sofa cushions.

The next hour passed in a fog. Jewel lost track of everything but the effort to keep her eyes open. Sara brought her a plate of chicken casserole and stood over her while she ate it, then helped her go out to her car, search fruitlessly for her toothbrush among the pile of bags, give up, and go back inside. She brushed her teeth with her finger and Sara's toothpaste, put on Sara's pajamas, and tumbled into the guest bed. The night swallowed her in blackness, and she slept.

Jewel woke, confused, at three o'clock in the afternoon. She stared at the clock through a tangled curtain of hair and felt a surge of panic. She had missed work! She lunged up in bed and saw she was at Sara's house. No, she hadn't missed work. She had lost Trevor to Selena Davis-Jones. A second surge of panic flipped her stomach into her throat. She pushed her hair out of her face and forced herself to take a deep breath. She was at Sara's house. No need to panic yet. She climbed off the bed and stood still, balancing on her feet, digging her toes into the fluffy white carpet. The whole room was white and fluffy. Carpet, comforter, lampshades. A bright red corduroy cushion on a rocking chair by the window made a splash of color, drawing the eye. Jewel looked at the rocking chair sadly and started for the door.

Downstairs, she found Sara in a bright green football jersey arguing with a sports commentator on ESPN, munching popcorn from a blue plastic bowl resting on her lap. She looked up as Jewel came down the stairs and reached for the remote, turning off the television.

"Sleeping Beauty lives! Did you have a good rest? You must be starving. I made French toast this morning, and I saved some for you. You want it?" Without waiting for an answer, Sara popped off the couch and padded into the kitchen. Jewel drifted after her and sat down in a chair at the dining room table. The townhouse was comfortable and well furnished, but small. The living room, dining room, and kitchen were arranged as a single large room. Sara had set her long leather sofa as a divider between the living and dining rooms, and there was a half-wall topped by a counter that separated the kitchen from the dining room.

The microwave whirred and beeped, and Sara brought a plate of French toast to the table, poured maple syrup over it, and handed Jewel a fork. When Jewel had eaten, they moved back to the couch, each going automatically to her favorite end and pulling a throw cushion or two around herself for comfort.

"So," prompted Sara, "tell me every single thing."

Full of French toast and almost twenty hours of sleep, Jewel found it wasn't so difficult to talk about what had happened. It was almost a relief.

"Trevor left me. Her name is Selena Davis-Jones, and she's a realtor. There are pictures of them kissing at almost every Seattle landmark. And feeding each other. You should see her, Sara. She's so sexy she's fierce. You can tell even without seeing her in person. And she called while I was packing my stuff. I just know it was her. I answered the phone, and she didn't even care. Can you imagine? Who are you if you aren't even worried that a woman is answering your boyfriend's phone?"

"Do you think she knows about you already?" Sara asked.

"I don't know. Maybe she does. She looks like the type who wouldn't care whose man it was, if she wanted him."

"Okay, I'm sorry, honey, but I just have to see her." Sara lunged over the end of the sofa and picked up her iPhone. "What did you say her name was?"

"Selena Davis-Jones, and don't worry, you can see it all. Her page is totally public. All the photos, everything. And since I found her from Trevor's page, that means probably all his friends know, too. There were some posts on his page that made it sound that way, anyhow."

Silence fell momentarily and Sara busily poked at the touchscreen on her phone. Then, "Hot mama! Look at her. I see what you mean. Those can't possibly be the lips she was born with. God wouldn't do that to anyone. Ditto on the boobs."

"Well, Trevor seems to like them."

Sara looked up. "Baby, I don't think it need concern you any more what Trevor likes."

"Oh, I know. Even I can see that."

Sara made a little sad face at her, full of sympathy. "So, when did he tell you?"

Jewel shook her head. "No, he didn't tell me, I just found out by myself. I've had a funny feeling for the last few weeks, maybe a little longer. He left his laptop home yesterday, logged in on the desk, because he left for work in a hurry. I got home before he did, and it was kind of an out-of-body experience. It was almost like I had a premonition. I sat down at his desk like I was pulled there by a string, and when I touched the mouse-pad, the screen came back on and there was his Facebook page. He has it set to never log him off. After that, all I had to do was click around a little and presto, Selena Davis-Jones." Jewel rested her head against the cool leather cushion behind her. "I don't know. I guess I should just expect this to happen. Sooner or later, it always does."

"Wait a minute," Sara held up her hand. "Wait, wait, wait. You said that Trevor left you."

"He did. How much more evidence do you need?"

"No, he didn't, Jewel. You left him."

Jewel stared at her.

"You—left—him," repeated Sara slowly. "Packed up all your stuff, hauled that rocking chair down the stairs, got yourself in your little car, and came to my house. You left him. Was he home when you left?"

"No, he wasn't." Jewel kept staring at her friend. She could see Sara was making a point. She waited, hoping for another clue, something to help her see what it might be.

Sara laughed a little and reached over to shake Jewel's knee affectionately. "You aren't getting it, are you? Let me say it again. You left him, Jewel. He didn't leave you."

Jewel sat up. "But he might as well have left. He's making out with Miss Fake Lips all over Seattle. The whole world found out before I did."

"But he hadn't left yet. For all you know, he wasn't even planning to. Selena may think she's God's gift to mankind, but it's just plain possible that Trevor was having a little fun on the side and is going to play her just as false as he played you."

Jewel felt stunned. "Are you telling me I should go back to him because he might still want me?"

Sara was horrified. "Don't you *dare* even *think* about going back to him! That's not what I'm saying *at all*!"

"I don't understand," said Jewel humbly. "What *are* you saying?"

Sara paused, tapping her finger on her lip. "Let me put it this way. I've known you since we were both still sucking our thumbs at night. I was there when Tony broke your heart, and then when Chris and Albert and all the other losers picked you up and dropped you. This is the first time, as far as I ever heard, that *you* got up and left. You always waited through the bitter end. You waited till Chris' new girlfriend threw all your stuff out on the driveway, and you waited till Albert actually hit you, and you waited till Justin left you all night at the bus station. It was like there was nothing too bad to live through. But look at you!" Sara surged up to her knees on the sofa, shaking her fists triumphantly over her head. "You didn't wait! You *left*! You didn't talk it over. He wasn't even home. He got no warning at all!"

Jewel's eyes widened and her jaw went a little slack. Sara began to laugh, and Jewel smiled faintly. Sara's laugh was contagious.

"Does it mean something?" she asked, when Sara had finished punching the air and settled back into her corner. "I did leave. I didn't even think about it. I just got up and started pulling things out of my closet."

"Excellent! You must be growing a survival instinct." Sara sat up. "I'm going to get us some lemonade. I wish they built houses with air conditioners around here."

Jewel sat quietly, waiting for Sara to come back.

"I left," she said to herself. "I left him. So, do you have a boyfriend? No, I left him when I found out he was cheating on me. I left. I didn't even notice it was me this time. I left."

She held out her hand for the tall glass of lemonade and drank thirstily. It tasted good, cold and sweet. A small corner of her mind noticed that it was still possible to take pleasure in something. Her life was a shambles, but lemonade was still refreshing.

"I left," she said again, a look of surprise dawning on her face.

"You left, baby! You left! What a step for you! There's been a coup, and you've come into power. What are you going to do with it?"

"Well," said Jewel, "I'm not going back, for one thing."

"Very good. That's the first thing you need to do in your new life. Not go back. So, you're going to be a single woman now. That's great!"

"A single woman?"

"Yes, we'll get you an apartment of your own. Have you ever lived by yourself? Let me answer that. No, you haven't. You went from your dad's house to that house we all shared in college, to whoever it was who came after that, ever since. It's time to have your own place."

Jewel was struggling with something. She wasn't ready for the conversation to move to apartment hunting yet. "Why did you never say all this before, Sara?"

Sara smiled ruefully. "I did, sweetie pie, or at least, I tried. You were always so destroyed by the time you confided in me that it was hard to do anything but be sympathetic. I would always tell you that you deserved better, but after a while, I realized that you thought I meant you deserved a better man."

Jewel drooped. "I don't think a better man would want me, at this point."

"That's not what I meant," snapped Sara, getting impatient. "You think you're dirt and you let these losers treat you like you're dirt. Of course you deserve a better man! You're a good human being. I think you deserve the best love in the world, from the best man! But what I'm trying to tell you is that going out looking for the man is what's killing you. I don't know how to say this nicely, so pleeeeease don't be offended. I love you so much, Jewel. You've been my friend forever. You always listen when I want to talk, you always keep me company when I'm lonely, you always help me get back up again when I fall down. But you don't take care of yourself in the same way. You're so desperate for love that you say yes to the first guy who offers it. It's like you don't believe you can survive by yourself, like you think anything is better than being alone. It's not, Jewel. It really isn't." She stopped for breath.

Jewel turned her face away, hiding it in the sofa cushions. With a sigh, Sara crawled across the couch and hugged her awkwardly. "Please understand, Jewel. I'm not trying to hurt you. It just seems like finally, it's the time when I can help you escape all this."

Jewel nodded dumbly, and Sara patted her back. "Jewel, you don't see yourself as you really are. You don't see how beautiful and smart you are. You could have it so much better than this."

"How?" wailed Jewel. "My life has always been like this."

"I know, love, but this is your chance. I'm sure it is! Yesterday, you did something you've never done before. Keep on going! Do some more things you've never done before."

Jewel moved restlessly. "Like what?"

"Hmm..." Sara sat back on her heels. "Well, start by getting your own place." She gasped excitedly. "The people three doors down from me are looking for a renter! It's perfect! It might only be for a few months, but I'm not sure. They bought a big place out in Snohomish, and they haven't been able to sell this one. Now they can't afford to wait any longer, so they're going to try for a renter to help them cover the first mortgage, just until the house sells."

Jewel began to look hopeful. "We would be neighbors."

"Yes, we would, so you wouldn't feel like you were completely abandoned, but you've got to promise me to make that place your own. Don't think of it as an extension of my house. Own it. Set it up. Turn the heat up and down. Play your most embarrassing favorite songs really loud and sing along. Do you see what I'm saying?"

Jewel wasn't sure, but she nodded. It didn't sound too hard, and Sara would be only a few doors away, if an abyss suddenly opened up in the floor and swallowed her.

Sara leaped off the couch and went to look for the number to call her neighbors and tell them she had the perfect renter for them. Jewel did not doubt that she would arrange everything. She had a long-standing confidence in the rightness of Sara's life, in the inevitability of things mostly going the way Sara wanted them to. Sara never needed much help.

Buoyed by a small but encouraging sense of accomplishment, Jewel cast about in her mind for something else to do, another step in this new direction Sara was envisioning for her. What else could she do to separate herself from everything in her life to date, to make some other kind of life? What other kind of life might there be? How could she get to it? Should she get a new job? No, her job was fine. Being a publications manager at a non-profit had nothing particularly to do with her love life. Fortunately, she had never been stupid enough to date anyone at the office.

Her wandering gaze landed on the front door and she thought of her car outside, still stuffed with her bags. In this heat, her makeup must have melted into liquid by this time. She'd have to get new makeup. Most of that makeup was a present from Trevor anyway...her mind leaped suddenly, hovering over a vision of her possessions, running through them item by item and realizing with a shock how many of them had been given to her by men. Those bags were full of designer clothes and shoes, and she had purchased less than half of them herself. All her underwear had come to her in pert pink gift boxes. So had her pajamas, if you could call them that. Her jeans, silk blouses, boots, sweaters, perfume were all tokens of affection, or what passed for it. Even her suits had been gifts from Albert, who thought career women were sexy. At least, he thought their clothes were sexy.

Jewel jumped off the couch and rushed to the kitchen. Sara held her off with a lifted finger, finishing her conversation with the neighbor. When she hung up, she said smugly, "I got it, of course. We'll go down and look at it when she's there tomorrow morning, and unless you make a complete idiot of yourself, it's all yours. She's bringing a contract. She said she had the same thing happen to her with the last man before the one she married, and she's sure if I vouch for you that you must be fine."

Jewel choked on the last of her lemonade and dropped the glass on the floor. "You *told* her?"

"Yes, I told her, and don't look so horrified. I know her. It was the right way to get her on our side. Don't worry, Jewel. It will be fine." Sara picked up Jewel's glass and wiped a drop of lemonade off the kitchen floor.

"Well, maybe, since you arranged it. It certainly wouldn't be fine if it was something I did. It's never fine, no matter what it is, if I do it."

"Hush, silly girl. Now tell me what you were so jazzed about when you came into the kitchen."

"Oh," began Jewel, starting to regain her enthusiasm, "I know what I need to do next. I want to get rid of all my clothes that came from men."

"All of them? Do you have something to wear when they're gone? Your wardrobe cost thousands, Jewel."

"Too bad," said Jewel, embracing rebellion. "It's all from men. All presents, like I was a walking doll that came with clothes you could put on and take off. I can't keep wearing them, Sara. I wouldn't feel like I had a new life at all. I would be getting up in the morning in my new life and putting on a bra that Albert gave me for Valentine's Day. How is that helpful? Let's get rid of them!"

"I'll help you sort them," Sara started for the door. "Can I have the ones that fit me?"

"No," said Jewel. "I don't want to look at you and think of Albert's bra."

Sara snorted with laughter and opened the door.

"In fact," said Jewel, becoming intoxicated with the possibilities, "I don't even want to take them to Goodwill. I want to burn them."

Sara swung around. "Come again?"

"In your fire pit," said Jewel, with relish. "It will be perfect. We can have a picnic on the patio while we throw my clothes in the fire."

"We better do it late tonight so the housing association doesn't see us," warned Sara.

At midnight, dressed in Sara's clothes, Jewel opened the sliding door and began pulling garbage bags of clothes out onto the patio. Sara came after her with a box of matches and a bottle of starter fluid. "Give me something really flammable, to get it going," she whispered.

"Pure silk, one hundred percent Victoria's Secret," hissed Jewel, tossing her a handful of panties. "You won't even need the match!"

Sara laid the panties ceremoniously in the fire pit and poured starter fluid on them. She lit a match and dropped it gingerly onto the pile, stepping back quickly. The panties caught fire instantly and began to burn. "Quick! Give me more, to feed it!"

"I want to do it myself," whispered Jewel, dragging the first bag over to the fire. She pulled out a handful of bras and flung them in, watching them ignite. The flames grew stronger, and she rolled up a pair of two-hundred-dollar jeans and shoved it into the pyre.

"This is awesome!" exclaimed Sara. She got a stick and poked the jeans further into the flames. "We should be whooping and dancing around the fire pit."

"No whooping," whispered Jewel, refusing to speak in a normal voice. "I don't want the housing association to come out here and stop me before I'm finished."

She stuffed the empty bag into Sara's outdoor trash can and brought over another one full of suits and sweaters. More jeans came next, then shoes and belts and a designer handbag that gave off a strange odor as it burned. Her melted makeup from Trevor went sizzling into the fire, along with a glittering handful of necklaces. She thought wistfully of the book of love poems abandoned on the sidewalk. It would have been satisfying to watch the pages incinerate.

By one o'clock in the morning, there was nothing left but a mound of charred fiber interspersed with scraps of blackened metal from buttons or jewelry. The air smelled acrid, unpleasant, yet Jewel breathed it deeply. It was the smell of battle, of carnage in a worthy cause. It was her first small victory.

Chapter 3

Anna Harris steered her blue Volvo neatly into a parking space along the sidewalk bordering the sloping, crescent beach by the Edmonds ferry terminal. She was five minutes early, and Xenia would probably stop to pick up a coffee on her way down from the shop. Anna settled a navy blue cap on her smooth, ash blond bob, frowning slightly at her reflection in the rear view mirror. Then she turned off the car, dropped her keys in her handbag, and climbed out into the heat, thankful for the insulated cup of iced coffee in her hand. The air smelled of salt water and sunscreen, an unfamiliar combination in a town where the water at the beach was too cold for swimming even in midsummer. She and Xenia Gregory had been coming here once a week in good weather for several years now. Xenia walked down from her shop on Main Street, and Anna drove over from her home in Lake Forest Park. It had started as a little celebration of Xenia's freedom when she hired her first shop assistant to cover the lunch hour, and when they decided to do it again the following week, it had become a habit. Sometimes they wandered along the sand, and sometimes they sat on a bench drinking coffee. Today, the sand was crowded with sun-starved townspeople. Without hesitation, Anna walked to her favorite bench, set under a scrubby pine tree by a curve in the sidewalk.

Anna sat down on the bench to wait for Xenia, looking cool and tranquil in a setting bursting with color and heat. Brilliant sunlight glinted like rhinestones on the gray-blue water. A flock of teenage girls in neon-colored bikinis roasted their skinny bodies on a rainbow of striped beach towels. Younger children raced barefoot across the sand or danced at the water's edge, hurling pebbles into the waves. A group of young mothers with their babies were sharing a picnic lunch under a red-and-white beach umbrella. An old man rested on a bench near Anna's, fingering the knobby end of a gnarled walking stick, his eyes staring toward the horizon. He seemed out of place today, a hold-out from the quieter crowd of regulars who came to sit on the benches or watch the sailboats from the jetty on days that were too chilly for sunbathers.

The ferry horn sounded, and Anna turned her head to watch the green-and-white ferry churn slowly away from the dock, bound across Puget Sound to the Olympic Peninsula. Her eyes strayed back to the sidewalk, and she caught sight of Xenia, striding through the crowd. Xenia was always striking. She was nearly six feet tall, big-boned, with long, generous lines and curves. Her strong, aquiline features, olive skin, and upswept raven hair gave her a slightly exotic look, accentuated by a supple contralto voice. It was the classic torch singer's voice, a little sad, yet still attractive, playing an oddly contrasting note to the graceless intensity of Xenia's eyes. Xenia's eyes drew the eyes of everyone who looked at her, even those of strangers passing her on the street. Anna had seen it, the casual glance and then the second glance as good manners gave way to the irresistible magnetism of such patent tumult. Xenia's eyes were like the eyes of a war orphan, Anna thought, deep, deep black and sorrowful.

"I'm late," said Xenia, greeting her.

"I'm early." Anna rose from the bench to hug her friend, and they sat down together.

Anna reached for her coffee. "What a gorgeous day! Look at all the people on the beach. You'd think the water was warm enough to swim in."

"They'll all be sunburnt before long," Xenia predicted, popping the lid on her own cup of iced coffee.

"Maybe some of them," Anna conceded. "Or maybe they're all wearing sunscreen, Xen. You can't tell by looking."

"Which is a polite way of telling me I'm a judgmental old grump."

Anna laughed.

"You're right, of course." Xenia sipped her coffee again, then set the cup on the bench beside her, folding her arms across her chest.

"How was your week, Xen?" asked Anna, undismayed by this belligerent posture.

"How was your birthday?" asked Xenia, pointedly ignoring the question.

"Very nice," Anna replied. "We had a four-course dinner at The Wild Ginger and an evening of Rachmaninov at Benaroya Hall. The symphony sounded wonderful." She smiled, remembering the night. Over dinner, George had fastened a fiery blue opal on a fine gold chain around her neck and told her that to him, youth had never been her chief attraction. It was so like him, to be driven near to awkwardness by the strength of his devotion. Anna sighed. "I'm forty-five, Xenia."

"Why shouldn't you be? I'm fifty-two," Xenia retorted. She ran a knowing eye over her friend. "Besides, you're aging gracefully. Trust me. I should know."

Anna laughed. "Yes, how are things at the shop?"

"The shop is doing well. My sales are up, I've increased inventory on my core lines and added a few new designers. There are enough returning customers that I'd say I have a following." Xenia snorted. "Ridiculous as that sounds."

"It's not ridiculous to acknowledge your success," said Anna indignantly. "It shouldn't be a surprise to you that you're doing so well at your work."

Xenia's dark eyes followed the flight of a bird. "It doesn't surprise me, at work."

Anna was silent.

"Why didn't you ever have a career?" Xenia asked abruptly.

"Well," Anna began, "I had plans, but things turned out differently than I expected."

"What do you mean?" asked Xenia, her eyes probing Anna's quiet face.

"We wanted children," Anna explained, her eyes on the mothers picnicking under the red-and-white umbrella, "and at first, I stayed home because we thought I'd be pregnant soon. It took several years to give up on that dream, and by that time, George was doing well at the university, entertaining a lot, traveling as a guest lecturer. We went on a teaching exchange overseas for a semester one year, and another year, he organized a big symposium on the East Coast. There's always something. It's a little like being the first lady, I'd imagine. I filled the extra time with church work and volunteering at the art museum and things like that."

"Is it enough for you?" asked Xenia curiously.

"More or less. I like what I do. But I wish I had something of my own, the way you do. Sometimes, I'm happy just the way I am. But sometimes, I get restless and try to think of something else to do, something to fill the void." Anna's eyes strayed back to the red-and-white umbrella. "If I could find one good thing, something I was sure I would love to do..."

Xenia frowned. "The more you think about it, the more you'll think yourself out of trying anything."

Anna laughed ruefully. "It's a failing in me, for sure. George says I'm the living personification of the old phrase 'lost in thought'."

"Well," said Xenia, to comfort her, "you aren't a total loss. You do more good than you know."

"I'm glad you think so, Xen. I wish I had your—your determination about things."

Xenia snorted. "Huh. You mean my bull-headedness. It's not a blessing, Anna."

"Well, it can be."

Xenia was not convinced. They were silent for a few minutes, hearing the chatter of voices on the beach and the whisper and slide of the waves.

"Oh, Lord, it's her," Xenia said suddenly. "And Dorothy, too. I hope they don't see us."

"Who?" asked Anna, looking around.

"Mrs. Edon," hissed Xenia, "over toward the ferry terminal. Look at them. They even wear dresses at the beach."

"I wonder why no one at church calls her by her first name," mused Anna, watching Mrs. Edon and her eighteen-year-old daughter step gingerly over the band of rocks and seaweed that lay just above the water line.

"Nobody wants to," said Xenia uncharitably.

"I'm sure she has friends at church, Xen. They've been coming for years."

"I don't even know what her first name is."

"Did you ever ask?"

"I don't want to know." Xenia folded her arms on her chest again, as if she had proved her point.

"Yes, I'm sure you don't," Anna said, making peace. "What is it, exactly, that she does to bother you so much?"

"Too much sympathy for Xenia, The Poor Widow." Xenia gritted her teeth.

"Dear me. That's unfortunate."

"You can't tell me you like her any more than I do."

"Well, I'm not always comfortable with her, but we seem to get along," said Anna, striving to be both tactful and accurate.

Xenia shifted on the bench, turning her back on Mrs. Edon. "Let's look at something else." Her eyes wandered over the beach. "There. Two girls standing in the waves eating ice cream."

"Where?"

"Straight down in front of us, a little to the left. In shorts, and with pony tails. A short pony-tail on the shorter girl, and a really long pony-tail on the taller girl."

"In their twenties, talking to each other?"

"That's them. Probably left their shoes in the car and burned their feet all the way down the sand to the water."

"It does get hot, on days like this. It's so funny to see a beach full of people who aren't wearing jackets and slacks," Anna laughed. "It could be Miami, instead of Edmonds."

"You clearly have never been to Miami," retorted Xenia.

"Well, you know what I mean. We should get ice cream and stand in the waves, Xen. It looks fun."

"We're too old for that. They don't have a care in the world, either one of them. Even if we were standing beside them, it wouldn't be the same for us." Xenia brushed her hands together as if she were cleaning dusty fingers. She stood up and reached for her handbag. "I should get back to the shop. My assistant does well enough, but I don't like to leave her for long. The customers get irritated if I'm not there to pamper their vanity."

"I'll walk you up the hill," offered Anna, rising and reaching for her own handbag. "I want to stretch my legs before I go home and tackle my garden."

As they started down the sidewalk, Anna's eyes returned to the two girls eating ice cream. One girl had finished her ice cream and was looking at her cell phone.

"Goodness!" Anna exclaimed.

"What?"

"That girl just threw her cell phone into Puget Sound!"

"What girl?"

"With the ice cream, the taller girl with the long hair. It wasn't an accident either. She did it on purpose, as hard as she could!"

"What on earth for?" cried Xenia, exasperated.

Anna threw up her hands. "How should I know?"

"Well! There you are. Now she *does* have a care in the world. She'll have to buy a new cell phone. And she better hope she didn't hit a scuba diver. The underwater park is probably full of them on a day like this."

Anna began to laugh. "Well, I didn't see anyone pop up waving his fists, so unless she knocked one out, she got lucky."

Xenia snorted. "People are idiots."

"They sometimes have their reasons," said Anna.

Chapter 4

"I can't believe I'm a renter," said Jewel, sitting next to Sara in the cab of Clay's red pickup, parked outside a large thrift store. "She just handed me a lease and I signed it. Just like that. Two bedrooms, two bathrooms, and the downstairs looks just like yours."

"The whole block is the same downstairs, and then some have more bedrooms or less, I think," replied Sara. "Now I'm just checking our list to make sure we didn't forget anything you need. I can never think straight once I'm actually shopping."

"I'm a renter," repeated Jewel, lingering a few minutes more in her own train of thought. "It can't be this easy, can it?"

"Why not? You're solving her problem for her," Sara pointed out. "I'm a practical person. That's why I can get things done pretty easily, most of the time. The key is to know who has a problem and who might be able to solve it. She can't afford two mortgages, and you want a place to rent. You both know me and trust me, so ta da! I fix you up together, and she gets help with her mortgages and you get a place to live."

"Maybe I should have let you fix me up with a boyfriend," murmured Jewel, but even as she said the words, she realized how tired she was of thinking about men. She could hardly remember a time when her mind had not focused, to the exclusion of all else, on her connection to a man and her efforts to remain in it.

"I must be so boring," she said suddenly. "Do I ever talk about anything besides men, even as a joke?"

"Men *are* a joke," retorted Sara. Her face softened. "All except Clay. Clay's almost as good as perfect. But to be quite frank, since you asked, no, you don't really talk about much else. You did when we were little, I think. Well, until your mom died. After that...."

"I know," Jewel sighed. "After that, I talked about my dad."

"Your dad is enough to make anyone obsessed." Sara grinned at her. "Just be proud, honey. Most people with your degree of provocation would definitely have gone to jail."

"I'm not in jail." Jewel gave her a half smile. "Not in jail. Well, it's something."

"Now here's my plan," said Sara firmly, bringing her back to the task at hand. "You need basic housewares, and you need your own clothes. Do you trust me to pick out dishes and stuff while you work on clothes, or do you want to do all of it yourself because this is for your very first house of your own?"

Jewel hesitated, waiting for Sara to give her some clue as to what her answer should be. Sara remained silent, returning her gaze matter-of-factly. Jewel opened her mouth and surprised herself by saying, a little too loudly, "I will do it all myself, even if it takes me all day. Unless you need to be somewhere," she added anxiously, recalling suddenly that she had not come in her own car. They had brought the pickup in case they found furniture. Jewel was starting at zero. She was setting up house with not much more than a winter coat, a broken rocking chair, and a toothbrush.

"I don't need to be anywhere but right here with you," said Sara affectionately, and they climbed out of the truck, ready to begin.

As Jewel closed the passenger door of the truck and stepped onto the curb, she heard a motorcycle pull up behind her. She jerked around, startled by the noise.

"Hey, baby. I knew I recognized you. You're looking good, Jewel. You know I always liked your hair like that." It was Albert, the man who hit her. Jewel felt her legs go soft, melting like wax into the hot gray sidewalk. Her eyes blinked nervously, without her volition. Her mind was empty. Albert leered at her and began to dismount from his motorcycle, balancing his helmet on the seat, coming toward her. Jewel stared at him, blinking.

"Hey, Albert! Hi! Wow! It's you," Sara charged onto the sidewalk beside her, hands on her hips. "It's been just ages since we saw you last. I wonder why that is. Oh, wait! That's right! The restraining order! Now get lost, Albert. I can dial 911 faster than you can say 'repeat offender'." Sara seized Jewel by the arm and dragged her down the sidewalk, past the door of the thrift store, to a large sporting goods store beside it. Without hesitation, she pulled the door open and propelled them both inside, past the check stands, deep into the store, coming to rest behind a large, dense rack of cycle shorts.

Jewel was shaking uncontrollably. With an exasperated sigh, Sara put her arms around her and hugged her tight. "Okay, okay, now just take one breath after another. He didn't follow us in here, and he doesn't know this wasn't where we were planning to go. In a few minutes, I'll go look out the front window and take a peek. If he's still there, I'll call 911 while you go into the restroom and splash cold water on your face."

"Go n-now, S-Sara," urged Jewel, through chattering teeth. "Go l-look. I w-want t-to know h-he's gone." She pushed her friend away and slumped forward, supporting her body by clamping her fingers around her legs just above her knees, struggling to control her shaking. She saw a store clerk coming toward her and sought wildly for some privacy. There was nothing to be had but cycle shorts. Instinctively, she shrank against them.

"Can I help you?" the clerk asked, coming up to her. He looked like he was about twenty and ran marathons.

Jewel shook her head. "I'm j-just l-looking." The words sounded ridiculously implausible to her, but he seemed to accept them. Probably he thought she had a speech impediment. Or a mental impediment. He withdrew to his checkstand, but she caught him glancing at her, keeping an eye on her.

Sara returned, looking triumphant. "He left. I don't see him anywhere. I even went out on the sidewalk and looked up and down. He's gone." She paused, then put her hand on Jewel's shoulder. "You've got to learn to protect yourself better, sweetie pie. What would have happened if I wasn't there to tell him off? You have a new life now, remember? Tell him to take a flying leap and go about your business. He doesn't have any power over you that you don't give him."

Jewel nodded, her nerves still twanging, her face hot with mortification. She stood up slowly and tucked her flowing hair behind her ears. A wave of depression struck her as she followed Sara out of the sporting goods store and back to the thrift store. Her path seemed strewn with booby traps and setbacks. Even now, as she was making her first real efforts to do better, she couldn't leave the house without being ambushed by her wretched past. It would happen again, without a doubt. Trevor was bound to pop out at her somewhere, any day now. She had not turned on her cell phone since she left the car dealership on Friday night, but she knew she was only putting off the inevitable. Sara could talk about making a new life. Sara had never had to make one. Was it actually possible for someone like herself? Could she ever be something more than a perpetual ex-girlfriend?

With loving obstinacy, Sara pushed her into the thrift store, acquired a cheerful red shopping cart for each of them, and started her into the housewares section.

"Look, honey. Dishes! Look at all this! It's like fifty estate sales happening in one place. I forgot how huge this store is. These are nice. No, that plate is cracked. No, not that one either. Here, how about this?" Sara pulled Jewel's arm until they were standing side by side in front of a shelf full of everyday china and stoneware. "Blue, green, yellow? I like this white set with the gold rims, but the rims look a little worn."

Jewel frowned at the dishes, and after a few seconds, she realized that she could concentrate again. Dishes. She was going to need dishes to eat off in her new house. "I'm going to make pancakes," she said suddenly. "Trevor hates pancakes. I haven't had them in seven months."

"Pancakes it is," said Sara encouragingly. "We'll get you a skillet in a minute. Here, this set is almost complete. I think it's short one saucer, but how often do you use saucers? It's kind of pretty. Blue and white flowers."

"Are there any sets that are perfect? That aren't missing something?"

Sara scanned the shelf. "I don't think so. But this one is, except for the missing saucer."

"I'll take it," said Jewel, listening to the decisive words being spoken in her own voice. She picked up the set of china, two pieces at a time, transferring it carefully into her cart. "Water glasses next. I like blue glass. I hope they have some blue ones."

For fifteen minutes, they moved slowly up one aisle and down another, acquiring four blue water glasses, a frying pan and a soup pot, three paring knives and a spatula, and a set of clean but rumpled placemats with matching napkins.

"I can't believe how inexpensive this stuff is," marveled Jewel.

"Yes, it's a great place to shop. I love buying stuff this cheap. It makes me feel like I outsmarted something."

Jewel pushed her cart to the end of the aisle. "We're out of housewares now. What's next? This looks like children's stuff."

Sara consulted her list. "Go all the way to the back. Shoes and bedding are back there, and then we'll tackle your new wardrobe."

"I don't have a bed."

"We'll see if they have a frame back there, and you can pick up a mattress new. Some things you don't want to buy second-hand."

Jewel shuddered, then her face cleared. "Is that furniture over there? Oh, let's do that first. I see a chair, a green arm chair." She pushed her cart up next to it, being careful not to jar her new china. "Only twenty dollars! Would this go in the truck, do you think?" She looked more closely. "It even reclines. Oh, it's got a little hole. I can put a cushion over that." She glanced up. "See? Here's a cushion for fifty cents."

"Hooray! I'll go get a clerk to mark it 'sold'. If you want, you can start on clothes while I see if there's anything worthy of your consideration in the bedding aisle."

Jewel nodded and turned back to the women's clothing section. It seemed enormous to her, like acres and acres of shirts, sweaters, running pants, dresses, pajamas, everything a woman could possibly wear and a few things she most definitely shouldn't.

"I'll just pick an aisle and start," she told herself. "I know what I'll do. I'll go to this side and go up and down till I come to the end. What is this...coats...well, it's summer and I have a winter coat, so I can skip that aisle. Next comes...dresses. I'll start here."

Jewel pushed her cart into the aisle, followed the markers until she came to her size, and stared into the tightly packed mass of garments hanging in front of her. "Whatever I want," she breathed, realizing she need not consult any taste but her own. "Do I want an orange dress, I wonder? Orange is a bright color. Do I like it? Does it look good on me?" She lifted down an orange cotton sundress with spaghetti straps and a short, flaring skirt. She considered its points. "I don't see how you could wear a bra under this. I think I'll only get dresses you can wear a bra under." She replaced the dress on the rack, pleased to have a made a criterion for herself. The next dress was a black jersey sheath that reached her ankles when she held it against her chest. She lifted it above her head, holding it against the light. "No, not this one either. Nothing you can see through. My underwear is my own personal business from now on." The next dress had a familiar look. "I had one like this before. Boobs falling out the front any minute. No more of that either." She made her way through several more, eliminating them for failing to meet her criteria. A white linen sundress came next, well-tailored, sleeveless without being strappy. Jewel held it against herself and touched the fabric. It felt smooth and cool. She checked the tag, making sure. "It's my size. I'm going to take this one to the fitting room." She laid it on top of the blue and white china. In a minute, a red wool suit dress followed it. It was the kind of dress that begged for a string of pearls. Definitely not Albert's style. She glanced at the white linen dress. Trevor wouldn't like that one. He hated white dresses. Jewel reached into the cart and patted the white dress as if it were a living thing. "It doesn't matter what they like," she said to the dress, with a little prickle of excitement. "There won't be anyone in the house but me."

Two hours later, Jewel and Sara balanced side by side on the rear bumper of Clay's pickup, stretching bungee cords over a lumpy mountain of bags and furnishings, securing Jewel's new belongings for the ride home.

"Clay is so prepared," Sara sighed rapturously. "I just love that he has his own bungee cords in his own truck box in his own beee-oootifully maintained red pickup."

"He makes your life simple," Jewel said seriously. "What's not to love?"

Sara considered this as they climbed down from the bumper and got into the truck. "In some ways he does, but it isn't that really." She turned on the truck. "My life is simple because he doesn't make it complicated."

"Isn't that the same thing?" asked Jewel curiously.

"Not at all," said Sara emphatically, pulling out of the parking lot. "Think about it. It's the difference between cleaning up a mess and not making the mess in the first place."

They drove for several minutes in silence, then Sara gave a little shout. "Ice cream! That's it! I was trying to think of the perfect ending, something to celebrate what we just did. We're going for ice cream, Jewelie my love. I know the perfect place. It's a tiny little shop about a hundred yards from the Edmonds ferry terminal. There's a beach there, remember? Let's get ice cream and eat it on the beach. We can take our shoes off and walk in the little waves. I think the tide is in right now."

Jewel's eyes lit. "That will be perfect! It's the kind of thing people do when they don't have a care in the world."

They parked the truck at the beach, high-fiving each other when they found a spot in the small, crowded lot, and they walked half a block from the parking lot to the ice cream shop. Sara chose two scoops of Praline Pecan with sprinkles. Jewel chose a scoop of Wild Mountain Blackberry and a scoop of Old Fashioned Vanilla. Returning to the beach, they left their shoes in the truck and stepped off the walkway onto the hot sand. Laughing and flinching, they ran down the brief slope of sunbaked sand and over the belt of seaweed covered rocks, licking the melting ice cream to keep the scoops from tumbling off their cones.

Jewel reached the water just before Sara. They splashed in together and stood side by side, eating ice cream and letting the lazy wavelets drift around their legs. Sea gulls floated by above them, calling into the breeze. A group of children launched a kite and ran with it, shouting as it dipped and jerked at the string. The ferry sounded its horn and started back across the water. Jewel swallowed the last mouthful of creamy cone and leaned over to wash her sticky fingers in the water. As she did so, she felt the flat metal body of her cell phone in the hip pocket of her shorts. She must have put it there this morning, out of habit. She stood up, closing her eyes, letting the wind blow through her. The air at the beach was never still. She thought of the Pacific Ocean, just out of sight on the horizon, with no land barrier between it and the cool water swirling around her. For a fleeting second, she felt limitless, balanced on the brink of the world, freed from all barriers, one with the water and the wind.

With a sigh, she opened her eyes and dug the cell phone out of her pocket. Sara saw it. "Go for it," she said, licking her fingers. "It can't bite you."

Jewel turned on the phone. For a split second, nothing. Then it came to life like a thing possessed: the screen flashed, the tone sounded, and the words "17 messages" flashed before her stricken gaze.

"Delete them," advised Sara, shamelessly reading over her shoulder. "Think how good it will feel."

Jewel started to press the key accessing her voicemail. The phone rang in her hands.

"Is that his number?" asked Sara.

"No, it's a number I don't know."

"Oh," said Sara. She sounded relieved. "Well, go ahead and answer it. I don't mind."

Jewel pressed the screen and held the phone against her ear. "Hello?"

"Jewel? It's Jerry. Someone just told me you and Trevor broke up. Are you okay?"

"I'm fine," said Jewel woodenly.

"That's good, baby, that's good. Listen, I never thought he knew how good he had it. You are far, far out of his league. I was wondering—I'm joining some friends for drinks tonight, and I'd like to take you to dinner afterwards, on my yacht, maybe talk a little about the possibilities."

Jewel took the phone down from her ear and jabbed at it with both thumbs. "Call ended" flashed on the screen. Jewel's hands tightened around the phone and her nostrils flared.

"Who was that?" asked Sara. "You look like you're about to—"

Jewel's arm swung back above her shoulder and she took a long, plunging step like a pitcher on the windup. Her arm snapped forward from the elbow and her fingers uncurled. The cell phone hurtled through the bright, sunlit air and plummeted into the shimmering waters of Puget Sound. A small "plunk" and an anticlimactic splash marked its passing for an instant. Then there was nothing left, no mark on the surface to show where it had gone.

Sara's mouth fell open.

Jewel's eyes returned to her friend. "Come on," she said. "I'm going to cut off my hair."

Chapter 5

On a bright summer morning, Jewel perched on a low brick wall in Edmonds' Centennial Plaza, immersing herself in the sights and sounds of the town's weekly Summer Market. Fresh herbs, berries, squashes, root vegetables, corn, green beans, tomatoes, peaches, cherries, snap peas, and lettuce were piled in colorful mounds on tables shaded by square tented booths. Brown eggs, cheeses, and organic meats were arranged in coolers, and there were banks of cut flowers, glowing and fragrant in the heat. Local artists and artisans displayed water colors, hand-made soap, wind chimes, garden statuary, jewelry, tie-dyed dresses, quilted handbags, or driftwood sculptures. The fragrance of sun-warmed fruit mingled with the scents of lavender and lilies and the aromas of roasting chicken and good coffee. The streets had been closed off in this corner of the little town, and people thronged the pavement, browsing the rows of booths, chatting with vendors, sampling a juicy berry or a sliver of barbecued meat on a stick. Many shoppers had brought the family dog along to be patted, discussed, and admired by friends and strangers alike.

Jewel had come early to the market, and the bulging canvas sack at her feet held a week's supply of fruit and vegetables. She had chosen as many unfamiliar things as she could find: red carrots, flat "donut" peaches, an oddly shaped squash, an onion still on its green stalk, two orange beets, and a "personal" watermelon. Jewel was certainly familiar with watermelon, but she had never seen such a small one, and the placard reading "Personal Watermelon" appealed to her. It seemed meant particularly for her, a joyful reminder that all her food was "personal" now, chosen and prepared to suit no one but herself.

In the two years that had passed since the day she had moved out on Trevor, Jewel had slowly ceased to fear her independence and had come to treasure it. She loved the domestic details of her life in the two-bedroom townhouse, where she still lived on a repeatedly extended lease. She loved venturing out alone into the town, looking for fun in the comfortable rhythms of its festivals and traditions. The Summer Market seemed like fairyland to her. She plunged into it each Saturday like a pearl diver, filling her burlap sack with the treasures of local farms and gardens, then resting on its shores, reluctant to be parted from its bounty. Reaching home, she would pile her purchases on the round oak table that now stood in her dining room, recalling the gorgeous radiance in which they had been discovered.

Turning her head, Jewel saw a man and his wife emerge from a garden art booth and begin their arduous journey down the sidewalk toward the street where their car was parked. Each grasped one end of a large rectangular mirror framed ornately in swirling bronze with a bronze water nymph, a naiad, mounted on its glimmering silver surface. The mirror looked heavy, and they coached each other anxiously as they strove to pass through the crowd without dropping it or knocking anyone down. As they came abreast of her, Jewel saw her own reflection scattered around the mirror, displaced by the nymph. She could see her black hair, pixie cut, just to the left of the nymph's rippling tresses. Her eyes were hidden behind the nymph's face, and her hands, folded in her lap, seemed to dangle from the nymph's belly. Slivers of her white peasant blouse and ruffled red skirt appeared in the spaces between the nymph's bare limbs and the rows of bronze waves. One garnet earring and part of her matching necklace could be seen, and her feet in black leather sandals appeared to be resting on the bronze frame around the bottom of the mirror as if she, too, were riding by within its confines. Jewel gazed at the image, disconcerted and fascinated to see herself, even in fragments, as someone else might see her. She had become so much accustomed to looking out at the world. Except for her weekly dinner with Clay and Sara, she spent her leisure hours in solitude, observing the world around her with interest, often with delight, but no longer with any sense that the world remembered her existence and might observe her in its turn. She wished, fleetingly, that the nymph had not been in the way. She might then have seen what Jewel looked like, sitting on a wall at the Summer Market, as much a person as the other members of the crowd she had been watching so attentively.

A gray-haired man in a long black robe appeared suddenly, a few steps away from her, and brushed a white handkerchief over his face. He took two wavering steps and sat down on the wall, too quickly, as if his legs could no longer hold him. He leaned forward, resting one hand on his knee and fanning himself feebly with the handkerchief.

Jewel stared at him for several seconds. His sudden appearance, his unusual clothing, and his evident distress startled her. Her instinct was to pick up her burlap sack and go home, but he was not a young man, and the heat was becoming oppressive. She couldn't walk away and leave him to faint on the sidewalk. Maybe she could find a glass of water, or someone who had come with him and could drive him home.

Jewel moved slightly on the wall, hoping to draw his attention. He put down his handkerchief, resting both hands on his knees and bowing his head. Jewel tried again. "Are you all right?" she asked in a shy voice.

He turned his head without lifting it and looked at her. She liked his face. It had a well-worn look, as if he had seen everything and could no longer be surprised. At the moment, he looked ill, but she could see smile lines around his dark eyes and in his cheeks above his gray beard. His voice was weak but clear, and the words were lightly stressed, as if he were more fluent in some other language. "Thank you, my friend, I think I am not quite well."

Jewel stood up. "Can I help you? Would you like some water, or did you come with someone?"

He nodded. "Yes, if you would. I am Fr. Nicholas, and there is a booth here—" he turned carefully and slowly lifted one arm to point into the crowded plaza behind them— "Do you see the booth with the blue roof? On the left? Four, or maybe five, booths up from the end?"

Jewel stood on the wall to get a better view. "Yes, I see it. There's one with a red roof right beside it, isn't there?"

"That's right. My church runs the blue booth each week."

Jewel jumped down from the wall and swung the straps of her bulging grocery sack awkwardly over her shoulder. "I'm going right now, and I'll bring someone to help you. Will you be alright here for a minute or two?"

He nodded without speaking, and she plunged into the crowd, holding her sack in front of her like a plow, dodging between elbows and strollers and people on cell phones. The distance seemed farther here in the pressing crowd than it had from her vantage point on the wall.

Reaching the booth, she paused. She could see several people inside, but she could not be sure which were in charge of the booth and which were visiting townspeople. As she hesitated, she heard a voice at her elbow saying kindly, "Can I help you?"

Jewel turned to see a blond woman, perhaps in her late forties, smiling and holding out her hand.

Jewel held out her own hand automatically. "Are you from this church?" she asked hopefully. "Do you know Fr. Nicholas?"

"I am, and I do," the woman smiled again. "My name is Anna. What can I do for you?"

"Oh, good," said Jewel, relieved. "I think he's sick. He sat down next to me on the wall down there, and he looks like he might faint."

Anna's expression changed immediately and she stepped quickly into the booth. "Xenia, can you hand me my purse? It's back there behind the table. I need to take Fr. Nicholas home. I wondered if he was well enough to come out in this heat."

Jewel heard what sounded like a snort from the interior of the booth, and a tall, dark-haired woman stepped out from behind a table. "It's a wonder he's not dead. Here, take some water. I'm sure he needs it." The tall woman thrust a purse and a bottle of water into Anna's hands and returned to her place inside the booth. Jewel realized she had been staring at the tall woman and stopped herself.

"Thank you, Xenia." Anna turned back to Jewel. "I'm so glad you came to find me. You lead and I'll make sure I don't lose you in this crowd," she said, and they made their way back to the wall as quickly as they could.

Fr. Nicholas was still sitting there with his head bowed. A few people stood near him on the sidewalk, watching him and whispering to each other. Jewel brushed past them with Anna beside her. Anna dropped down on her knees and laid her hand on Fr. Nicholas's shoulder.

"Fr. Nicholas, you look awful. Here," she offered him the water bottle. 'I've got this for you from Xenia, who says it's a wonder you aren't dead." This drew a faint chuckle from Fr. Nicholas. "I'm going to take you home now. Have a drink, and then we'll help you get up."

She rose to her feet and turned to Jewel. Jewel nodded in response to her unspoken question and stepped closer to Fr. Nicholas. When he set down the water bottle, he offered them his hands and let them help him to his feet. The whisperers on the sidewalk withdrew a few paces, still watching over their shoulders. Jewel frowned at them, and they withdrew again, dispersing into the crowd.

Fr. Nicholas was perhaps a head taller than Jewel. Copying Anna, she drew his arm around her shoulders, encouraging him to lean on her. He was a slender man, but exhaustion lent weight to his body and the heat added to their burdens.

"Come along," said Anna cheerfully. "My car isn't far, just a block or so from here. We can go nice and slow, and if you need to stop and put your head down, just squeeze my hand." She leaned forward to look past Fr. Nicholas at Jewel. "I'm so glad you came to find me. I'm sorry, but I didn't catch your name."

"My name is Jewel. It's nice to meet you, both of you." Jewel adjusted her grasp on Fr. Nicholas' arm and tilted her head to look at his face. "It's too bad you aren't feeling good on such a hot day. There isn't much shade here, except in the booths."

Fr. Nicholas smiled but did not attempt to answer her.

"He likes to go out and talk to people around the market," said Anna affectionately. "He knows almost everyone in the town, and their dogs, too. We're almost there now. See the blue Volvo up at the corner?"

Jewel nodded, feeling the trickle of sweat down her back. She could imagine how hot the sun felt to Fr. Nicholas in his black robe.

When they reached the car, Anna kept one arm around Fr. Nicholas while she unlocked the door, and then she and Jewel helped him into the front seat. He leaned back and closed his eyes, and Jewel stood quietly beside him with her hand resting on the open door, letting the hot air escape from the car while Anna went around and got in on the driver's side. Anna started the car, turning on the air conditioner full blast. After a moment, Fr. Nicholas opened his eyes.

"Thank you both," he said, "my old friend and my new friend. You have been very good to me." He sat up and reached for something from the outside pocket of Anna's purse, which was balanced on the console between the driver's seat and the passenger's seat. "You will not mind me taking this, for Jewel. Here," he reached out of the open door to hand Jewel a glossy red postcard. "This is our church. Come and see us. I would like you to come. Not everyone will show so much kindness to an old man who is a stranger. Bless you." He lifted his hand, the fingers bent, and traced a shaky cross in the hot air. "Bless you," he said again and closed the door.

Jewel stood on the sidewalk, clutching her burlap sack with one hand and the red postcard with the other, watching the car drive away.

Chapter 6

Jewel called Sara when she got home from the market and invited her to bring Clay along for dinner. "I'm going to make red carrot salad, and you can each have a slice of my personal watermelon. Oh, and there's chicken, too."

"Your personal watermelon?" Sara laughed. "Was it monogrammed?"

"There was a sign right next to it, and it said 'personal watermelon'. It's really cute. You should see it."

"If it's really cute, Clay will be able to swallow it whole without slicing it. We have a big watermelon here, so I'll bring that and my famous pasta salad with sundried tomatoes. That way you can have your personal watermelon all to yourself."

"Well, all right. I was going to make everything myself," said Jewel, disappointed.

"It's no trouble, sweetie. You know I like to help," said Sara comfortably.

"I like to help, too," persisted Jewel.

"Then I'll only bring the watermelon," said Sara. "Seriously, Clay loves watermelon, and we'll need more than just yours."

Jewel gave in and hung up, surprised at how much the conversation had irritated her. She had depended on Sara for most of her life, and she loved her more than any other living person. But Jewel had her own house now. It would have been nice to make the whole dinner by herself. Oh well. It would be a pity if Clay ran out of watermelon.

She browsed her shelf of cookbooks for a carrot salad recipe, couldn't find one, and decided to make one up. Sara would tell her if it wasn't any good. Clay would eat anything. She made her own pasta salad, a little guiltily, and unpacked the rotisserie chicken she had bought at the market. It didn't look as large when she thought of Clay eating it, and she added a basket of bread and a plate of butter to the table.

Sara and Clay knocked once and let themselves in, and there was the usual flurry of greetings and hugs.

"Hi there, neighbor!" Sarah hugged her, then put up an inquiring finger to touch Jewel's necklace. "Is that a new one? You made it, didn't you?"

"I do that now," said Jewel, secretly proud. "It's my new hobby."

"Good for you, honey. A hobby's a great idea."

Sara stopped to tighten her pony tail, and Clay held out an enormous watermelon to Jewel, a rueful smile on his face. Clay was an easy-going man with bright red hair, a beard, and perpetual grease stains around his finger nails. His Texas accent was exactly what you expected to hear coming out of his mouth, and if anything in life had ever upset him, Jewel had never heard of it. Clay's idea of dressing for dinner was to put on a clean T-shirt, but he was a welcome guest in her house because he happily ate whatever was put before him and said thank you like he meant it.

They sat down around Jewel's oak table in their accustomed places, Jewel passed the food around, and they started eating.

"Are these carrots in the salad?" asked Clay conversationally.

"Red carrots," said Jewel, "I got them at the market. Did you know there are yellow carrots, too? The man had all of them together on the table, red, orange, and yellow, with the green feathery part still on. It looked pretty."

"They're good," said Clay, taking another bite. "So's the chicken. It's great food, Jewel. Thanks for making dinner."

Jewel smiled at him, then turned to his wife. "How was your day, Sara?"

Sara laughed. "My day was fabulous. I went down to the beach this morning and had coffee at that ice cream shop. I brought a novel and sat there at one of those little tables on the sidewalk, drinking coffee and reading my book. Then I came home and napped half the afternoon. I love summer vacation!" She took a bite of the carrot salad. "Hmm. Not like regular carrots exactly, but not bad. What's the dressing?"

"I made it up," said Jewel. "Is it good or bad?"

Sara chewed meditatively. "Good. I would have put in more salt, but that probably means I'll have high blood pressure before you do. It's good, Jewel. You should write down the ingredients and make it your trademark dressing. When people ask you to bring something, you can always make a salad with this dressing."

Jewel frowned. "And who would these people be, the ones who are asking me to bring something?"

"Us, for one," retorted Sara, but her face softened. "Don't worry, sweetie. Look how far you've come. You needed some time to be by yourself. You'll start adding people back into your life any day now."

Clay nodded at her in a friendly way, adding his support to Sara's. A little silence fell, broken by the sounds of forks on plates and water glasses rising and settling back on the oak table.

"Speaking of people," Jewel said suddenly, "I met some at the market today." Seeing the looks of surprised interest on the faces of her friends, she hastily amended her statement. "I mean, it wasn't exactly meeting, not in a social way. But I was sitting on that little brick wall, down at the bottom of the plaza, enjoying the sights, when an older man suddenly sat down next to me, and I thought he was going to faint. He was wearing a long black robe, all the way to his ankles and with long sleeves, and he didn't have a hat or sunglasses."

"In this heat? No wonder he was about to faint," exclaimed Sara. "Why was he wearing a long black robe? Who was he?"

"I bet he was a priest," said Clay.

"Priests don't wear long black robes outside in the summer, do they?" asked Sara. "I teach at a Catholic school. I should know this."

"Catholics aren't the only ones who have priests," said Clay, with a little grin at his wife.

"Yes, exactly," said Jewel, recalling their attention to her story. She had a specific reason for wanting to tell it. "I found out later he was an Orthodox priest, but that's telling the story backwards, so just listen. He looked so unwell that I thought I should offer to help, and I asked him if there was someone who had come to the market with him who could take him home. His church has a booth at the market every week—"

"Do they sell things?" interrupted Sara, "or is it like a mission?"

"I don't know," said Jewel, "I wasn't paying attention to that. I went to the booth and found a woman named Anna, and she came back with me, and we almost carried Fr. Nicholas all the way to her car. When he was leaving, he gave me a little card with information about their church, and I think he gave me a blessing, too."

"For helping him out, I'm sure. That was nice of you, Jewel. Do you have the card? Is that how you found out he was Orthodox?" Sara, ever curious, held out her hand as Jewel got up to bring the postcard from where she had laid it on the kitchen counter. Sara glanced at the picture and flipped it over, reading the back.

"This is only about fifteen minutes from here. Who knew? We go to the big Greek festival at the church downtown most years, but I didn't realize there were other Orthodox churches around here." Sara handed the postcard to Clay, who flipped it back over to look at the picture on the front.

"The picture looks like something from a museum," observed Jewel.

"Maybe it's something they have hanging in the church," suggested Clay.

"Oh, probably," said Sara enthusiastically. "You should see the big church downtown. Huge mosaics, covering entire walls. It's very colorful. Not your standard pews-and-pulpit type church at all."

"He invited me to come to his church," Jewel told them, watching their faces.

"That was nice," said Clay.

"You should go," said Sara eagerly. "You might meet some nice people. Here's your chance to get asked to make your famous carrot salad."

"Do you think so?" asked Jewel.

"Sure, why not?" Clay smiled at her and handed her the postcard. "You're as nice as everyone else is."

Jewel had a feeling this was not quite the point. "I'm not really a church person, am I?" She looked intently at Sara, uncertain whether she was hoping Sara would agree with her.

"What's a church person?" Sara laughed. "Look at me! I teach at a Catholic school, so does that make me a church person? I'm right here eating dinner at your house, so if I'm a church person, you must be one, too."

Jewel smiled faintly. "Well, I just meant that I haven't been to a church in...have I ever been to one? Maybe when my mom was alive?"

Sara thought for a moment. "You got me. I have no idea if you've ever been to church. You weren't Catholic, so you never came with me, back in the day. You could come with us now, if you wanted to. We don't go all the time, but we do go some of the time."

Jewel hesitated, remembering her childish jealousy of Sara's church friends with their plaid school jumpers, slumber parties, and reliable parents. She shook her head. "No, thank you, I'm still not a Catholic, but it's nice of you to offer, Sara." She felt awkward, no longer willing to confide the trend of her thoughts. She was off balance, out of tune with her well-intentioned friends. She would think it all over later, after they had gone. Rising from the table, she gathered their empty plates and headed into the kitchen, saying over her shoulder, "Let's take that watermelon outside so you two can have a seed-spitting contest."

Clay and Sara began to laugh, their eyes meeting across the table. Jewel stacked the dishes by the kitchen sink and went to open the sliding glass door. She wished there were not quite so much watermelon. The thought of sitting next to her happily married friends while they ate it and joked over it, one piece at a time, made her tired.

Chapter 7

Eight days later, Jewel crept into the church of Fr. Nicholas and Anna. The heavy door closed behind her, creaking and sighing. A few steps away from the door, Jewel saw a wide marble shelf built into an alcove in the wall. Rectangular wooden boxes filled with sand bloomed with beeswax candles tipped in clear, smokeless flame. Pictures like the one on her postcard were propped against the wall behind the candles. Jewel tiptoed closer, gazing at the warm colors and distinctive faces through the flickering glow of the flames.

As she stood there, a solemn little boy with a blue bowtie came up next to her. He picked a candle from a basket on a low table nearby and raised himself on tiptoe to touch the wick to a candle flame on the shelf above him. When he was satisfied that his candle was lighted, he pushed the wax end down into the sand and crossed himself, round forehead, chubby tummy, small shoulders. Jewel withdrew to one side as his parents came up beside her. Another family came after them, a young woman with long blond hair and a long dress, who looked just like her mother, and a thin boy with glasses, who looked just like his father. Secure in her chronic belief that she was mostly invisible, Jewel stared at them intently, observing each detail of their appearance and actions as they came to light their candles. She noted the mother's arm around her daughter's shoulders and the way the father bent his head to hear a whispered comment from his son. All four of them looked neat and comfortable, as if they were in their proper place here. They moved away in a group, and Jewel saw them open the door into the sanctuary, a glass door set in a glass wall.

For the moment, she was alone. She took a quick step, reached for a candle from the basket, and stood perfectly still, touching the wick to the flame of someone else's candle, waiting for it to light. Then she pushed the wax end down into the sand. Her eyes rested on the pictures again. The heat of the candle flames reached up to touch her cheeks. Hearing the creaking door open behind her, she moved away from the candles and went to peer through the glass wall at the sanctuary, now more than half full of people. They were all standing, and Jewel could hear their voices through the glass. *I run to you, O Lord. Teach me to please you, for you are my God.* It was singing, but something about it was slightly foreign. The melody did not resolve itself into the customary phrasing of western music. It seemed to flow on and on, one line dissolving into the next, as if it were not a song at all, but a conversation.

Jewel took a deep breath. It would be silly to come all the way up to the door and run home like a rabbit without ever going in. She opened the door and stepped inside. A few feet away, against the glass wall at the back of the sanctuary, she saw an empty chair. She tiptoed over to it, sat down, and then stood up because everyone else was standing. She felt something brush her elbow and turned nervously. The tall, dark-haired woman from the Summer Market booth was standing there with a printed program and a book, pressing them against Jewel's arm to get her attention.

"Oh! Thank you," whispered Jewel, setting her purse on the chair behind her and accepting the book and program with two hands.

The tall woman took the book back from her and flipped it open. She rested a firm finger at the top of a page. "Here," she whispered. "Just follow along, and when you don't know what's happening, check the program." She stepped away before Jewel could thank her again, going back through the glass doors into the lobby.

Jewel slipped the program between the pages of the book and began to read, skimming down a few lines until she found words that matched what the people around her were singing. She turned the page, reading along, concentrating, and then turned another page. After a few minutes, she closed the book. The effort to follow the words was distracting. She wanted to listen and let her eyes wander around the room, examining the faces of the people near her and of those pictured on large golden panels around the walls. She heard bells and saw Fr. Nicholas standing at the front of the room in a sumptuously embroidered robe, swinging a brass censor toward the people, who bowed their heads toward him. She saw the puffs of smoke drift with the motion of the censor. Incense. She opened her mouth a little, breathing in, tasting the fragrant air.

Behind the glass doors, Xenia stood with her handful of programs. Five more minutes, and she would lay the rest on the table by the door. People who came in this late could pick up their own programs. She glanced toward the door, then toward the candles. Her eyes snapped back to the solitary figure of the young woman at the back of the church. Xenia noticed that she was no longer following the service in the book. Gave up already, apparently. Still, she did not look restless. Xenia watched her turning her head from side to side, leaning a little to the left, perhaps to see up the center aisle. Something about her was vaguely familiar, but Xenia couldn't place her.

Anna did not see Jewel until the service was over. She and George were making their way slowly to the back of the church, nodding and smiling at their friends, when Anna glanced ahead and saw Jewel, the girl who helped her rescue Fr. Nicholas, sitting on a chair near the door. Jewel's eyes were on the flood of people surging through the doors into the narthex. She seemed to be waiting for the doorway to clear. No one was talking to her, and she did not appear to be seeking anyone's attention.

Anna let go of her husband's hand. "Go find us some food and a seat, George. I'll be right with you. I see that girl who helped me with Fr. Nicholas at the market..." Her voice trailed off as she parted from George, plunged through the current in front of the door, and landed beside Jewel on the other side.

Anna laid a friendly hand on Jewel's shoulder. Jewel started and looked up at her. "I'm Anna, Jewel. Do you remember me from the Summer Market? You helped me rescue Fr. Nicholas."

Jewel pulled the strap of her purse over her shoulder and stood up. "Oh. Oh, yes, I remember. He must be feeling better now." She glanced over her shoulder toward the altar.

"He is. It was just the heat, and he had been sick the week before and wasn't really well enough to be there yet. But he does love to go." Anna began to move toward the door, and from politeness, Jewel followed her, not able to break away until the conversation was complete. They pressed through a gap in the crowd and found themselves in the narthex, not far from the alcove where Jewel had lit a candle.

Jewel settled the strap of her purse more securely on her shoulder. Her eyes strayed toward the door.

"Come and eat with us," invited Anna, pointing toward a double door that opened into a large fellowship hall. "We have a meal and coffee, and you could say hello to Fr. Nicholas. He was really touched by your kindness to him. My husband George is here with me. You can sit with us."

Jewel's eyes darted from Anna's face to the fellowship hall. "Oh, no, thank you, I think I need to go home. But it was nice." She blushed a little. "The service, I mean. It was very interesting."

"I'm glad you liked it," said Anna, smiling. "Come back and see us again soon. It's good to have you here." She pressed Jewel's hand and let her go. Jewel's step slowed for just a moment as she passed the alcove. Then she disappeared through the creaking door. It closed behind her with a sigh.

Chapter 8

"Fr. Nicholas?" Anna poked her head around the door of his office and smiled at him when he looked up from the book he had been reading. "It's good to see you looking so well again. May I come in for a minute? I wanted to let you know what we're doing about the robes for the altar boys."

"Yes, yes, come in." Fr. Nicholas came hastily around the desk, setting a chair for her with old-fashioned gallantry. Anna sat down on the edge of the chair, resting a pile of folded robes on her lap, and Fr. Nicholas went back to his seat behind the desk.

"The altar boys looked like scarecrows last Sunday, my dear. I'm glad to hear you are going to do something for them. What is the plan?"

"The robes are in good condition, but most of them are too big for the boys who are currently serving," Anna explained. "I went back there this morning and sorted the whole collection. I've set aside some of the bigger robes because we do have one or two older boys who serve, but I'm taking these four home to hem. They've been using masking tape and pins, probably thinking that a permanent hem is a waste when the boys will only be growing larger. But if I just tack the fabric in place, the stitches can easily be snipped out later."

"And then the robes won't be longer on one side than the other," finished Fr. Nicholas. "Could you do something about the sleeves, do you think?"

Anna nodded. "Good idea. It would reduce the number of near misses with candle flames."

"Yes, that is what I am thinking. Thank you for taking care of this." Fr. Nicholas leaned back in his chair and rested his hands behind his head, as he always did when he wanted to talk. Anna settled herself into the chair.

"How are you, Anna? What is happening in your life?"

"I'm well, Father. Thank you for asking. Nothing much is happening in my life, or at least nothing particularly new. We spent a week at Lake Chelan at the beginning of the summer, and George got a good rest. I like to get him away from the university right at the end of the school year. As soon as his grades are in, we escape!" She smiled, thinking of George at Lake Chelan, asleep on a deck chair in the middle of the day.

"And you? What are you doing, aside from what you do for George? He is a lucky man."

"He knows it, too," said Anna saucily. After a moment, her face sobered. "I'm doing a little of this and a little of that. I'm feeling restless again. I know I shouldn't be. I'm grateful for my blessings."

"Take on something new," suggested Fr. Nicholas. "In fact, I will tell you about a new project of mine, and maybe you could think of some way to help me with it."

Anna looked doubtful. "I always have plenty of projects, Father. They just don't seem to fill the void."

Fr. Nicholas nodded understandingly. "I will not press you if you are not interested, but let me tell you about it before you decide."

"Fair enough," said Anna. "I'm listening."

Fr. Nicholas folded his hands on the desk in front of him, leaning forward. "Everyone is lonely," he said. "In the world, I see it wherever I look. It fills me with sadness. I see it here at church, too. There are groups of friends, but on the edges, there are people who come and go alone. Nobody attaches to them, and they attach to nobody. Why does this happen? Are they difficult people? Do they prefer to keep to themselves for some reason? Sometimes I ask the parish council to consider it, but it is not a problem to solve with policy, I think. So instead, I have decided to ask some of my parishioners to help. I have asked three or four people, and some are already making a start. What I have in mind is for you, if you are willing, to come up with a shared activity that could be used as an excuse to meet regularly, perhaps once a month. And then to go out into the hedgerows and invite the lonely people to join you in doing it. For example, one gentleman has decided he will start a formal grounds crew for the church property. Before, the parish council took turns mowing and the gardens had to fend for themselves. But this man likes gardening, and he has invited two other men to help him. One has been coming to church for only six weeks, and the other has come for years but never talks to anyone. The silent one was in the forestry service before he retired, and he has already started work on the trees around our property."

"Did the man who invited him know he was a forester?" asked Anna, interested.

"No, it was a surprise to him. He asked him because he could see he was lonely. It makes me wonder what other surprises await us," Fr. Nicholas said eagerly. "Now, I know you are a good hostess. I have been to wonderful parties at your house. You are comfortable with people, and you are comfortable at church. Would you consider starting a group? You must give them a task. Shared work always breaks the ice."

Anna was silent, thinking it over.

"You have a soft spot, Anna, for lost lambs," said Fr. Nicholas. "It might fill the void, for a time at least."

"I like the idea very much, Father, but I'm trying to think what I would have them do. I can think of several people to ask, but I think they're mostly lonely because other people find them difficult, as you were saying."

"Something will come to you," said Fr. Nicholas confidently. He stood up, seeing she was ready to go. "I will look forward to hearing what it is." He held out his hand, and she kissed it.

"Thank you for thinking of me, Father," she said. "I'll do my best to come up with something." She started toward the door, then turned back to him. "Did you see Jewel on Sunday? Your rescuer from the

Summer Market? She came. She was all the way at the back, and I only talked to her for a few minutes before she ran away. But she did come."

"I did not see her!" exclaimed Fr. Nicholas with genuine regret. "I will pray she comes again."

"She's one of your lonely ones, I suspect," mused Anna.

"Then you must ask her to join your group," said Fr. Nicholas triumphantly, and Anna laughed, accepting her mission with good grace.

Chapter 9

Jewel did not go to church the next week. She meant to go, but Sara and Clay invited her to go to the lavender festival on the Olympic Peninsula, and she couldn't refuse the invitation without explaining that she had somewhere else to be. They went every July, and Jewel had gone with them for the past two years. They knew she had no life. If Jewel said she couldn't come, Sara would wonder why. So Jewel went to the lavender festival, making no mention of where else she might have been. For now, the church was a secret, a place where no one knew anything about her, a world with no past.

The following week, Jewel went to church. She arrived earlier this time and walked through the door with greater confidence. She lit a candle and was just turning toward the sanctuary when the young woman with the braid and her mother seemed to rise up out of the floor in front of her. They stood side by side, with their identical braids draped across their shoulders, wearing crisp cotton sundresses that covered their shoulders and almost reached their ankles. They smiled at her, and Jewel realized with a crinkle of nerves that they were about to speak to her. So much for her invisibility.

"Good morning," said the mother, with a pleasant smile. "Welcome to our church. I'm Mrs. Edon, and this is my daughter, Dorothy. Did you get a program?"

She held one out to Jewel, and Jewel took it with a little bob of her head.

Dorothy smiled at her also. "I'm in college at the U. Do you live around here?"

Jewel nodded again, her mind unaccountably blank. She glanced from one to the other, making her own lips smile a little. Dorothy's eyes were blue, and her cheeks were as smooth as rose petals. Jewel noted the real pearl necklace and earrings she wore. Unoriginal design, but stunningly good quality. She made a little sound in her throat and pointed to Dorothy's necklace. "Those are beautiful," she said, making conversation.

"My pearls?" Dorothy's fingers touched them lightly. "Thank you. They were a gift from my parents when I turned sixteen." She glanced toward her mother, and a smile passed between them. Jewel's face began to feel stiff.

"We're going in now," said Mrs. Edon. "Would you like to come with us? I think my husband and son are already inside."

Jewel did not want to sit with them. She wanted to sit by herself. "Thank you, that would be nice," she said.

"I'll stand next to you and point out where we are in the book," said Dorothy, smiling at her again. "It's a lot of flipping back and forth if you aren't used to it."

Jewel bobbed her head at Dorothy and followed her through the glass door. They walked around to the right side of the church and found seats near the front. The father and son were there, and they shifted one seat to the left to make room for Jewel at the end of the row. They stared at her curiously until Mrs. Edon gave her husband a look, widening her eyes and lifting her brows, after which he leaned forward to nod at Jewel. The son was reading something in the back of the prayer book, his nose wrinkled up to hold his glasses in place. He took no notice of Jewel or, perhaps, of anything outside the book.

"Here," Dorothy whispered, putting a book into Jewel's hands and then opening it and turning several pages awkwardly, trying not to bump Jewel with her arm as she did so. "This is where we are. I'll let you know when you need to turn to the back for the apolitikion and things."

Jewel wondered what an apolitikion was. She stared in front of her and saw a red straw hat on the head of an older woman. The woman's hair was coiled in a neat chignon under the hat. Two large men sat on either side of her. Jewel couldn't see much beyond the hat. She pretended to focus on the book in her hands, uncomfortably conscious of Dorothy chanting from memory beside her. *She's going to see if I put my book down. She'll think I'm not paying attention. I don't want her watching me. I want to be by myself and do what I want. Why couldn't I stop myself from sitting with them?* Jewel's fingers rubbed nervously around the cover of the prayer book, making it quiver. Dorothy glanced at her questioningly. Jewel tightened her finger joints, commanding herself to be still.

The service was longer than she remembered. Dorothy helped her find every song and cued her standing and sitting. Mrs. Edon smiled and nodded. She seemed pleased. Jewel couldn't focus on the service. She felt lost in a sea of unfamiliar words, never quite able to predict when Dorothy would pounce on her with instructions. Jewel wanted to go home.

As the service ended, Dorothy leaned toward her and whispered, "We have a nice brunch now in the fellowship hall. The food is mostly homemade, and it's always good. Would you like to join us?"

Jewel was ready for her. "Thank you, and thank you for your kindness during the service, but I have to be somewhere in half an hour, so I'll have to go now." She stood up, clutching her purse, prepared for a quick escape.

Mrs. Edon reached around Dorothy to shake Jewel's hand. Jewel shook hands quickly, feeling herself begin to smile and nod again. She sidled out of the row of chairs, saying goodbye, and made her way to the back of the sanctuary, where she encountered the crowded doorway and felt herself caught. She ran her eyes over the crowd, looking for an opening, and there was Anna, directly in front of her. Anna had gotten her out before, and for some reason, it seemed natural to touch her arm, to ask for her attention.

Anna's face lit with a welcoming smile. "Jewel! I'm so glad to see you again. I looked for you when I came in, but you must have been seated already."

Jewel's face assumed a cautious expression. "Oh, yes, some people invited me to sit with them." Her hand waved vaguely behind her. "I'm going home now. I just saw you, and—" She stopped, realizing she was about to confess that she wanted help getting out the door. Anna had already drawn her into the current. They floated through the door and the current dropped them near the alcove again, as it had done before. Jewel kept her back to the people flowing by behind her. She didn't want to see Dorothy and her mother again.

"I'm glad you saw me," said Anna. "How was your week?"

"It was nice," said Jewel. "Did you have a nice week?"

Anna laughed. "I did, thank you. Nothing unusual happened, but there's no harm in that." She smiled, and Jewel smiled back, fascinated by her gracious air.

"Did you see Fr. Nicholas this time?" asked Anna, after a short pause. "He was so sad to have missed you last time you were here."

"Oh, no, I didn't," Jewel frowned slightly, not sure how she would go about seeing Fr. Nicholas. Everyone surged around him at the end of the service. She still had his postcard in her purse, but she wasn't going to stand around trying to make conversation with

Dorothy for all the time it took to make it through the line to speak to him.

"You know, I'm noticing your lovely jewelry," said Anna, recalling Jewel's attention to the conversation. "It looks handmade and quite original."

Jewel felt a tingle of excitement. "Thank you," she said. "I made it. I make jewelry. It's not my job," she added, correcting any false impression. "It's what I like to do."

"Oh, that's wonderful! I would love to be so creative. Did you design it, too?"

"Yes," said Jewel, feeling her face grow warm. Her fingers moved along the intricate beading at her throat, lifting the necklace a little so Anna could see it better. Anna reached out her hand and touched the necklace delicately with one finger. Then she clasped her hands together and drew in a breath as if an idea had just occurred to her.

"Jewel," said Anna confidentially, bending her head toward Jewel and lowering her voice. "I'm starting a little group, just four or five women from church. We're going to bring our knitting, or any craft project we like, and we're going to meet once a month to work on our projects and spend time together. I think I'll make it a dessert potluck. Would you come? I would love to have you. It would be so interesting to see more of your work, and to get to know you better."

Jewel blinked at her. A personal invitation to join a group of Anna's friends and do craft projects together.

And all because Anna thought her jewelry was beautiful. Jewel felt a shock of delight, followed by a prick of doubt. "Really?" She heard her voice say the ridiculous word before she could stop it. Her face flushed. "I mean," she shook her head slightly, clearing her brain. "I mean, thank you."

"No, really," said Anna, almost urgently, "I'm quite serious. I want you to come. We don't live very far from here. Look, I'll give you my card, and you can call me if you need directions." She smiled ruefully. "I used to give people directions automatically, but everyone uses GPS or MapQuest these days."

There was something about Anna's smile that inspired an answering smile in Jewel. Anna sounded serious. She might actually want Jewel to come. Jewel held out her hand for Anna's card, a tastefully feminine visiting card printed on thick, cream-colored stock. Jewel felt a twinge of awe.

"I could come," Jewel realized. "It sounds very nice, Anna. Thank you for inviting me. I want to come."

Chapter 10

From her kitchen window, Anna could see the lake, a sparkling sapphire reminding her of its presence with flashes of reflected sunlight. It was her favorite view from any window in the house, the glimmering water beyond the stretch of woods that bordered the grassy lawn. A yellow seaplane bustled into view like a noisy guest, seeming to graze the treetops in its eagerness to make a bumptious landing on the rippling blue. Anna sighed unconsciously and turned her attention to the pile of clean china and crystal slowly accumulating on the drain board beside her. She began on the silverware, her thoughts drawn away from the sunlit lake by the familiar pleasure of touching these old treasures, dinged and polished with age, wearing their rose blossom pattern with the jaunty grace of an old woman who has never forgotten her dancing days.

Turning to pick up a linen tea towel to dry some of the more fragile dishes, Anna saw herself reflected in fragments all over the kitchen. Her head and shoulders appeared in the glass doors of the hanging cupboards. Her slim figure, grossly inflated, rolled across the shiny steel breadbox. Her pale khaki skirt showed dimly on the glass window in the oven door. Only her feet were absent from this distorted body that could only move its parts in weird independence of each other, simultaneous but not coherent.

Anna's mind evolved a meaning for this kitchen metaphor as she returned to her dish board. *A broken body*, she mused, placing a dry crystal goblet on the counter and reaching for another, *or a body that only appears broken because you aren't looking at the body itself but only at the way it's reflected by the distorting surfaces around it*. She placed the second goblet on the table and picked up a third. *I know*, she thought, *the body is only alive when it's whole, so this is a metaphor for spiritual wholeness…the parts make no sense alone but only in relation to each other*. She set the third goblet down. *Or it's just a bunch of reflections that have no other meaning at all*.

It was a habit of hers, to work smoothly and competently at her task while her mind traveled miles away from her surroundings and her face wore its habitual expression of gracious serenity. For Anna, the inner world was sometimes more real than its visible counterpart.

Anna presented the appearance of a fortunate woman, no longer in her first youth, but wearing time lightly, like a shawl she might lay aside, if she chose. Her bright hair had faded to a tasteful ash-blond. Creases showed in the corners of her gray-blue eyes and stood like parentheses around her smooth pink lips, but a little makeup, skillfully applied, could still do wonders. The khaki skirt and white blouse she wore this afternoon were like the rest of her clothes, conservative and well made, attractive in a quiet way.

George saw to it that she had real jewelry, even for casual occasions, and she tried to wear it regularly, to please him.

Anna's house looked well-dressed, too. Wherever the eye wandered, it fell on a pleasant scene of domestic comfort and unpretentious elegance: polished wood, pristine glass, crimson or blue upholstery accented with gold brocaded cushions. Green philodendron trailed heart-shaped leaves from window sills and occasional tables, its tendrils interspersed sometimes with candles or small statuary. In one corner of the living room, a single, hand-painted icon of the Holy Theotokos and the Infant Jesus hung above a small dresser on which stood a red pillar candle that matched the robe and lettering in the icon and was always lit when Anna was at home. The other paintings on Anna's walls were signed by personal friends and lent a charming novelty to an otherwise conventional atmosphere. The house smelled faintly of rose petals and cinnamon, lemon soap and furniture polish.

Anna knew that to her friends and George's colleagues, her life was acceptable, even enviable. Yet she had not realized how quickly time would pass for her, how quickly she would be beyond the age of easily resisting the strength of the familiar, beyond the age when her whole life still lay ahead of her, ready to be shaped to any dream she chose. She had not realized that she would reach her forty-seventh birthday, as she had this month, and find herself still filling up her days with whatever stood in front of her, still diverting her attention to George and his career until she could figure out what she wanted to focus on in her own life. George periodically suggested that she hire household help, and Anna always replied that she liked the ritual of her domestic efforts. Now, in her secret soul, she suspected herself of clinging to these little tasks to frame the hours of her life in purposeful activity. Sometimes she permitted herself to wonder what might come to take their place if only she could make up her mind to go looking for it.

The telephone rang. She lifted the receiver and heard her own gracious telephone voice saying, "Hello?" as her mind returned to the evening at hand.

"Hello yourself. It's Xenia. Are you still going through with this tonight?" Xenia clearly was not using her gracious telephone voice.

"The other ladies are coming at seven, Xen. You know I'd love to have you here. There ought to be at least one person who actually knows how to knit!" She laughed lightly.

"Well, it certainly won't be you!" Xenia snapped. "I don't know what possessed you to start a knitting circle, but I'll come and help you." There was a pause. "Shall I bring cookies, or something?"

"Bring your ginger cookies, if you have time to make them," said Anna, tactfully. "Or if you don't, just bring some other light dessert that's easy to pick up on your way here."

"I will," said Xenia, and hung up.

Anna made herself a salad and a cup of soup, and ate her dinner in snatches as she set the dining room table for a dessert buffet and placed the tea things on the kitchen counter. She had sent George off to the Seattle Tennis Club for a few matches and a late dinner with a longtime friend. He would enjoy that far more than lurking in the den while his house filled up with church women.

Xenia arrived before the others, letting herself in the front door and calling to Anna as she walked through the entryway into the kitchen. She kicked off her shoes as she came and set a Delft-blue china platter of ginger cookies on the dining room table before turning to give Anna a fierce hug of greeting.

Xenia was only seven years older than Anna, but Anna often felt herself to be decades younger than her friend. Anna knew what little of Xenia's story Xenia was willing to tell, and she knew some of the older women at church remembered it, but to the younger generation, Xenia was a puzzle with no solution, a source of endless energy, a tower of stamina in all good causes, and a vortex of thinly veiled rage. Anna remembered the first years of her friendship with Xenia, the years when she believed that the sharp edges of Xenia's nature were the effects of grief. Xenia was a young widow then. It was natural that her pain should still be raw and unmanageable. But the longer Anna knew Xenia, the more she began to sense some other emotion mingled in the pain, some darker force that would not let the wound begin to heal.

Anna emerged from Xenia's hug with a smile, brushing her hair back into place automatically and glancing up at her friend's face. "Thank you for the cookies. I have a lovely strawberry cheesecake George brought home for me, and some of the other women have promised to contribute, so we should do very well."

Xenia seated herself on a bar stool by the counter with surprising grace, folded her hands, and inquired resignedly, "What other women? Whom did you invite?"

Anna perched on the other bar stool. "Well, Fr. Nicholas asked me to seek out a few people I thought would welcome a chance to—to belong, to be part of a group. A few turned me down, but there are four who told me they were coming. And another person who thinks he would like to join us also."

Xenia raised her eyebrows. "He?"

Anna nodded. "Do you know Timothy Paulson, the chanter? Brown hair, glasses, probably in his early thirties?"

"Timothy knits?"

"I don't know," Anna replied doubtfully, "but why else would he want to join? He was very polite about it. He overheard me inviting someone else, and he stopped me in the parking lot to ask if he could join us. He said he expected it was meant to be a women's gathering, but he thought that might be because most men don't knit. He said that of course it should be our decision, but he asked me to put forward his name because he wants to join us if he would be welcome."

Xenia almost snorted. "Oh, *Timothy*. I know who that is. Well, it's a little odd for a man to join a women's group, but I doubt it'll make any difference if he's present or absent. He never opens his mouth."

"You may be right," said Anna, after a moment, "but I'm going to honor his request and ask the other ladies to confirm that they would be comfortable having a man present."

Xenia made a face indicating that she didn't think a speechless knitter was a "man" worthy of the name, but she refrained from further comment, smoothing the countertop with her hands for a few moments before asking, "Who are the women you know are coming?"

"Elizabeth, and Barbara, too, of course, and also Jewel, whom you might not remember. She was the one who came to get me when Fr. Nicholas was ill at the Summer Market. She hasn't been coming to church for more than a month." Anna got up to turn on the burner under the tea kettle and switch on the coffee maker.

"Elizabeth and Barbara, Elizabeth and Barbara. Wherever Elizabeth leads, Barbara follows," remarked Xenia.

Anna smiled. "I think it's sweet, Xen. Barbara's such an introverted person, and Elizabeth is so comforting. She grandmothers everyone who crosses her path.”

“So Elizabeth bear-leading Barbara, Timothy the man-knitter, Jewel who I don’t know from Adam, and who is the fourth woman?” inquired Xenia, pushing out her stool and standing up.

“Dorothy,” said Anna meekly.

“Ah, yes. Miss Sanctimonious herself. What a crew. I wonder if it’s safe to let us all have knitting needles. The temptation to stab each other might overwhelm us.” Xenia’s laughter always came suddenly and ended before the listener could believe it had happened at all. Within seconds, she was frowning. “Is there a St. Dorothy?”

“I think she’s named for Dorotheos of Gaza, the ascetic.” Anna lifted the whistling kettle from the burner and began to fill her china teapots.

“She *would* be!”

“Would be what? Named for an ascetic?”

“You know what I mean,” Xenia persisted. “She’s just like her mother. Holier than the priest. I doubt her feet even touch the ground when she walks. A plain old saint wouldn’t be good enough for her.”

“She’s twenty, Xen. We all took life too seriously at that age, didn’t we?” Anna hesitated. “Besides, from what I remember, Dorotheos was more interested in Christian community than in being holier than the priest.”

"Ten to one, she doesn't know that," said Xenia, unconvinced. "Or she thinks he didn't mean it!" And with this parting shot, she moved into the dining room, where she rearranged everything on the table, a little absently, as if her mind were elsewhere. Anna watched her, resigned, after years of friendship, to Xenia's chronic inability to let things be.

The doorbell rang.

"Here they come," said Anna, giving the counter a swipe with the towel before heading to the door. "Could you turn on a little quiet music for me, Xen? In the living room?"

Xenia left the dining room table to its fate and went purposefully up the two steps into the living room, reaching it just as Anna reached the front door and opened it.

Jewel stood on the flagstone porch, the overhead light gleaming on her chic black hair and flicking the tiny diamond on a fragile silver chain at her throat. In one hand, she held a plate of lemon bars evenly dusted with powdered sugar. In the other, she carried a flat, rectangular case made of red leather with a silver clasp. Anna wondered fleetingly what it was before she reached out her hand for the lemon bars and said, "Welcome, Jewel. I'm so glad you could come. These look delicious. Come right in, and we'll put them on the table."

Jewel stepped into the front hall and closed the door carefully behind herself. Anna had gone a few steps further, to place the lemon bars next to Xenia's cookies, and was just turning back to Jewel when a vigorous rendition of Stravinsky's *Firebird* burst from the adjacent room, followed by Xenia, looking satisfied with her choice. The music was so loud and startling that Anna could think of no tactful way to respond to it. "Xenia!" she shouted, waving her hands frantically. "Find something else! And turn it down, quick!"

Jewel's eyes followed Xenia's flight back into the living room, then returned to Anna's flustered face. The music ended as suddenly as it had begun.

Anna laughed, a little breathlessly, and brushed her hair back from her face. "Where were we?" she asked Jewel apologetically.

Jewel directed a cautious glance toward the living room. "Shall I put my case in there? Is that where we will be meeting?"

The opening notes of a piano concerto on low volume sounded from the living room.

"Yes, you can go right in and find a comfortable spot," said Anna, with relief. "I thought we'd work for a while and then relax while we have our dessert."

The doorbell rang again, so Anna turned away to answer it while Jewel found a sofa corner next to an end table with a good lamp.

Elizabeth and Barbara had arrived together. They came through the door like an ocean wave, floating along on Elizabeth's warm laugh, hugging their hostess at almost the same moment, and then receding into the dining room to deposit two plates of brownies and some cup custards on the table before surging into the living room and coming to rest, side by side, on the red sofa at the far end of the room, near the icon.

Dorothy came next, a bright expectancy written on her face, her long honey-blond braid and full-skirted sundress swinging with every step. She handed Anna a sweating jar of homemade rosemary lemonade, hugged her affectionately, and, glancing over Anna's shoulder, saw Jewel sitting in the sofa corner by the lamp. Bringing her wide blue gaze back to Anna's face, she offered, "I'll keep an eye on Jewel for you. I'm not shy, and she doesn't really know anyone, does she?" Watching Dorothy cross the rug and sit down next to Jewel with a friendly smile, Anna brushed away a flash of uneasiness at the idea of Dorothy gathering under her wing a woman who was likely ten years her senior and a stranger.

Anna slipped into the kitchen for a glass of cold water and a moment to collect her thoughts before returning to the living room to begin the evening's business. She paused on the threshold to take stock, wondering how what had seemed a graceful arrangement of furniture could look so disjointed when all her guests were seated on it. *Should I have escorted them in one by one?* she wondered. *Or is it just because they're all so different from each other?*

The room looked fractured, resembling a series of individual encampments more than a single group met for a single purpose. Xenia, seated in the red and gold overstuffed chair to Anna's left, had already begun to knit, and her lap and her mind were wholly occupied by a copious turquoise shawl. Her needles clicked and her lips murmured the stitch count. She glanced up at intervals to survey the other guests, but she made no attempt to talk to them. Elizabeth and Barbara each held a workbag on her lap, but their heads were turned away from the room as they admired the icon on the wall behind them and waited for Anna to give the sign to begin. Jewel sat in her sofa corner with her hands folded on the red case in her white linen lap and her feet flat on the floor. Her eyebrows were slightly lifted and her eyes slightly dilated as she listened to Dorothy making cheerful conversation that seemed to require no response.

Anna stepped fully into the room and seated herself in the chair that matched Xenia's. She felt the smooth brocade under her palms as she rested them on the arms of the chair, and she realized her hands were empty. She had forgotten to provide some handwork for herself, the woman who hosted a knitting group but did not know how to knit.

"Let's get started, shall we?" Anna began, and the conversations ceased as all eyes turned to her. She folded her hands together in her lap and made herself smile. "Thank you all for coming and helping me to get this group started. I hope we'll have many happy evenings together and make many beautiful things. I thought we could open with a little prayer for our time together, and then I'd like each of you to introduce yourself to the group. Some of you know each other, but some of you don't, and it's always nice to start fresh in a new setting. But before we do that, Elizabeth, would you lead us in a prayer?" She had chosen Elizabeth instinctively, because she was the oldest woman present and the least likely to be nonplussed by the request.

"Certainly," said Elizabeth, getting to her feet. "Let's all stand and look to this beautiful icon Anna has here while we pray." She turned to the icon as she spoke, crossing herself, and began to pray in her warm, Southern voice. She spoke unhurriedly, as if her words were rosary beads and she gave each a little polish, pronouncing it fully, before counting it over on the string. "In the name of the Father, and of the Son, and of the Holy Spirit. O blessed Christ our God, be with us here in this welcoming home. Open us to your love as we enjoy fellowship with one another. We offer you our grateful thanks for the good food and good conversation we are about to enjoy. Amen!" She lifted her hand to her lips and kissed her fingers to the icon as they all echoed "Amen."

When everyone was seated again, Anna continued. "Thank you, Elizabeth. I want to say a little about our purpose here, and then we'll get started with our introductions. As you know, Fr. Nicholas has been encouraging the parish to make opportunities for fellowship outside the church setting. Our knitting group is an attempt to meet this goal. I hope we will enjoy our time together, especially as we grow to know each other better." She shifted in her chair, glancing around at their listening faces. "And now, let's get to know each other. When it's your turn, tell us your name and who you were named for, what you do for a living, and one thing you'd like to share about why you're here. I'll get us started. My name is Anna, and when I was baptized, I took the name of St. Anna, the mother of the Theotokos. You might say I don't have a 'real' job, but I keep busy with volunteer work and friends, and with looking after our home. I don't actually know how to knit, but I'm looking forward to spending time with all of you. Now Dorothy," she said, turning to her right, "you're next."

Dorothy sat forward on the sofa, flipping her braid back over her shoulder. "I'm Dorothy, and I'm named for Dorotheos of Gaza, who was a famous instructor of monks. I go to college for a living, and I'm here because I plan to have a home of my own some day and I want to start making things to put in it." She sat back again, smoothing her skirt.

Anna nodded. "Thank you, Dorothy. Jewel, you're next."

Jewel glanced around at the group before returning her attention to Anna. "My name is Jewel," she began. "I'm a visitor at church, really, but I'm hoping to use my time in this group to pursue my hobby. I'm a publications manager for a small non-profit, and," touching the red case in her lap, "I like to make jewelry on the side." She glanced around the circle again, pausing when her eyes fell on Barbara, who came next.

Barbara shifted toward the front of her seat, still holding her workbag with both hands. "I'm Barbara, and I'm named for St. Barbara who was the friend and cell-keeper of St. Elizabeth the New Martyr. They actually went to their deaths together. I'm a pediatric nurse at a practice in Everett, and Elizabeth and I make blankets for a non-profit that distributes them to children in traumatized circumstances."

Barbara sat back and Elizabeth sat forward, her brown eyes moving around the circle, making friendly contact with everyone. "I'm Elizabeth, and I'm named for the St. Elizabeth who was martyred in the Russian revolution, with St. Barbara and some others, as Barbara says. I worked at the university library for many years before I retired, and my occupation now is keeping company with all the good friends and neighbors God sends to me. I came here to knit. I like knitting. Xenia, you're next."

Xenia put down her knitting for a moment. "I'm Xenia. I was named for Xenia of St. Petersburg, a fool for Christ. I own a little shop in downtown Edmonds, and Jewel, I'd be interested to see what you're making, if you're good at it. I sell hand-made jewelry from several local artists."

"I could get up, if you'd like to sit here?" offered Dorothy. "Then she could show you—"

"No, no," Jewel half rose, then sat down again. "I'll bring it over as soon as we begin working."

All eyes returned to Anna.

"Please," Anna lifted her hands to them, urging them on, "go right ahead and get started. I'll just check on the tea and be with you in a minute." She stood up, saw all of them opening bags and adjusting needles and yarn, and went down the two steps into the dining room, where she rearranged all of Xenia's rearrangements on her way to check the tea and pour the decaf into a carafe. She lingered in the kitchen, mentally searching the house for something to do with her hands for an hour while the other women knitted. *In my closet, I think. That counted cross-stitch kit Aunt Sabina sent me a few years ago...the crown jewels, or something like that...did she get it in England, I wonder? I haven't embroidered in years, but something is better than nothing.*

A few minutes of rummaging in the neatly labeled baskets on her closet shelf brought the project to light. It was still sealed in the original packaging, but she saw that it came with an appropriate needle, so all she needed to find now was a pair of small scissors. When she discovered them, perched on the shelf over the sink in the master bathroom, the round silver handles of the scissors reminded her of Timothy's glasses, and she realized that she had not mentioned his request to the other women yet. *I'll wait for a natural opening,* she decided, *or I'll make an opening, once I get this unwrapped and have something to do with my hands.*

Returning to the living room, Anna established herself in her chair, unwrapped her project, and in a few minutes, had a needle threaded and felt more like a credible member of the group. Looking around, with the needle in her hand, she saw Elizabeth and Barbara trading neatly rolled balls of yarn to match colors and textures for the two blankets they planned to crochet for school-age children, Elizabeth's for a boy, Barbara's for a girl. Dorothy had pulled a half-finished red crocheted scarf out of her bag and was explaining to Jewel that she was trying a new stitch she had learned from her grandmother. Jewel, excusing herself politely to Dorothy, was stepping across the room to Xenia, who laid aside the turquoise shawl to make room for Jewel's case on her lap. Anna decided to wait a few minutes before bringing up Timothy.

Jewel knelt by Xenia's chair and undid the silver clasp of the case, opening the lid and laying it back so that Xenia could see all the contents in good light. Dorothy craned her neck, visibly curious about what the case contained, but perhaps sensing that she had not been invited to look over Jewel's shoulder. Elizabeth caught Jewel's eye and smiled encouragingly. Barbara went on sorting yarn.

Anna, sitting next to Xenia, could see that the case contained two trays, the top one subdivided into twelve small compartments full of colorful beads of many textures, sizes, and shapes, the lower one subdivided into six rectangular compartments holding wire, thread, chain, clasps, earring hooks, and some small, shiny metal tools. Under the second tray, Jewel had stored her work, a half-finished necklace and a bracelet complete except for the clasp.

"This isn't all my work; I only brought what I planned to work on tonight," Jewel explained carefully, lifting the bracelet out so Xenia could examine it closely. Xenia laid it across her palm, testing the workmanship, letting the light play on the variegated shades of green and blue sea glass, interspersed with tiny gold beads and fine gold wire.

"What type of clasp are you planning for it?" Xenia asked, reaching for her glasses and peering at the bracelet again through the rimless half-lenses.

Jewel extracted a small square of drawing paper from the case and handed it to Xenia. "I want to make one of my own design, like this. I apologize for the quality of the sketch. I know what it means, but...these are seahorses, facing each other, and the actual clasp will be between their fins, midway down the body of each. I'm still experimenting with construction and deciding how much beading to add. Probably just a small bead for the eye of each seahorse." She shifted slightly on her knees.

Xenia nodded. "It's good," she said, placing the bracelet back in the case. "Come see me at the shop. It's on Main Street, in downtown Edmonds. I'll give you my card before I leave tonight."

Jewel clasped her hands together once, firmly. "Thank you, Xenia. I'll come this week." She rose to her feet, gathered up her case, and returned to the sofa corner beside Dorothy.

Seeing Dorothy about to make a congratulatory remark that would be awkward for Jewel to respond to in front of Xenia, Anna chose this moment to introduce Timothy's request. "Ladies," she said clearly, before Dorothy could speak, "could I have your attention again for just a moment?" She rested her sewing in her lap. "How many of you know Timothy Paulson, at church?"

"Is he a chanter?" asked Elizabeth, rubbing her chin, "In his middle thirties, maybe?"

"Brown hair and glasses," added Barbara.

"That's him," said Xenia, flipping the turquoise shawl and stabbing in her needle to begin the next row of stitches. "You never get a word out of him unless he's behind the chanter stand."

"He is a quiet person," Anna agreed, putting Timothy in a positive light.

"I like quiet people," remarked Dorothy.

"Timothy has asked me to ask you ladies whether he would be welcome as a member of our group. Apparently, he knows how to knit, and he would like to join us if we feel comfortable having him." Anna took a stitch or two at random and waited for their response.

"What difference could it make? He never opens his mouth," said Xenia.

"The invitation to join the group was extended only to women, wasn't it?" asked Barbara, frowning.

"Oh, there now," said Elizabeth comfortably, "where's the harm? He's probably lonely. Most shy people are. And if he can knit, he probably can't find any congenial company for doing it because most men don't know one end of the needle from the other." She chuckled, and they all relaxed a little.

"What do you think, Anna?" asked Dorothy.

"I think the decision rests with all of us, but I agree with Elizabeth that he won't do us any harm," Anna replied.

"It won't be the same with a man present," Barbara said. "I mean, women talk more freely together when only women are present, usually."

Xenia grunted. "The conversation hasn't been flowing freely in this room full of women. He can't disrupt something that isn't happening." She caught a startled expression on Jewel's face across the room and asked bluntly. "Do you have an opinion, Jewel?"

Jewel shook her head quickly. "I don't know him."

Xenia directed another of her fierce glances at Barbara's disapproving face and abruptly lost her patience. "Oh, come on, Barbara! It's just Timothy! Let him come."

"Hear, hear!" Elizabeth sang out, as if seconding a motion. Barbara looked hurt.

Anna made a final try for consensus. "We aren't abiding by Robert's Rules of Order here, so let me just say, does anyone have a strong objection to Timothy being invited to join?"

Barbara pursed her lips but said nothing. Dorothy seemed faintly excited, but she too said nothing.

"You go right ahead, Anna," encouraged Elizabeth. "We'll all welcome him if he wants to come, won't we ladies?" There was a general murmur of consent, and with that Anna had to be content. Registering a fervent hope that she wasn't letting Timothy in for a bad time, she put her sewing on the table and invited the ladies to join her for dessert in the dining room.

Closing the front door on the last guest an hour later, Anna dropped into the nearest chair and let all the air escape from her lungs in a long, exasperated sigh. She heard the garage door opening and George's car pulling in. Anna gazed at the cake crumbs and teacups on the dining room table. George never ate breakfast, certainly not at the dining room table. He drank his coffee standing in the kitchen, then followed her around, up and down the hall, munching a piece of toast and chatting about his day until it was time for him to drive to work. Anna got up and turned off the dining room light. She stepped into the hall and opened the door for George. He must have showered and changed after tennis, she noticed. He was wearing a sky blue polo shirt and khakis, and his gray hair was parted on one side and combed back neatly. He smelled like soap. She smiled. He kissed her from the doorstep, and she took his arm. "Come in, darling, and come to bed. The church ladies wore me out."

Chapter 11

Jewel sat on the red tweed couch by her living room window. Her jewelry case sat on the couch beside her. It was beautifully made of tooled red leather with a silver clasp, and the neat arrangement of shelves and compartments inside it fascinated her. She had found it in the thrift store, the same store where Sara had taken her to buy her first furniture and replace her clothes after her bonfire. She wondered about the case, about its history before she found it on the thrift-store shelf. There was a small burn mark, shaped like a half moon, on the underside of the case in one corner. How had it come there? Who had owned the case, and why had the owner decided to part with it? She would never know, but she felt a foolish affection for this inanimate thing, as if it, too, knew what it meant to have a past.

Inside the case lay her prized collection of tools and her supply of beads, wire, chain, glass, buttons, and other odds and ends that struck her fancy. She had come to this hobby wholly by accident, in the early days of her independence. By the end of her first week alone, she was frantic for something to occupy her mind and fill the quiet nights when sleep eluded her. Stopping at the library one afternoon in search of light reading, she saw a table near the door with a display of books on various hand crafts. There was one book about beading with a brightly colored photograph on the front, showing a beautiful necklace in the hands of the woman who made it. The necklace would have graced the jewelry counter at Nordstrom, and the woman had the contented, prosperous look of one whose goals are attainable and whose dreams come true. Jewel checked out the book on the spot and bought her first beads the following day. For a week, she came home each night, swallowed her dinner, and opened the book with the sensations of a fairy-tale knight requesting a mission. She copied each piece pictured in the book as well as she could with her limited skills and supplies, and gradually, the work became easier and her dependence on the book lessened. One night, she had an idea for a bracelet before she had even come home from work. She did not open the book at all that night. She made the piece from her own imagination. It was a night of enchantment.

And now, almost two and a half years later, she was facing her first chance to sell her work to real people in a real shop. Jewel got up quickly and went into the bathroom to look at herself in the mirror. Her hair was neat. Her makeup was tasteful. She was wearing jewelry of her own design, a necklace of antique silver filigree beads with matching earrings, and a navy blue dress that looked businesslike but not, she hoped, un-artistic. She stared at her face in the mirror, grasping for the meaning of this moment in her life. She felt its importance instinctively and wished she could articulate it, even though there was no one listening.

"I make jewelry," she said aloud to her mirrored image. "It turns out I'm very creative, which nobody ever knew, but I might be able to sell my work now at a shop in Edmonds. Of all places. People have money in Edmonds. It's not the same as putting out a blanket at a street market in Seattle. Xenia's customers aren't crunchy people who hope their stuff looks homemade." Jewel sighed. There was more to it than that, but she could not put words to it. "It's like singing a song you don't know the end to," she said. "Maybe Xenia won't buy my things. But it still matters that I'm trying, I think. Doesn't it?"

Jewel rubbed the palms of her hands nervously down the front of her skirt and went back to the living room to pick up her case and her purse. She locked the front door behind her, backed the car carefully out of her driveway, and turned toward downtown Edmonds, where people bought real jewelry and wore it.

Xenia was expecting her at four thirty, when the shoppers would be thinking of dinner and Xenia would have a moment to look through the items Jewel had culled from her stock and brought for inspection. She drove down the winding road, making herself watch the patches of sun-dappled tree shade on the pavement, the mailboxes by the sidewalk, a woman playing with a dog on a driveway. She preferred not to tangle with hope or skepticism. It was important to keep the day's events in perspective. After all, she didn't need to sell the jewelry. Her job paid well enough to support her and her one-person house. It would just be a sideline, a little creative outlet in her careful, orderly life. Jewel sighed and parked the car outside Xenia's shop, a small well-kept establishment with the name, *Top Drawer*, in gold calligraphy on the large bow-window that made up her storefront on this street of exclusive little shops and well-filled restaurants. Jewel stood by her car, gazing at the window display for a moment, then stepped over a little curbside garden onto the sidewalk and entered the shop with her case in her hands.

Xenia sat behind a glass display case, reading a document in an open manila folder. Her rimless half glasses perched on her nose, and she glanced over them at Jewel as the door swung shut behind her. "You're here," Xenia said.

"I am," replied Jewel. She laid her case on the glass counter top, and Xenia opened it. She gazed silently at each piece, handling it carefully but confidently, testing its construction and missing no detail of its design. Jewel stood quietly beside her, awaiting her decision.

"Could you make sets of jewelry, perhaps a necklace and a bracelet or earrings, in colors that would coordinate with the various clothing lines I carry each season?" inquired Xenia. "That garnet red pant suit, for example. What could you do for that?"

Jewel considered it for a moment, her head tilted to the side as her fingers explored the texture of the fabric. "I could make a necklace and a bracelet for this. These are three-quarter sleeves, so a bracelet would show. I might use garnets, but it would be more interesting to use something multi-colored, don't you think? Cloisonné would be nice, or maybe gold filigree, alternating with something colorful." She turned to look at the displays around her. "Could I make a set for this one and that turquoise shantung over there, on approval?"

Xenia nodded firmly, settling it. "Now wander around the shop and familiarize yourself with the styles I carry here so you know how to play along." A customer entered the shop, taking Xenia's attention from Jewel, leaving her free to wander as ordered, browsing the racks and the glass cases of jewelry displayed around them. The shop seemed to cater to mature women with substantial discretionary income and flawless taste. While many of the styles were conservative, each creatively expressed an attractive natural artistry. Rich color, fine fabric, and hand-crafted decorative touches gave the collection the flavor and diversity of an island art festival transported to this staid little mainland town. In the window display, Jewel recognized the turquoise shawl Xenia had been knitting at Anna's house. In Xenia's lap, it had seemed excessive, too large and woolly to be wearable in public. But draped over a dressmaker's form in the shop window with a remarkable carved stone necklace, Jewel could see its transparency, the ephemeral intricacy of its stitches. *It's all hers*, thought Jewel. *She must choose the whole collection, and she's artistic enough to create some of it herself. This is one of those shops that people come to because they admire the proprietor's personal taste and can buy it here.*

She was still standing by the window, contemplating the shawl and the necklace, when Xenia returned to her.

"I make these myself, in shades that coordinate with the fabrics I carry in some of the clothing lines." Xenia led her to a rack near the window, and Jewel caught her breath at the array of colors and textures, crimson, metallic orange, aquamarine, lemon, fuchsia, emerald. She turned to Xenia impulsively. "Let me make jewelry to go with every color you knit, Xenia. You choose the yarn, and I'll find beads to match. We could make it a feature, like a set of accessories. A shawl, and maybe earrings and a necklace to go together. Even a bracelet, if I can do it fast enough. You could bring me snips of yarn and pattern sketches when we go to Anna's, and I'll work from those. What do you think?"

Xenia held out her hand. "If you can keep up, it's a deal." They shook hands pleasantly, awkwardly, then Jewel gathered up her case and said goodbye. Outside, she waited until she was safely inside her car to clasp her own hands together and shake them triumphantly over her head.

Chapter 12

Xenia parked her car in the same spot every time she came to church. She drove straight to the end of the parking lot and pulled in next to the recycling bins. Today, rain soaked the pavement and blurred the windshield almost faster than the wipers could clear it. Fr. Nicholas's car, parked near the church entrance, was the only other car in the lot, but Xenia had long since ceased thinking about where she parked. She always parked in the same spot, so where was the sense in thinking about it? She snapped open a gray umbrella and stalked up the walkway to the church door.

The creak of the door still jarred her, tightening nerves all over her body, summoning unwanted memories. Xenia was coming to confession, and her hatred of this sacrament was only exceeded by her need of it. The sound of the door opening on the empty vestibule, the silence of a church devoid of visible people, reminded her of each individual confession she had survived in the years of widowhood that had passed over her so heavily. She had not come to church for five years after her husband's untimely death. Unbridled grief and fury had torn her from the tenuous pleasantries of her erstwhile spiritual life. It had taken the long, hideous slide into an almost suicidal darkness to draw her, still resisting and blind, to the door of Fr. Nicholas' office five minutes before he went home one Friday night. When he saw her face, he put his keys back on the hook and walked her into the sanctuary. They sat down in front of the icon of Christ because Xenia could not stand, and they stayed there for two hours while Xenia struggled to form a single word.

For weeks after that, Xenia strove to confess to Fr. Nicholas, coming almost daily to do battle against herself in painful silence before the icon of Christ. After three months, she managed the first word: "ANGRY." Fr. Nicholas offered the full sacrament immediately and restored her to communion. He tried to give Xenia holy unction, but she walked away, shaking her head violently, crying in a strained voice, "Not healed yet!" No explanation of the sacrament as a means of healing, not a reward for healing, had any effect. Xenia could not bear to risk herself under the touch of the blessed oil that might tear her anguish from her and heal her against her will. Xenia sought resolution and justification, a satisfactory answer to all she had suffered, but most of all, she longed to be comforted, and she feared God would never comfort her if He had the opportunity to heal her first. In her ruthless way, Xenia acknowledged to herself that if she were truly healed, she would not need comforting any more. Yet still, to her own disgust, she begged God feverishly for consolation.

For the fifteen years following that first word, Xenia had come to confession on the first Friday of every month, the anniversary of the day when she learned of her husband's death. She had not planned it that way.

It happened because she could never overcome her dread of that day, which seemed to recur with horrifying freshness every month. Time, the great healer, could take no pity on Xenia, so she offered her sins desperately to God, unable to contain so many wounds in a single heart.

Fr. Nicholas learned to expect her each month at the same time. He would enter the sanctuary minutes ahead of her, with time to light a candle at the icon before the heavy church door creaked open upon her arrival. She would find him standing there, his gray head bowed, his lips moving in prayer, and she would stand next to him, gathering her strength in the few moments before he finished praying. Then they would labor through the opening prayers of the sacrament together, he with his head still bowed, she grasping her handbag like a drowning woman seizing a raft, and they would wait for the sound of Xenia's voice.

In fifteen years, Xenia's confession had progressed from the first painful word to sentences, a litany of the effects of grief. She confessed to suicidal thoughts, to despair, to resentment and frustration. She did not refer again to anger.

Xenia found the personal pronoun to be the most difficult word in any confession. She recoiled from it each time, hating the way it forced her to touch that inner wound and recognize it as her own, a marking on herself brought about by everything she most longed for and everything she most despised. Sometimes, she would stare frantically at Fr. Nicholas, her eyes entreating him to say the words for her. Fr. Nicholas understood this look and had once explained to Xenia, as gently as he could, that he could not speak for her. Fr. Nicholas knew enough about Xenia and about human nature to guess at the roots of her anguish, he said, but he deliberately withheld himself from such conjectures. He strove instead to hear everything she could tell him about what was actually happening to her, that nothing might dull his ability to help her speak the full truth to God and to herself.

Today, Xenia came into the sanctuary slowly, trying to fold her wet umbrella and snap the band around it with trembling fingers. She gave up as she reached the icon and let the umbrella drop to the floor. Her hands closed around her purse automatically, and she forced her gaze to meet the dark eyes of the iconic Christ. The candle flickered between them, lighting His face and perhaps hers also if she could have seen it reflected somewhere in the sanctuary.

Fr. Nicholas began to chant the opening prayers of the sacrament, leaving a little silence in the places where Xenia should respond. When he reached Psalm 50, he handed the prayer book to Xenia and allowed her to read it in silence. This small act of trust both relieved and irritated her. She knew that speaking the whole psalm aloud was beyond her, but she felt that this lack in herself somehow constituted a lack in the performance of the sacrament. Irrationally, she both expected and resented this allowance being made for her.

But the feeling faded quickly before the great, encompassing dread that poured over her as they reached the moment for her words of confession. She had come today because she always came, but for some reason, she could not think of anything to say. She had confessed everything she felt able to say, over and over again for fifteen years. Today, there was nothing left, nothing but the unspeakable.

Xenia looked down at her hands, focusing her mind on each individual knuckle and the little dips between them. She moved her attention slowly from her hands to her mouth, trying to skip over the heart and lungs, trying not to travel far enough to reach the brain. She felt her dry lips parting slowly, sticking, but not tearing.

"Angry." She cleared the gravel from her voice and breathed a few times. "Father—" No, that was worse. Focus on the icon. Pretend Father isn't there. Breathe. Or maybe focus on Father and pretend the icon isn't there. Xenia felt panic rising to close her throat and wrenched her hand upward in a crude gesture of rage and frustration. "My husband, Father! My husband!" Her purse crashed to the floor and spilled its contents as she lost control of her voice and covered her face with trembling hands. Fr. Nicholas started awkwardly, patted her back, and then abruptly, out of the thick silence she felt pressing in around her, Xenia heard his voice, chanting. It sounded like part of a psalm.

*Answer me in Your Righteousness;
do not enter into judgment with
Your servant, for no one living shall
become righteous in Your sight. For
the enemy persecuted my soul; he
humbled my life to the ground; he
caused me to dwell in dark places as
one long dead, and my spirit was in
anguish within me; my heart was
troubled within me. I remembered
the days of old, and I meditated on
all Your works; I meditated on the
works of Your hands. I spread out
my hands to You; my soul thirsts for
You like a waterless land.[1]*

When Fr. Nicholas lifted the epitrachelion[2] and laid it over Xenia, she heard the break in his voice, speaking words of blessing and forgiveness, and knew his eyes were wet.

---

[1] Psalm 142:1-6.

[2] The priest's stole, worn as a symbol of his priesthood. At the end of the sacrament of confession, the priest places the end of his stole over the penitent's head for the prayer of absolution and blessing.

Chapter 13

The second meeting of the knitting circle at Anna's home took place at the end of a perfect late-summer day. The afternoon heat lingered into the evening, softening the little puffs of wind and the drowsy flowers scenting the air in Anna's front garden. Anna went barefoot until a few moments before her first guests arrived, taking unexpected delight in the cool floor tiles and thick pile carpet under her toes. When the doorbell rang, she stepped reluctantly into her sandals and braced herself for the onslaught of mismatched personalities and an evening spent trying to do counted cross-stitch in a room full of agitated knitters.

Anna opened the door to find Jewel on her doorstep, with the jewelry case in one hand and the lemon squares, perfectly dusted with sugar, in the other.

"I'm so glad you came first, Jewel," Anna said, holding the door wider to welcome her into the house. "I didn't get a chance to visit with you last time. You can put the case in the living room and the lemon squares in the dining room. Thank you for bringing those. Lemon is so refreshing on a hot day." Her urge to make Jewel feel especially welcome was giving way to the suspicion that she was babbling. Jewel seemed so contained. Every detail of her appearance gave an impression of neatness and silence. Who could guess what thoughts might be passing behind that careful politeness?

Preferring not to put herself and her shy guest through the ordeal of a question-and-answer conversation, Anna seized the kitchen shears and sent Jewel back out to the garden to cut flowers for the table. Jewel met Dorothy at the door as she was going out.

"Me, too, Anna! Can I do something to help?" asked Dorothy, hugging Anna with one arm and clutching her full pink skirt with the other to let Jewel pass. She dropped her brown workbag in the living room and came expectantly into the kitchen. Anna gave her a light bulb and a small step ladder, and sent her out to replace the bulb in the front porch light. It was the only thing she could think of. She preferred to make her own preparations in the kitchen.

Five minutes later, Anna returned to the front door to check on her helpers and found that a third guest had arrived in her absence. She stood quietly, observing the scene, unnoticed by any of the three people so absorbed in their tasks in her front yard.

Dorothy balanced on the top step of the ladder, bracing herself with one hand against the wall of the house and reaching above her with the other to twist in the new bulb. Anna could see her feet, on tip toe, in pink ballet slippers. The old bulb lay on the porch, precariously close to Timothy's foot. Timothy stood below Dorothy, steadying the ladder with both hands and leaning back slightly to escape the swirling pink skirt of Dorothy's sundress. His eyes, however, were not on Dorothy.

A few feet away, like a porcelain statue rising from the artistic tangle of wild roses bordering Anna's yard, stood Jewel. The fragrant air ruffled her smooth hair but left her face untouched, strangely still. Jewel's whole mind seemed bent on cutting roses, her nimble fingers eluding the sharp thorns and lifting each scarlet blossom from the brambles with all its velvet petals intact. As Anna watched, Jewel gathered her bouquet gingerly together and came toward the house. Dorothy gave the bulb a final twist and came gracefully down the ladder. Timothy lifted the ladder and stepped back to let Dorothy pass. Dorothy paused on the doorsill to thank him. Jewel paused on the porch step, uncertain whether to walk past Timothy or wait for him to go in ahead of her. Timothy took another step back and turned to Jewel. Anna couldn't see his face, but Jewel gave a little nod and went quickly past him into the house. Timothy took one more step and crushed the burned-out light bulb still lying on the porch.

Anna came out of her trance abruptly. "Oh, Timothy! I'll get a dustpan. Just stand still a moment. I don't want the glass to get into your sandals." She raced into the kitchen and back. Timothy took the dustpan and brush and crouched on the porch, brushing up the glass and lifting his feet to be sure no fragments clung to his sandals. He stood up slowly, and Anna led him to the kitchen trash can, where he emptied the dustpan and held it out to her apologetically. Anna couldn't help smiling.

"Don't feel bad, Timothy. It wasn't the new bulb! Thank you for cleaning it up and for holding the ladder. Would you mind stepping out again to move the stepladder off the porch? Oh, there's the doorbell. I'll come with you, and we can just fold it away." Anna started for the door and Timothy followed her, looming behind her silently as she opened the door to Elizabeth and Barbara.

"Is this for us, honey?" laughed Elizabeth, shaking her workbag at the stepladder.

Anna heard a movement behind her. "Timothy's just coming to put that away for me, Elizabeth. We were replacing the bulb in the porch light. Come right in. Those pies look delicious!" Somehow she got the two ladies in the door and Timothy out of it. Elizabeth and Barbara surged happily across the dining room, each leaving pies on the table, and receded into the living room to subside onto the sofa at the far end of the room. Anna came back to the door as soon as she could and saw Xenia striding up the path, eyeing Timothy askance as he stood on the porch, folding the stepladder.

"Humph," said Xenia, crossing the porch. Coming in the open door, she hugged Anna fiercely and whispered, "I saw it all from the road. I'm going to outstay everyone!" before walking calmly into the living room with her knitting.

Anna found herself alone in the hall, slightly mussed, and full of a powerful conviction that those who thought Timothy would drop into the group and disappear like a rock in a pond were sorely mistaken.

He's enormous, for one thing. He didn't look that big at church, did he? Why does he look bigger standing on my porch staring at Jewel in my garden? Look at me. I forgot my sewing again. I'll just run back and get it. They're still settling in there. Enormous. Well over six feet. I can't believe he knits. Where is he going to sit where he won't bump the elbows of the ladies beside him? Ah, here it is. Back I go. Oh wait, he's got that wretched ladder. He hasn't said a word yet.

Anna met Timothy in the hall and held out her hand with a laugh and a smile. "Welcome to our home, Timothy. You can prop that ladder against the wall here. I'll put it away later. Did you bring your knitting?"

Timothy grasped her hand. He had a deep baritone voice. "Thank you, Anna. I think I left it on the porch. I'll get it. You go on in."

Anna envisioned Timothy facing a room full of sharp feminine appraisal. "It's no trouble. I'll take you in with me."

With a nod, Timothy went back to the porch and returned with a paper grocery bag. A humorous grin lit his face and he bent his head to Anna, lowering his deep voice to a whisper. "It'll be worse when they see I carry my knitting around in a paper bag."

Anna laughed again, relieved that he knew what he was getting into and could take it so lightly. She put her hand on his arm and led him into the living room, feeling like a tugboat guiding an aircraft carrier into port.

All conversation ceased as they entered the room. Anna used the silence to make introductions, hoping it looked natural that way.

"Ladies, this is Timothy Paulson. He's a chanter on Sundays, and he runs the financial aid office at the community college during the week. Timothy, this is Xenia here on my left, and the two ladies on that sofa are Elizabeth and Barbara. Jewel is sitting by the end-table there, and Dorothy is beside her." She paused, gazing quickly around the room full of gracious nods, looking for somewhere Timothy could sit. Timothy stood beside her, solemnly nodding back at the ladies and holding his paper bag tightly.

Xenia came to the rescue. "Here, Timothy," she said in her brusque way. "Sit by me." She pushed the matching ottoman away from her chair with her foot, moving it a little to one side so that it came to rest in front of where Timothy was standing. He nodded to her again, and sat down on the ottoman, settling the paper bag between his large sandaled feet, and drawing out the beginnings of a green knitted blanket. Fishing out his knitting needles, he began to knit, watching each stitch form between his large square fingers.

Anna sank down into her chair beside him and scrabbled through a tangle of embroidery silk in her workbag before she pricked her finger on her lost needle. A brief glance showed her that the others had returned to their work, but she caught every one of them peeping over her knitting at Timothy. Except Jewel. Jewel's deft fingers flitted in and out of the case, choosing a tool or setting one aside, assembling a lacy scrollwork bracelet with crimson beads and gold wire. Beside her, Dorothy knitted industriously. Her cheeks seemed flushed to Anna. The pink ballet slippers tapped the floor occasionally as if, somewhere in her own mind, Dorothy was dancing.

Conversation languished. Elizabeth and Barbara chatted to each other, and occasionally, Elizabeth tried to draw Jewel into the conversation. Jewel smiled and answered yes or no, but soon returned to industrious silence.

Timothy did not say a word. He sat obediently where he had been placed and took slow, even stitches. His big hands wielded the needles a little awkwardly, but he made no errors, and his knitting, surprisingly, looked no different than anyone else's.

Anna counted stitches, thankful that her work could appear so absorbing and save her the necessity of speaking to anyone. Despite the lack of conversation, the room seemed full of hidden messages. The air felt charged, as if a high-powered electrical current flowed through it, ricocheting off the quiet bodies of her guests until even the silence seemed loud. *It's their thoughts,* mused Anna, picking out an unnecessary stitch with her needle. *They aren't saying anything out loud, but I know their minds are chattering like magpies. Xenia can't wait to tell me what she saw in my garden. Dorothy is looking way too pink and pretty, and she wasted a whole lot of graceful femininity on that burnt-out light bulb. Barbara's probably telling herself she* knew *Timothy would make things different, and Elizabeth's probably thinking he's a good-looking man and wondering who she can match him up with.* Anna glanced around the room, and her eyes fell on Jewel's quiet face and busy fingers. *I wonder what Jewel's thinking. I'm always wondering what Jewel's thinking. I never saw such a contained person in my life. I wonder if she even noticed that Timothy was watching her out there in the garden. Was he really staring at her, or am I making too much out of that?* She snipped her thread and reached for a thin silver strand. *The advantage of a crown-jewels cross-stitch is some fun thread colors. But still...it looks silly. Like something a tourist would buy. Oh, good. It's eight o'clock. I can get dessert started.*

Anna set aside her work and stood up, with a wave of her hand toward the dining room. "Time for dessert, ladies and Timothy."

Timothy stuffed his knitting into the paper bag and stood aside politely for Anna and Xenia to pass him. Elizabeth was whispering to Barbara, and Jewel was carefully repacking her case. Dorothy jumped to her feet and smiled engagingly. "Come on, Timothy. I'll show you the food." Timothy gave her a little smile and a nod, and followed her docilely from the room, the paper bag in his hand.

Elizabeth and Barbara were cutting the pies, and Anna was pouring tea into Royal Albert Violet Cameo cups. Beside her, Xenia was dropping a cream puff and a strawberry onto each glass dessert plate.

Elizabeth smiled at Timothy as he came in. "Here, honey. I never yet knew a man who didn't like a slice of pie around this time of the evening. Pass it to him, Dorothy," she said, pushing the glass plate across the table. The strawberry fell off. Dorothy flipped it back on and handed him the plate with a little grin.

"Thank you, Elizabeth and Dorothy," said Timothy, balancing the plate carefully on the palm of one hand as he set down his paper bag with the other. He took an instinctive step back as Xenia came around the table to start passing teacups, and he came to rest with his back against the wall and the paper bag between his feet.

"Tea?" inquired Xenia in a voice that suggested it was just the beverage for a speechless man knitter.

"No, thank you," answered Timothy, taking a bite of pie.

"Eat, everyone," urged Anna, noticing that everyone was standing around the table watching Timothy, who was beginning to show signs of strain.

Dorothy giggled and turned to pick up a plate of pie. Barbara took a cup of tea and started a conversation about synthetic fabrics with Elizabeth. Jewel ate a single cream puff in three small bites and wiped her fingers on a red linen napkin. Anna brought her cup of tea around the table and stood beside Timothy and Dorothy, feeling that he might need her help.

Dorothy bit into her strawberry and looked up at Timothy. "Mmmm! Strawberries taste like summer. These are so good, Anna."

Anna smiled. "They are good, aren't they, and I wish I could take the credit. Those are from Xenia's garden. They're so different from the California strawberries that they almost seem like a different fruit."

"They're certainly sweeter and softer," agreed Dorothy, reaching for another from the crystal bowl on the table beside them. "My mother likes to use local fruit when she can, so we grew up eating these. I remember the first 'store strawberry' I ever had. I thought it wasn't ripe, it was so much harder and more acidic."

Anna nodded. "They often are, but they can be very good as well. It's just a different flavor and texture. And they certainly last longer. These little local berries have to be eaten almost as soon as they're picked. But I think it adds a little something to their appeal, that knowledge that you have to snatch their moment of sweetness before it's gone." Anna took a sip of tea. She was getting tired of strawberries. Timothy had finished his pie and was standing quietly, holding his plate, unable to reach the table to put it down without bumping into the two berry-obsessed women conversing in front of him. Anna excused herself to refresh the tea pot and left Dorothy to entertain him by herself. It was probably what she was hoping for in any case. Returning with the tea, she heard Timothy's voice. Dorothy seemed to have been talking animatedly about something, and when she paused for breath, he said politely but clearly, "May I have a lemon square, please?" Anna saw that the plate of lemon squares lay directly in front of Jewel, who still stood quietly by the table, watching the others talk.

"Certainly, Timothy!" Dorothy's face showed that she found his request a little unexpected but inexpressibly cute. She turned swiftly, leaned in front of Jewel, and lifted a lemon square with a small silver spatula provided for the purpose. Turning again, she whisked it onto his plate and smiled up into his face, happy to have given him what he wanted. Just behind her stood Jewel, looking intently at the lemon squares and refolding her linen napkin.

She could at least have told him that Jewel made the lemon squares, thought Anna, refilling Barbara's empty tea cup. *She's probably too caught up in the moment to wonder if he deliberately asked for something Jewel could reach.*

Thirty minutes later, Anna stood by her door, saying goodbye to each guest. Jewel went first, ending a silent evening with a few words of thanks. Anna watched her walk down the steps, carrying her jewelry case against her hip with the empty lemon-squares plate pressed on top of it, her car keys in her other hand.

Anna turned back to the hall, holding out her hand to Timothy, who shook it warmly. "Thank you for your hospitality, Anna." His eyes strayed to the open door. Anna knew he could see Jewel, walking through the garden on her way to her car parked at the curb. He shifted the paper bag to his other hand and bent his head to Anna, addressing her for the second time in the evening in his deep, confidential whisper.

"Who is that, Anna?"

Anna did not pretend to misunderstand him. Jewel had been introduced like everyone else. "I don't know her story, Timothy." She hesitated, wondering what else she could say. "She's been coming to church for two months, maybe a little less. I don't think she was raised Orthodox."

"Hmmm," said Timothy.

"Will you be coming again?" asked Anna humorously.

"It wasn't so bad, most of it. I expected they would be talking more. Maybe that will come when they all warm up to each other."

Jewel's car pulled away from the curb as he walked out the door. Anna saw his head turn, looking after it, as he crossed the garden.

"We cleaned up your kitchen, Anna," called Elizabeth, coming into the hall with Barbara and Dorothy behind her. They all kissed each other good night, and Elizabeth started out the door. Barbara leaned toward Anna and whispered, "Do you think it will be better next time? It seemed so awkward tonight, with him just sitting there, not saying a word."

"Here's hoping," whispered Anna, with an encouraging smile. She closed the door behind them, knowing there was no point in waiting for Xenia to follow them. Xenia had promised to outstay them all, and she always meant what she said.

Xenia was waiting for her in the living room. Two cups of tea steamed on the table between their customary chairs, and Xenia looked ready to pounce. Anna sat down and kicked off her sandals. Each took a sip of tea. Xenia set down her cup.

"That man might as well have been a brass band, right here in your living room, Anna."

Anna choked on her tea. "And you were the one who said it would make no difference at all if he was here. You convinced me, Xen."

Xenia sniffed. "He's a chanter, and he never stays for coffee hour. How could we know?"

"Well, to be fair, he didn't do a thing tonight," Anna pointed out. "He just sat there being male."

Xenia snorted. "Did you see what happened outside before they all came in?"

"I thought I might be making too much of that," mused Anna.

"If you ask me," said Xenia, "Miss Dorothy thinks a chanter would be just the sort of pious husband a righteous girl would like. Especially a big handsome chanter."

"Don't make it sound so nasty, Xenia. You know she doesn't mean it like that. She's just so darn young she thinks a mutual interest in Orthodoxy is sufficient basis for romance."

"Love by formula," snapped Xenia. She paused. "I don't mean to be unfair to her. I hope she won't make a fool of herself."

Anna shook her head. "There was nothing wrong with anything she said or did tonight."

Xenia sighed. "Well, she's not as transparent to him as she is to us. Whatever his animal magnetism, he doesn't come off as the sharpest knife in the drawer."

Anna disagreed. "Oh, he's sharp enough, Xen. He just keeps his own counsel." She laughed suddenly. "And feeling awkward in a crowd of staring women doesn't mean you're stupid!"

For a few moments, they drank tea in companionable silence.

"I'm tired," said Anna.

"Are you going to keep this up? I notice you're doing a ridiculous cross stitch you can't possibly want to finish."

Anna sighed. "It's definitely awful, but it gives me something to do. I don't know how to knit, remember?"

"You should learn," Xenia answered bluntly.

Chapter 14

Jewel lay in the dark, listening to the patter of raindrops on the roof above her, too tired to remain awake, too wound up to fall asleep. She had been meeting publication deadlines at work every night since the evening of the knitting circle, and her mind felt like a noisy committee clamoring for her attention, demanding time to process what she had tried not to think of since she drove home from Anna's house. Half-heartedly, she strove to single out the sounds of individual raindrops, but even this familiar meditation failed her. With a groan, she rolled on her side and gave herself up to the puzzle of her emotions.

Dorothy, first of all. *She bothers me so much. Even the first time I met her, I wished she would go away. I don't want to go to church any more when I think about sitting with her and Mrs. Edon. I'm so stupid. I should stand up for myself. Other people sit by themselves in church. There must be some way to drive her off without being horribly rude. But she still comes to the knitting group, and I can't get away from her there.*

Jewel envisioned the dancing pink slippers, the wide blue gaze, the cheerful voice, the smug security radiating from the real pearl necklace and the church-girl pink dress. *Is it because she's so obvious? Is that the word I want? She can't possibly be natural, can she? Is anyone actually like that? Maybe they are, if they can be. It's not that what she's doing is so wrong, it's that you can always tell she's doing it. She would never be my friend if she wasn't trying to make me join her church. She wouldn't even like me as me. She's too pleased with who she is to have any use for someone like me.*

Jewel's thoughts dwelt bitterly on the lemon square. It was embarrassing to think she cared about that. She hunched her shoulders uncomfortably in the darkness. *I wish I never had to see her again. I wish she would stop coming to Anna's. Maybe I should stop coming. But I want to come. And that makes the second time I've almost decided not to go back to a place because Dorothy would be there. There are other people there, too. And I was invited. Anna wants me to come. She acts like she likes me every time I see her. And Xenia is going to bring me swatches and yarn samples. I have to go. I have to be okay around people who bother me. Otherwise, I'll be giving up what matters to me to save myself from dealing with Dorothy Edon, and what does that make me? It makes me nothing. It makes me a big fat loser who lets everyone dump her.*

Jewel sat up in bed, without turning on the light, forcing herself to relive each detail of the evening at Anna's, from the bramble roses through the lemon square to the ride home. She visualized each member of the circle, recalled their comments and gestures, the thick silence and her own one-word answers to Barbara and Elizabeth. Jewel had not wanted to talk. She had wanted to immerse herself in her work, eluding the complexities of her position among church-going strangers.

It's because I'm not the right kind of person to be in a church. That's why it's hard to be with them and why everything is awkward for me. If I was just like them, it would be easy. I wish I was like Anna. She knows what to say and do. And Xenia has her own store. I bet Xenia tells everyone where to get off. They know who they are, that's what it is. They can do something about their lives because they know. Even Dorothy knows who she is. She's just a little too pleased about it. I know who I am too, but it's not the same because who I am is all messed up.

Jewel drew a long breath and released it slowly as she felt the click of two ideas coming together in her mind. *That's why I can't stand Dorothy. Because I know I'm messed up and she isn't. She might be socially awkward, but she's never done half the stupid things I've done, and I bet she never will. Why shouldn't she act like she's better? She is better. She makes me feel like a moron. She never lived with anyone, and she never would. Her mommy wouldn't let her. Her daddy wouldn't let her. But it's not even that. She can't imagine being me. She'll never have any idea what it's like out here where people aren't so protected. My old friends would have made so much fun of her, and she makes my skin crawl, but who am I to throw rocks at her? Who ever really loved me? About two people, in my whole life. And whose fault is it that I lived with six nightmares, one after the other like it was fun? Mine. It's my fault. I could have done so much better than I did. Why didn't I? Why couldn't I stop needing to try it one more time?* Memories surged around her, accusing her. Her flaws tangled her like vines in a jungle. She had cut herself free from them, but she could not escape the feeling of their writhing arms tripping and binding her.

Anna's knitting circle was the first social activity Jewel had attempted since she moved out of Trevor's apartment. Her weekly dinners with Sara and Clay did not count, in her own mind or in theirs. After the first meeting at Anna's house, Jewel had felt that it would be a nice way to get out in the evenings without complicating her life. *But that was before Timothy. Nothing can be simple if there's a man around. I didn't realize it would matter with church people, but I should have. And Dorothy is a perfect church girl, and he's a handsome chanter, and they will fall in love right there in front of me. It's like a Hallmark movie happening in real life. It will make a great story for them to tell their grandchildren. But why do I have to watch?* Imagination drew the scene for her with sickening clarity, the little shared glances, the low laughter, the respectful courtesy of the big silent man toward the blue-eyed girl. Jewel pressed her fingers against her eyes, blotting out the picture. She did not want to see it up close, where she couldn't ignore it. If she couldn't be one of the lucky ones, she'd rather not know exactly what she was missing. *It's the ultimate vicious circle, isn't it? Good girls get good men, and bad girls get bad ones. I should have been a good girl while I still had the chance.*

With a deep, sad sigh, Jewel sank into her pillows and stared at the darkness until, out of sheer physical weariness, she slept.

Chapter 15

Xenia paused, the glass door to the sanctuary still held open by the palm of her hand. Fr. Nicholas was waiting for her, as always, but today, he sat in one of two chairs facing the icon of Christ.

"What's this?" croaked Xenia, letting the door bang to her shoulder as her hands instinctively clutched her purse.

"Come sit with me," answered Fr. Nicholas, beckoning.

Xenia walked slowly to the chair. Fr. Nicholas held out his hand to her, helping her to seat herself without dropping her purse.

"When you came to me last month, you confessed that you are angry," began Fr. Nicholas. His eyes rested on her face for a moment. "It reminded me of your first confession, after Andrew's death, and I think that you have never mentioned this anger since. What is it that you feel you cannot say, Xenia?"

Xenia did not answer him.

"Let us have a conversation with Him this time," said Fr. Nicholas. "Tell Him the whole story, from the beginning, and let Him decide what part is a sin. I will say a prayer, and then you just start talking."

Xenia's dark eyes flickered toward the icon and returned to Fr. Nicholas. Fr. Nicholas bowed his head and began to chant, in a low, clear voice, the Troparion of St. Xenia of Petersburg, in Tone 8.

*Christ the Lord has shown forth in
thee a new mediatress and
intercessor for our race;/ thou didst
will to endure evil in thy life and
didst lovingly serve both God and
man./ We zealously run to thee in
misfortune and sorrow,/ we hope in
thee and cry from our hearts:/ Put
not our hope to shame, O blessed
Xenia.*

The last note lingered in the air. Fr. Nicholas folded his hands.

Xenia plunged into speech like a prisoner rushing toward a rapidly closing door. "People think I'm angry with God, for Andrew's death. I let them think that, but the truth is that I'm angry with Andrew. He's dead, Fr. Nicholas, and I'm so angry with him that I can't grieve. At first, I tried to excuse what he did so that I could tell myself there was no reason to be angry. But I couldn't get around the fact that he really was to blame. I feel like he deserved my anger, and so I can't let go of it. I can't feel my love for him. It's like a second death. My husband died and my love died too, and that's almost worse." Her voice was hoarse and painful. Her eyes fell on a glass of water standing at the base of the iconostasis. Fr. Nicholas had thought of everything. She let go of her purse with one hand and picked up the water glass, drinking eagerly, almost choking. She wiped her lips on the back of her hand in a long-forgotten gesture from her childhood.

"What did he do, Xenia?" Fr. Nicholas asked calmly.

Xenia put down the glass of water and sat back in her chair. Her hand returned to grasping her purse. "He drank too much at a party with his military friends, and he drove home."

"Is that what caused the accident, when he died?"

Xenia began to shake. Her hands tightened on the purse. "He took three other people with him, Father. One of his friends was riding with him, and they crashed into another car head on. My husband was driving on the wrong side of the road, on Highway Ninety-Nine, at seventy-five miles per hour. There were two people in the car he hit, a man and his wife. The woman was airlifted to Harborview, and she died that night. Everyone else died instantly. They were already dead when the police arrived..." Xenia's voice trailed off. The sweaty print of her palm was plainly visible on her suede purse as she reached for the water glass again.

"Lord, have mercy," said Fr. Nicholas softly.

"But I can't, Father. I can't feel any mercy," cried Xenia.

"Was he an alcoholic, Xenia?" asked Fr. Nicholas, after a moment.

"No, he wasn't. He was a social drinker, but he usually stopped after a few drinks. He was just—" Xenia let out all the air in her lungs and gasped it in again. "You never met him, Father. He was one of those people who are loveable even though they aren't perfect. His intentions were always a little better than his actions. He meant so well, and he had such a hard time living up to...to my standards, at least. He was always friendly, he was too generous with money and time for his own good, and he would go to any lengths to help a friend."

"Do you think that's why he was driving his friend home on the day he died?"

"I don't know, Father. It sounds like something he would do—great intention, complete lack of judgment." Xenia rested her head wearily on one hand, propping her elbow on the purse in her lap.

"Before this happened, Xenia, did you love your husband?" asked Fr. Nicholas gently.

Xenia nodded, unable to speak.

"But you were often angry with him, weren't you?"

Xenia lifted her head. "I thought I could fix him, Father. I thought if I explained often enough what he needed to do to get his life in order, he would do it. But he never did, and it killed him. I didn't even want him to go to that party. I knew the group of men who were throwing it, and I knew what their parties were like. But his friend was going. His friend was an alcoholic, and my husband tried to convince him not to go, and then when he couldn't, he decided to go with him and try to save him from the worst."

"He sounds like a loyal friend, with his friend's true welfare at heart."

"Yes, but he wasn't fit for the task!" Xenia's voice began to rise. "He didn't know his own weakness, and instead of saving his friend, he killed him and himself, too. It's my worst nightmare, his stupid lack of judgment finally bringing him to the worst possible fate. I was always afraid something would happen to him, and it did! He died because he wouldn't listen to me! He said I didn't see the best in people, that I didn't give people a chance. He didn't want to be like me, Father, and now he's dead because he wasn't."

Xenia's purse slid to the floor as she crushed her face in her hands, wailing aloud. Her dark hair fell around her shoulders like a black cloud, hiding her. The terrible sound of her grief filled the church.

After a long time, Fr. Nicholas spoke. "Fr. Seraphim Rose of Platina said, 'Do not trust your mind too much; thinking must be refined by suffering, or it will not stand the test of these cruel times'."

"What does that mean?" sobbed Xenia.

"It means that you are angry because you believe your thoughts about your husband, Xenia."

Xenia straightened, and her hair fell back from her face. "What else can I believe? I know what happened, and I know why it happened. There's no easy answer to this, Father! Believe me! I've been looking for one for decades!"

"Don't get angry with me, Xenia. I am not offering you an easy answer. Listen to what I said again. I said you are angry because you believe your thoughts about your husband. So what is the answer? What am I asking you to do?"

Xenia's eyes flashed with rage, the tears still streaming down her face, but she took a deep, sobbing breath and kept silent.

Fr. Nicholas continued, keeping his voice calm and low, speaking carefully. "I am asking you to stop believing your thoughts about him. I want you to actively consider what you might not know about the situation and about your husband's spiritual life. I do not know much about your marriage, only what you have told me, but it sounds as if you were the standard of rightness in the marriage. You, instead of Christ. You saw your own way as orderly and your husband's way as foolish. You say he meant well, but you do not seem to value that. As I was listening, I thought of your saint, Xenia of Petersburg. She was a fool. A *fool* for Christ. Have you never thought of your husband in this light?"

"St. Xenia did not kill herself and three other people because of an error in judgment, Father!" Xenia shouted, brushing fiercely and ineffectually at the tears on her cheeks.

"I am not saying your husband was perfect, Xenia. I am simply asking you to look at him from another angle. You must do it as an exercise. Each day, set aside some time to think about your husband as a man who was on his way to becoming a fool for Christ.”

“But he never got there, Father! He never got past being just a fool!”

“How do you know that? How can you wash out every good act of his life in the stain of his final error?”

“The error was too great! It was death!”

“Death is the absence of God, Xenia. Your husband, however poor his judgment in doing so, died trying to help a friend. How can you be sure God was not there?”

“How can you be sure he didn’t die in sin? How can you know what happened and not see that he gave into temptation and died before he could recover himself?” Xenia’s hands were clasped together, palm to palm, every knuckle white. Her voice was strident, and her tears washed down her ashen cheeks like rain.

“We were not there, Xenia, either one of us. So you have no more proof for your argument than I do. In fact, I could say that you have less because you are so angry. Your anger is thinking for you, and angry thoughts are never trustworthy. They come from the wrong source. We cannot solve this problem from knowledge of the situation. We have to solve it from knowledge of God.”

“And what does God say, Fr. Nicholas?”

“‘For whoever desires to save his life will lose it, but whoever loses his life for My sake will find it’. Matthew 16:25. Just suppose God looked at his heart. Suppose God looked at what he was trying to do, not just at what he did. Suppose that every time you were saying 'You are falling short', God was saying, 'Keep trying, you are almost there'."

Xenia reached a trembling hand to lift her purse off the floor. She slung it over her shoulder, stumbled away from the chair, and left the church without speaking again, letting the heavy door slam shut behind her. She drove her car home with a fierce carefulness, making each motion a slap against the carelessness of her dead intoxicated husband, a confirmation that her priest had sided with the enemy. She parked in the center of her own driveway. Her trembling hands tried three times to unlock the front door. She slammed her palm against the door panel, unable to believe that even the small relief of entering her own house easily could be denied her.

Once inside, Xenia drew her chair close to the sliding door, bringing her face near the glass, selecting individual raindrops for attention, letting her gaze slip down the pane along each silvery trail until the drops, one after another, lost cohesiveness and dissolved into the indiscriminate wetness, the gray day. She breathed lightly, withholding the moisture-producing warmth of her breath from the glass so that it would not obscure her concentration. She knew, too well, that in a matter of moments this meditation would fail her and her being would vibrate with painful, tingling rage.

As the pain began, she strove to direct it, to stoke the new flame of her rage against Fr. Nicholas. She had read, in old prairie stories, of men fighting fire with fire, setting a blaze to fend off another blaze not of their own making. But she had never understood the art of it, the reason why flame could drive off flame, and she wondered if it was truly possible or simply another example of the flawed science of the long ago, the less enlightened. Whatever the science, it must be the act of desperation. Who would set a blaze without first abandoning hope that the original fire could be quenched in any other way?

With a long, shuddering sigh, the breath escaped from her lungs and with it the space between her raw nerves and the hot surface of her pain. The raindrops blurred, the glass lost its sheen, and Xenia groped for the heavy gold drapery, pulling it closed, hiding her uncontrollable grief from the passing world.

Chapter 16

Strawberries, one last time. A taste of summer, with autumn approaching. Anna set the crystal bowl in the center of the table and arranged red linen napkins around it like petals, making the fruit her centerpiece. As she did so, she remembered Timothy backed against her dining room wall while she and Dorothy went on and on about strawberries. She thought of his large, silent presence disrupting the meeting and of Jewel staring at the lemon squares behind Dorothy's back. *What will happen next? Do I even want to know? And I suppose I'll have to go on with that wretched cross stitch.* Anna sighed deeply and started down the hall to look for it. *I should learn to knit, but would that help? I can't seem to muster any patience for this group. We've only had two meetings. It will take some time for them to coalesce, won't it? But you'd think people who all go to the same church wouldn't be so awkward with each other. I thought this was a good idea before I started it, but it isn't turning out well, is it?* She glanced at her watch, the habitual gesture of a woman who sees each day as a series of tasks and hopes to find a sense of fulfillment in their timely accomplishment. At the moment, a day of dusting and polishing, of compiling a tastefully arranged dessert buffet and ironing a tastefully arranged outfit had left her moody and tired. Her day reminded her of juice from an over-squeezed orange, a little faded and watery. *My trouble is that I keep squeezing the same orange over and over again. I do the same things over and over again. No wonder there isn't any flavor left. But where do I get another orange? Or should I try another fruit altogether?* She smiled a little at the ridiculous comparison, but the feeling of weariness persisted. She had drifted to a stop partway down the hall and stood now just outside the little powder room across from the kitchen. Stepping inside, she gazed inquiringly at herself in the mirror.

"So," she said aloud to her reflection, "what is the problem here?" Her own blue eyes returned the question, brows a little lifted. She crossed herself and closed her eyes, breaking off one conversation to begin another. "Dear Father, I've been a hostess to one person after another for as long as I can remember. I'm tired out. What am I doing wrong with this group? Is it me? Is it them? Is it going to be better tonight and will I feel like I was making a mountain out of a molehill? Why are there so many molehills with these people? What shall I do?" She sighed. "In the name of the Father, and of the Son, and of the Holy Spirit, Amen." She crossed herself again and sat down on the edge of the sink, staring at the small watercolor painting on the opposite wall depicting a pre-Raphaelite woman, her flowing hair and clothing weaving themselves into the leafy vines climbing around her. Her face seemed expressionless to Anna, as if she found nothing strange about her predicament or perhaps misunderstood it.

What an annoying picture, Anna thought. *I wonder why I chose it.*

The doorbell rang. Anna stood up, shouldering the burdens of the moment. But she took the picture down before she went to answer the door.

Timothy stood on her doorstep, the paper bag in one hand, a box of cream puffs in the other. "I came first," he said. "I want to pick my own chair."

"Understandable," Anna replied, struggling against a wild giggle rising in her throat. "Come right in. But I wouldn't advise you to take that red armchair. Xenia always sits there when she comes to my house, and I don't know what she might do if she found someone else in her place. Now if you'll pardon me for a minute, I need to dispose of this."

"What is it?" asked Timothy curiously, closing the front door behind him. She held out the painting, and he set down his bag, took the picture in one hand, and lifted his glasses to peer closely at the entangled pre-Raphaelite woman. "Not my type," he said with unexpected humor, returning the picture to Anna. "Too much hair and not enough wit to cut the ivy down."

Anna laughed freely, thankful for the chance to let the wild giggle escape, and left Timothy to find his own chair while she stowed the witless lady and her ivy in the coat closet and laid Timothy's cream puffs on the dining room table. The other guests were not expected for another twenty minutes, so she came into the living room, curious to see what chair he had chosen for himself.

Timothy had taken a chair from the dining room and placed it next to the end table. On his right stood the sofa where Elizabeth and Barbara always sat, and on his left stood the end table next to Jewel's habitual spot. "You needed one more chair," he explained. "I'll start knitting now." He opened the paper bag and pulled out the blanket and his needles. Anna watched him setting the needles in his hands. It was difficult to place him, to find a category he might fit into. His glasses and his musical training suggested an intellectual. His ponytail and sandals, and the Swiss Army knife in a well-worn case on his belt, suggested an outdoorsman. His red polo shirt and khaki shorts suggested a businessman at leisure. His big-boned, muscular body suggested an athlete. His clean, quiet hands, knitting, suggested an artist or an ascetic. There was something incredible about those big square fingers making such neat, even stitches. And without the female gaze and tension around him, Anna noticed the essential quietness of his presence. *If we had ever had a son, I might have sat with him like this, waiting for guests. We might have talked things over. He can knit. George can't knit and neither can I, but sometimes the next generation solves what the last generation only fumbled with.* Almost without meaning to, she said, "Timothy, what can I do to make things go well tonight?"

He stopped knitting and looked up at her face, where she stood in the middle of the room. "You mean you want people to be more comfortable?"

Anna nodded.

"Are you comfortable yourself?" he asked, and something about his deep voice made the question courteous, not impertinent.

Anna grimaced. "Not very, and I don't know why. With my husband's work, I've been hostess to every kind of social gathering for so many years I could do it in my sleep. And I know these people. They know each other."

"That's what it is, then," said Timothy, going back to his knitting. "Everyone is uncomfortable because everyone is uncomfortable. Except Elizabeth. And maybe Dorothy. She's too young to be uncomfortable, and Elizabeth's too old." Again, the deep, quiet voice gave the words a respectful quality.

"If I could just get a conversation started," Anna mourned, "it would help. But each time, something happens that absorbs my attention or upsets someone else, and my mind goes blank. Or else," she added wryly, "the only things I can think of to say are not appropriate."

"Maybe," said Timothy, surprising her, "I should just start telling knock-knock jokes to Xenia."

Anna shouted with laughter and went to answer the ringing doorbell.

One by one, the women drifted in, all showing by some little gesture or expression that they noticed Timothy's new position and the addition of another chair. Elizabeth and Barbara, whether by accident or design, switched places on their sofa so that Elizabeth, not Barbara, sat next to Timothy. Elizabeth seemed pleased, settling herself into the comfortable seat with a grin and a friendly greeting as she hauled the half-finished afghan from her bag.

"Hi, young man. I see we didn't scare you off last week," she remarked, taking her first stitch. Barbara frowned over her knitting, but Timothy took this bluntness in stride.

"I don't scare easily," he replied in his deep voice, turning his head away from her briefly as Jewel sat down on the other side of the end table.

"Hi, Jewel," said Timothy, watching her.

"Hi," said Jewel, opening her case. "Hi, Dorothy," she turned to greet her couch-mate, "how's the scarf?" She shifted slightly, hiding her face from him.

Timothy turned back to Elizabeth, bent his head toward her confidentially, and whispered, "Did you bring pie?"

Elizabeth chuckled. "Blueberry pie and ice cream, too."

Timothy grinned. "If you weren't already taken, I'd ask you to step out with me."

"It's still the quickest way to a man's heart," she returned, leaning towards him in her turn, with a wink. "I haven't been married forty years for nothing."

Anna, watching from across the room, saw Timothy glance warily at Barbara before leaning back in his chair. She suspected he was trying to warm things up in his corner, but Barbara appeared to be beyond him. She was frowning again, and during his banter with Elizabeth, Anna was sure she had seen Barbara sniff disdainfully and shake her head. Elizabeth was easy, God bless her. Jewel was listening intently to Dorothy's every word. It only needed Xenia, who was a little late this evening, to cast a fierce and tactless eye on the scene and drop a lightning bolt to start the fire.

Silence reigned for a few moments as Dorothy finished describing her day to Jewel. The doorbell rang once and Xenia could be heard letting herself into the hall. "I'm here, Anna!" she called and followed her voice into the living room, making straight for the red armchair and opening her workbag as she came. Anna watched her friend, thinking she did not look well. Xenia's hair streamed down her back. She wore a gray linen dress, and her skin seemed only a few shades warmer. Dark smudges under her eyes gave her face a bruised look. A murmur of greeting came toward her from the group, but she only nodded sharply and began to knit.

Dorothy's bright young voice broke the awkward silence. She put down her knitting and sat forward on the sofa, looking around the group. "Since this is a church group, and we started by mentioning our saints, I thought it would be nice to read something sacred at the beginning of every meeting."

Anna gazed at her youngest guest, feeling in the back of her neck that Xenia's eyebrows had gone up and her nostrils flared. "Did you?" she said inadequately, forestalling Xenia's famous snort. "What did you have in mind, dear?"

Dorothy smiled, plainly considering this an invitation. "I brought a little reading from the writings of my patron, Dorotheos of Gaza. Can I read it after we say the prayer?"

Anna realized guiltily that she had forgotten all about her plan to start with a prayer. Apparently, so had everyone else. No one had noticed the omission last time. They had been too busy wondering where Timothy would sit. Dorothy's mention of it now almost looked like a reminder. Anna felt flustered. "Certainly, Dorothy. Shall we pray now?" She stood up and looked around the room for a likely person to lead the prayer.

Before Anna could speak, Dorothy, who had also jumped to her feet, leaned forward a little to see past Jewel to Timothy. "Since we have a chanter here, could we ask you to chant our prayer, Timothy?"

Timothy got to his feet, still holding his knitting to keep his place, and looked to Anna for guidance.

"If you don't mind, Timothy, that would be lovely," said Anna, apologetically.

Timothy set his knitting on his chair. The other women rose and crossed themselves as he did. Timothy closed his eyes, breathed deeply, and began to chant the prayer from Psalm 140.

> *O Lord, I have cried out unto Thee,*
> *hear Thou me. Hear Thou me, O*
> *Lord. O Lord, I have cried out unto*
> *Thee, hear Thou me. Give ear to the*
> *voice of my supplication, when I cry*
> *out unto Thee. Hear Thou me, O*
> *Lord. Let my prayer be set forth*
> *before Thee as the incense, and the*
> *lifting up of my hands as the*
> *evening sacrifice.*
> *Hear Thou me, O Lord.*

He chanted slowly, his deep voice cherishing each word, lingering unselfconsciously for each full note. The sound filled the room. When the prayer ended, no one moved. They stood in a circle, their heads still bowed, eyes closed, breathing the resonant air.

Dorothy opened her eyes first, and the small sounds of her braid sliding forward and her blue gingham skirt rustling against the upholstery broke the silence as she turned again to Timothy, smiling. "Thank you," she said, and everyone stirred, crossing themselves, sitting down, searching for knitting, while Dorothy reached into her brown bag for the reading she had prepared.

Anna said nothing, but she caught Timothy's eye across the room and gave him a little nod, smiling. It didn't seem right to thank him, as if the prayer had been a personal favor.

Jewel excused herself suddenly and started toward the door, reaching it just as Dorothy opened her book. Dorothy paused, and Jewel paused. "I'll just be a minute," Jewel said, speaking to Dorothy as if the rest of the group were not also staring at her escape. "You go ahead."

Dorothy frowned a little. "I could wait," she began, but Jewel shook her head.

"Do it now. It will be nice to have it right after the prayer." Jewel vanished into the hall.

Anna decided to take a hand. "That's right, Dorothy. You just start. We'd all like to hear what you brought."

Somewhat reassured, Dorothy opened her book and began to read in her clear, bright voice. "Imagine that the world is a circle, that God is the center, and that the radii are the different ways human beings live. When those who wish to come closer to God walk towards the center of the circle, they come closer to one another at the same time as to God. The closer they come to God, the closer they come to one another. And the closer they come to one another, the closer they come to God." She closed her book. "That's from his instructions for monks. I thought it was nice to think about people coming together when we're here in a group."

Xenia coughed.

"Thank you, Dorothy," said Anna.

"That was nice," added Barbara, speaking for the first time. Elizabeth nodded and smiled at Dorothy kindly, seconding the motion.

"That's a great metaphor," commented Timothy. Dorothy smiled at him and put the book away in her bag.

Jewel came back into the room as he spoke and crossed quickly to her seat. She opened the red case on her lap and immediately became absorbed in attaching hooks to a pair of green sea-glass earrings. Dorothy opened her mouth to say something to Jewel, then seemed to change her mind, and started knitting.

Anna glanced at Xenia taking sharp, jabbing stitches, her hair falling like a curtain around her. Her lips moved silently, and from long years of friendship, Anna could guess what she was saying. *As long as she keeps it to herself. Well, at least until the rest of them go home. I'm exhausted. Do I really have to do counted cross-stitch? What time is it? I can't believe they've only been here fifteen minutes. I'll just sort my thread or something. I'm too tired to focus on anything so silly. I wish I could just turn on some quiet music. Piano. Celtic harp. Something with no words. But that would be admitting defeat because no one would try to talk over it. Not that they're trying now.*

Anna fussed with the thread and pretended to check her pattern for another forty-five minutes before, glancing at the clock for the twentieth time at least, she saw with relief that it was time to move the tea things into the dining room. Stuffing the cross-stitch untidily into its bag, she escaped to the kitchen. As the murmur and rumble from the living room told her that people were putting away their knitting, she heard someone behind her and turned to see Timothy coming into the kitchen, this time without his bag of knitting.

"I saw lemonade on the table," he said. "Do you have a tall glass?"

Anna was puzzled. "There are tumblers on the table by the pitcher, aren't there?"

"I was hoping for a pretty one," he answered solemnly.

Surprised, Anna opened the glassware cupboard and stared into it, seeking inspiration.

"That one," said Timothy, over her shoulder, and she stepped aside as he reached a large hand into the cupboard and lifted a hurricane glass carefully from the shelf. "I saw mint in your garden..."

"Help yourself," she offered, and watched as he went purposefully out the front door. A few minutes later, from the dining room where she was pouring tea, she saw him return with a sprig of mint in his hand. He came through the dining room, collecting a handful of strawberries from the centerpiece.

"Timothy has the right idea," said Dorothy, setting down her pie to spoon some strawberries onto her plate. "Would you like some, too?" she asked, gesturing toward Barbara across the table with the spoon. Barbara held out her plate.

"Where's Jewel?" asked Elizabeth. "I've cut pie for everyone else, and a big slice for Timothy so he won't carry me off!" She grinned mischievously at Anna beside her.

"She'll be along in a minute," said Anna. "I think she's just packing up her case. All those small parts, you know."

Timothy returned from the kitchen and passed through the dining room without stopping, the hurricane glass in his hand. Anna's eyes widened. She saw cut strawberries and mint in the lemonade, and sugar crystals clung around the rim of the glass. Was he a lemonade connoisseur, or…Anna thought she caught a murmur of voices in the living room. A minute passed. She realized she was holding a plate with a piece of pie on it, so she picked up a fork and took a bite. Xenia was still in the living room, too. What was going on in there?

Timothy returned to the dining room without the glass of lemonade, bringing Xenia with him and holding his paper bag. "Here's Xenia for some pie, and I've got to take mine on a paper plate tonight because I'm meeting someone at the airport."

"Oh, did they get you to pick up the priest for this weekend?" Elizabeth asked. "It's about time Fr. Nicholas went on vacation. His brother always covers for him, you know, and he always covers for his brother."

Xenia's face became alert at the mention of Fr. Nicholas, but she said nothing. Anna handed her a cup of tea and went to open the door for Timothy, whose hands were full of bag and pie. As he said goodbye on the doorstep, her curiosity overcame her. "What happened to the lemonade?" she asked, in a conspiratorial whisper.

"She drank it," said Timothy, and he walked down the path through the garden to his truck at the curb.

Chapter 17

Xenia took the plate of blueberry pie Elizabeth was holding out to her and the cup of tea from Anna. The cheerful clatter of voices and silver spoons brushing crystal plates grated on her ears, and she turned carefully, balancing the tea and the pie, and went back to the red armchair and the comparative quiet of the living room. Across from her, Jewel was just closing the red case. A hurricane glass with a sprig of mint and a slice of strawberry in it stood on the end table beside her. Xenia sat down and drank her tea, making no attempt to talk. If Jewel had wanted chatter, she would be in the dining room. Jewel stood holding her case for a moment, glancing toward the door to the hall and the door to the dining room. With a quick breath, she said, "Good night, Xenia," and chose the door to the hall.

Xenia leaned back in her chair and closed her eyes, letting the pie stand un-tasted on the small round table beside her chair. She held the tea cup between her palms, nursing the warm china and the sweet flowery scent. They would all go soon. Timothy and Jewel had gone already. The others would not stay long. She could hear Elizabeth offering Dorothy a ride. Any moment now, the house would be empty of guests, except herself, and she knew that her friendship with Anna had reached the point where she was no longer a guest.

It was strange to think that someone like Anna should have become so close a friend to her, so necessary to her daily sanity, such as it was. Anna was so calm and gracious. She knew what to do every day, and she did it. Anna's life was tidy. Anna's husband was alive. And yet, there was something comforting about her. Talking to Anna was soothing. You felt that she understood more than she had personally experienced, or perhaps it was just that whether she understood or not, she sympathized, quietly and sincerely, without gushing.

Xenia heard the door shut and realized the house was quiet now. Anna drifted in, kicking off her shoes as she came, and sank into her chair beside Xenia's, a cup of tea in her hands.

"Lord have mercy," said Anna succinctly, and took a long drink of tea. She got up to turn off the overhead light, leaving the incandescent glow from the floor lamp behind their chairs. She sank into her chair again and sighed. "You look as tired as I feel, Xen."

"That girl," said Xenia, without bothering to name her, "has no sense."

"It was certainly awkward," Anna replied. "I don't know why it bothered me so much. She's among friends, church friends at that. It shouldn't be wrong to suggest that we start with a prayer."

"If that were all she did, maybe not, although the way she did it came off like a criticism of you because you're the hostess of these 'church friends' and that means it's your place, not hers, to lead the group." Xenia took another sip and set down her cup, warming to the subject. "But that wasn't the worst of it. She set Timothy up! What could he do but say yes? The man is already sticking out around here like a sore thumb without her calling attention to him and making him perform. She thanked him, like it was a personal favor or something, like she was his hostess or the chairwoman of the meeting!"

Anna sighed, drank her tea, and sighed again. "It's probably because I'm doing such a bad job of being the hostess, Xen. Seriously, I can't remember ever having a group that failed to come together like this one has. This is our third meeting, and look at us! It's like a middle school party with everyone too embarrassed to talk to everyone else."

"It's not embarrassment, it's Timothy!" snapped Xenia.

"It's not Timothy," Anna contradicted, "it's the rest of them. He's not doing a thing. It's everyone else getting wound up in their own personal issues because of him. There's Barbara, sniffing and snorting at Elizabeth, and there's Elizabeth, practically flirting with him, but that's just her way. But Dorothy—Xen, have you ever seen anything so *transparent*? And I don't think he sees her that way at all. She's just a kid to him."

"She's just a kid, period," said Xenia, "and if she doesn't figure it out by next time, she's going to embarrass herself. And won't that be fun for us all."

"Figure what out? That he isn't interested in her?" asked Anna, setting down her empty cup and drawing her feet up under her in the chair.

"More than that. He's not only not interested in Dorothy, he is interested in Jewel."

Anna sat upright. "What makes you so sure?"

"Lemonade," said Xenia, with one of her strange, shattering bursts of laughter. She pointed to the empty hurricane glass, which still stood on the end table by Jewel's customary place.

"It was for her?" cried Anna. "You were both still in here, so I wondered, but I wasn't sure. Tell me what happened. Did you see it?"

"I saw everything. He went right past me when he came in, but he knew I was there, and he didn't care. Why should he? Who cares what I think? He handed her the glass, and you should have seen her face. He saw it, that's for sure, but it didn't stop him. He stood right there, waiting for her to taste it, so she set down her case and held out her hands for the glass."

"Well!" said Anna, plainly torn between discretion and rampant curiosity. "And I thought I was imagining things when I caught him staring at her in the garden."

"The man has a plan," Xenia decided. "He set his chair next to her, and he made her lemonade."

"He went all the way out into the garden to get fresh mint to make her lemonade," Anna burst out. "Xenia, this makes my day. If nothing else comes from this wretched knitting group, maybe Timothy and Jewel will fall in love. How satisfying that would be."

Xenia frowned. "If it works out, it might be."

"Why wouldn't it work out?" asked Anna, disinclined to see obstacles in the way.

"Sometimes, love doesn't," answered Xenia, and her face darkened.

Anna leaned across the arm of her chair and grasped her friend's hand, cherishing it between her own. "Oh Xen, I am so sorry for your grief. I wish there were something I could do for you. Is it worse again?"

Xenia looked away from her, into the far corners of the room. "It is. If Fr. Nicholas had just let things be…"

Anna patted her hand, but said nothing.

Xenia stirred a little. Tears slipped from the corners of her eyes. "I did love my husband, Anna," she said, with difficulty, "but…" There was a long silence. Xenia lifted her tea with her free hand, and took a sip. "I don't think love is enough. It can't have been enough. It wasn't for us, or I wouldn't be here, like this, so many years after his death."

Anna hesitated, about to speak but weighing her words, and Xenia knew her friend was trying not to say the wrong thing. Her mouth twisted a little at the knowledge that Anna could see how close she was to falling into a million pieces.

"What did you want love to be enough *for*, Xen?" asked Anna carefully.

Xenia frowned at the dark window panes at the far end of the living room. She felt Anna's thumb absently soothing the back of her right hand.

"Who is Jewel?" Xenia said, after a silence. "I'll grant you she's attractive, or she would be if she wasn't wound up so tight. But why is she wound up so tight? What makes her such a mouse around us? Why is she visiting our church, instead of going to a church where she grew up? Timothy's an attractive man, but he might as well be a lump of coal for all the notice she takes of him. Why is that? Do you see what I mean? We don't know the answers to any of those questions, and as far as I know, neither does Timothy. If he did, would he still be interested? Can he actually take her on, with everything that might come with her?"

Anna nodded slowly. "I see what you mean. We're all a package deal, Xen. Nobody comes without some problems."

Xenia shook her head. "I think there are problems and there are problems. I'm sure you aren't perfect, but it can't be that hard for George to be married to you. Can you imagine a living man who would be brave enough to take on *me*?"

Anna looked shocked. "Would you want one to?"

"No, that isn't my point. The Lord knows I'm not looking for romance. But my point is, while both you and I might be said to have problems, mine are more than your average man could cope with. He might fall in love with me, but I would destroy him and his love, when he got close enough."

"What makes you think Jewel has problems, Xen?"

"I don't know that she does, Anna. I'm not arguing with you. I just can't look. I can't watch and believe, like you can. It rubs my last nerve to see people fall in love." Xenia bowed her head.

Anna was quiet for a few minutes. Then, "I missed you at church on Sunday, Xen."

Xenia's throat tightened. "I can't go there, Anna. Fr. Nicholas tried again—" her voice failed.

"He's on vacation this week, remember? Timothy's getting the other priest at the airport tonight." Anna spoke softly, like a mother patiently reasoning with a frantic child.

"I just can't, Anna. I can't."

Xenia turned her face to her friend, unable to speak, and they sat quietly in the lamplight, holding hands, staving off the darkness.

Chapter 18

Jewel stood in the bathroom, her toothbrush in one hand, staring into the mirror over the sink. She had made it this far—out of Anna's house, home in the car, into her house, out of her clothes, into her pajamas—by singing the alphabet song in her head, over and over, shutting out thought. But now, her glance caught in the mirror, her hand frozen in midair, the whole evening washed over her like a towering wave crashing down to the sand.

I'll have to warn him off. I don't know what he's doing, but I'm the wrong girl. She's already in love with him. It can't be me. I'm not going to do this. I'll have to warn him off.

She saw him again, so vividly that the walls and the mirror in front of her faded into mist. He came toward her from the doorway, the dark eyes behind the clear lenses watching her intently. He held a glass of lemonade, a beautiful glass of carefully prepared lemonade, lemonade with fresh mint, with sliced strawberries, and sugar crystals clinging to the moistened rim. She was sitting on the couch, just closing her jewelry case, but he seemed so enormous crossing the room that she stood up instinctively, trying to find equal footing with him. She had been so slow to react, so completely unprepared for him. None of her standard defenses had sprung readily to mind.

She could smell the mint as he held out the glass. His voice was so deep. "I made this for you, Jewel," he said, using her name.

Mesmerized, Jewel saw her hands come up to take it. She felt his warm fingers, slipping away on the cold glass as her hands closed around it. The sugar melted on her lips as she tasted the lemonade, laced with mint and strawberry. She saw, over the rim of the glass, that he stood silently in front of her, unembarrassed by Xenia's presence in the chair behind him. He was waiting to see if she liked what he had made.

She took a long drink, letting her mouth fill with slices of strawberry and a mint leaf, glancing up at him and feeling shy over the awkward business of chewing the fruit.

"Thank you," she said, almost whispering. "I like it."

His quick smile flashed across his face like light, a little relieved, a little triumphant. He stood still, waiting for her to finish the lemonade, so she drank it all, trying not to gulp, and set down the empty glass. Her eyes returned to his eyes, and she saw his glance moving slowly over her face, noting every feature. Then he swung around and was gone, taking Xenia with him into the dining room.

Jewel stared at herself in the mirror. Eyes, nose, lips, chin, blush. What had he seen? What stunned, awkward face had she made, watching him and his lemonade come toward her? How could she prepare for something so unforeseen and forestall it? What could she do about it now? Need she do anything?

Dorothy had almost stepped around her to get to Timothy, to get him to chant for her in front of everyone, at a gathering Dorothy wasn't even hosting. A man might not have been able to read Dorothy's face, but everyone else there knew Dorothy had a crush on Timothy. Jewel was sure of it. She was equally sure they would all approve of the match. So why had Timothy made lemonade for her, for Jewel, the girl who wasn't named for a saint? All her wicked knowledge of the male sex told her it was not from pity or pious charity. It was so deliberate, so intricate and intimate. Yet he had not touched her. He had stayed away, with his hands by his sides, with Xenia directly behind him. He was a chanter at a church. He was a man who knitted. Perhaps, after all, he was a type outside her experience, if such a thing existed.

Whatever he was, he remained a man, and there was only one thing to be done. She couldn't be friends with him, and she couldn't be more than friends with any man. There was no place for chances in Jewel's lonely fortress. If he showed any further signs of interest, she would tell him, politely but firmly, to go away.

Besides, he would lose interest quick enough if he knew more about me.

A vivid image of Dorothy, complete with sound effects, burned across her inward vision, the blue gingham dress and the pearls, the bright voice, the holy book, the personal thanks for a chanted prayer that Jewel could not let herself remember, even for a second. She bit her lip and tasted the lingering sweetness of sugar crystals and strawberry lemonade. A lump welled up in her throat. She grabbed the toothpaste tube, squeezing it too hard, spilling a little. She brushed her teeth, her tongue, the roof of her mouth, and her lips, especially her lips, vigorously, roughly, until the toothbrush slipped out of her fingers and she bent to turn on the spigot, burying her face in handfuls of cold water, gasping for breath.

In the morning, on her way to work, Jewel put on her headset and called Sara from the car.

"I'm driving to work, babe," said Sara's voice in her ear as she pulled out of the driveway. "Did something happen? Is Albert after you again?"

"No, I'm fine. I just wanted to call…" Jewel's voice trailed off. It suddenly seemed like an enormous task to tell Sara about Timothy and his lemonade.

"Are you okay? You sound funny," said Sara. Jewel could hear her drinking coffee. Sara never drove to work without stopping for coffee at the little drive-through stand at the end of their street.

"I just wanted to vent, I think. There's this girl who makes me absolutely crazy, and I was hoping you would think she was crazy, too." Jewel felt nervous and guilty. It was true, of course, but it was a massive evasion.

"What girl? Someone at work?"

"No. I went to that church, and then I got invited to join a knitting group. First the girl was at the church, and now she's at the knitting group. I wish she would go away," said Jewel vehemently.

"Ummmm....what? You went to that church? Why didn't you tell me? That's great. Wow. So you must have made some friends there. Who invited you to knit? I didn't know you were a knitter."

"No, no, I don't knit. I do my jewelry there. Most of them knit, but you can do any craft you like. The woman who invited me is really nice. Her name is Anna, and I think she likes me. But Dorothy gives me a rash."

"Tell me again who Dorothy is?" Sara took another sip. "I don't think the caffeine has reached my brain yet."

"I could call you later," suggested Jewel, merging onto the interstate.

"No, no, you can't do that. You've got me all curious now. You have to explain. There's still a good fifteen minutes before I make it to school."

"Okay. I went to that church, the one with the priest who almost fainted at the Summer Market. When I was there, I met the woman who drove him home. Her name is Anna, and she was friendly to me. Then the second time I went, she told me that she has a little group of friends who meet at her house to do crafts together. I was wearing some of my own jewelry, and she asked about it, and when I told her that I made it, she wanted me to come to her group."

"That's so great!" Sara sounded genuinely enthusiastic this time. "Look at you going out and making friends! And getting a little air time for your fabulous handiwork, too! I'm so proud of you, Jewel."

"Well, I'm glad you are. But the problem is Dorothy."

"Ah, we're back to her again. I'm sure she's a real stinker, but will you please tell me who she is?"

Jewel paused. How could she put this in terms Sara would understand?

"Dorothy is—" prompted Sara.

"She goes to the church, too. She and her mother invited me to sit with them the second time I was there, and I think they're trying to be nice, but...if you could see her, it would help. She's blond and blue-eyed, she wears real pearls all the time, and she has these long dresses that are always pink or blue. She's always so good, and she knows she's so good, and everyone around her knows it, too."

"Wow, she sounds like a pill," said Sara helpfully.

"Maybe it's me that sounds like a pill," Jewel said remorsefully. "She's only about nineteen or twenty, and her life is so different from mine. Maybe I'd be like that too, if I had two doting parents following me around."

"No, you wouldn't," said Sara with conviction. "My parents love me, but you don't see me going around in a pink dress doing good to the heathen, do you?"

Jewel giggled. "But wait, Sara, it gets worse. There's this guy who started coming to the group."

"What for? Men don't knit."

"He does. He has these great big hands and he does it really slowly, but he knits. It's kind of amazing. But the point is that he's a chanter at the church and looks really clean-cut and everything, and Dorothy has a crush on him."

"W-w-wow!" Sara could hardly get the word out, through her laughter. "Let me get this straight. You're going to a church-person knitting group with Miss Pink-and-Blue and her knitting chanter boyfriend? And how's that going for you, may I ask?"

"Well, but he's not actually her boyfriend. At least, I don't think he is. It's her that likes him," said Jewel incoherently. "I really like Anna, but I don't want to sit there and watch Dorothy's love life happening right in front of my face. If it does happen. Which it probably will. You can see nothing's ever gone wrong in her whole life."

"So she likes him, but he doesn't like her? Wow. This gets better and better. How do you know he doesn't like her? Is she embarrassing herself? Or did Anna tell you?"

"Well," began Jewel, thankful that Sara couldn't see her face, "I think he might think that he likes....I mean, I might be wrong, but he made me lemonade." Her voice choked itself off just in time to clear the line for an explosive shout from Sara.

"It's *you*! He likes you, not her. She must be so mad. Am I right? Are you telling me that chanter boy is coming for *you*? That *will* be a first!" There was a pulsating moment of silence during which Sara apparently realized what she had said. "Oh, Jewel, you know what I mean. I didn't mean that as hurtfully as it sounded. I'm sorry, honey. You know I love you."

"It's okay," said Jewel, humbly. "It would hurt my feelings except it's completely true. Seriously. Who could picture me with a church guy?"

"Oh," wailed Sara, "that's exactly how I don't want you to feel. My stupid mouth runs away with me. Your life is so different now. It makes sense that a new kind of man would want you, right?"

Jewel felt a surge of embarrassment creeping up her neck into her face. "Sara, honestly, I don't know whether he even likes me. He made me this really nice glass of lemonade, with mint and everything, and brought it to me and stood there waiting for me to drink it. That's all. I don't know anything about church guys. Probably he was just being nice. My only point is that Dorothy is much more his type than I could ever be. Much, much more."

"If Dorothy is anything like you say, that doesn't make me think too highly of him."

"Oh, he's not like Dorothy at all," explained Jewel.

Sara laughed. "Babe, you make no sense. First, you say she's awful, then you say she's just his type, and then you say he's nothing like her. How does this add up? How do you know she's his type? Did he say so?"

Jewel felt a headache gathering behind her right eye. "I can't think all this through while I'm driving," she said. "If you say it doesn't make sense, I'm sure you're right, but it made sense to me. I mean, he might think he likes me, but that's just because he doesn't know me. I get the feeling he might actually want more in life than—than—"

"Than your other boyfriends did?" supplied Sara. "Well, good for him. If he has that much sense, he might not be as excited about Dorothy as you seem to think he should be."

Jewel's headache was moving around the side of her eye, on its way to her forehead. "Well, I have to hang up and drive now. I'm at the part with the one-way streets."

"You have to keep me posted, okay?" urged Sara. "I just know something interesting is going to happen."

"Fine," said Jewel. "I hope I left some Advil in my desk at work."

She hung up and caught her own eye in the rearview mirror. "What on earth was I thinking?" she asked. The girl in the mirror made no response.

Chapter 19

Barbara would not be coming this time. Anna hung up the phone with a guilty surge of relief. One down. One less irritant, one less set of preferences to be accommodated. She had seen right through Barbara's thin explanation of commitments at work, of being too tired. With any luck, the commitments would go on indefinitely, and Barbara and her disapproving sniffs would never come back.

Anna sighed and let herself droop, resting her head on her arms on the high counter at the front of the kitchen, where she sat on a bar stool by the telephone. She turned her head so she could look out the window at the brilliant red leaves of a tree, glinting and dancing in the steady rainfall that began in autumn and seemed to last, uninterrupted, until late spring. So many people complained of the rain in Seattle, but Anna loved it. She loved the soft sound, pattering on the roof, and the soft gray glow seeping into rooms cosseted by lamplight. She loved the deep verdant color it brought to the grass and the garden.

What can I do to make the knitting group feel special tonight? How can I bring the comfort of this rainy day to them? Somehow, the removal of Barbara had lightened the burden enough that she felt willing to try again. Not inspired, exactly, but able to see that the group might have potential.

Soup, she thought. *It's a perfect day for soup. I'll call and tell them to come to dinner. George can stay, for dinner at least, and that will give Timothy some company.* With renewed energy, she lifted her head and started telephoning, holding the phone with one hand as she rummaged for a pot and assembled meat, barley, stock, and vegetables on the counter. She selected fresh herbs from a basket harvested earlier in the day, crushing a few leaves in her fingers, relishing their pungent scent. If she started now, their savory blessing would greet her guests as they opened the front door.

George came home just as she finished sautéing the meat and dropped it into the pot.

"Mmmm," he murmured, sniffing the air and stooping to kiss the back of her neck. "Soup for a rainy day. Will you save some for me, or is it all for the irritable knitters?"

Anna turned into his arms, pressing her face gratefully against his chest, breathing his clean scent. *This is one thing I did right*, she thought. *I may be a childless perpetual hostess, but I love my husband, and he loves me.*

"Do you mind?" she asked him, still muffled in his shirt. "Do you mind that we never had a child and I had a vicarious career?"

George's arms tightened, and he rested his cheek against the top of her head. "I love your vicarious career!" They were silent for a moment, holding each other close. "I would have liked a daughter," he said, breaking the silence. "Your daughter would have been—special." His voice was strained, and she felt tears stinging her eyes. She found the neat white handkerchief she tucked into his pocket every morning and blew her nose. There were guests coming. She turned back to her soup pot, but George remained where he was, close behind her.

"You're invited tonight, my love," said Anna over her shoulder. "I'm trying to reset the tone. Barbara quit, and I feel like this is my chance. We're having dinner together. I reached everyone on the phone except Jewel, who probably wasn't home from work yet. Here, you stir this while I try her again."

Anna handed him the spoon and made for the phone, returning for a moment to kiss his cheek because he looked so sweet standing by the stove stirring the soup with his coat still on and his briefcase on the floor by his feet.

Jewel answered just as the voicemail recording began to play. There was a moment of confusion as she disengaged it. "Yes? This is Jewel."

"It's Anna, Jewel. Come early tonight, and don't bring anything you haven't made already."

"What's happening?" Jewel sounded wary.

Anna decided on an honest answer. She was tired of politeness. "I'm making soup, and we're going to sit down to dinner together and try to get to know each other before we knit. I'm hoping we can all relax a little. I've felt like things were getting strained."

"Oh." Jewel didn't speak for several seconds. Anna wondered if she, too, had been planning to stop coming. Anna did not want that to happen.

"Just come, honey. My husband George will be joining us, and we'll be very informal. I would love to have you."

"Well—" Jewel started to say something, stopped, then blurted, "Can I sit next to you and your husband?"

Anna's eyebrows flew up, and George raised his own, questioningly, watching the conversation from across the pot of soup. Despite her expression, Anna's voice was calm.

"Of course you can. Whatever makes you most comfortable. In fact," she added, scribbling the conversation down on a pad of paper and pushing it across the counter to George, "why don't you come over now? The others are coming a little later, but you can help us make the salad and we can get acquainted." There. Jewel wouldn't be able to wriggle out of that invitation without downright rudeness, and Anna doubted she was capable of that.

"Thank you," said Jewel's voice, carefully. "I'll— I'm—I'll be there in fifteen minutes."

"See you then!" Anna hung up the phone, perched on the bar stool, and told her husband everything she had been too tired to tell him before, starting with the burned out porch light and ending with the lemonade, laughing when he let out a long, expressive whistle at the end of her story.

"Wouldn't it be fun if they fell in love?" she finished, running her fingers through her hair and straightening her blouse.

"So long as they just plain fall. So long as they aren't pushed!" said George, gazing upon his erstwhile dignified wife in humorous astonishment. "Since when have you become a friend to the lovelorn? A Matchmaker is worse than a Church Lady."

"I just want everyone to be as lucky as I am," Anna came around the counter to take his coat and briefcase. "I want to do something that matters permanently to someone, George."

"Pure altruism," remarked George.

"It is!" countered Anna. "How could it be selfish to want them to be happy?"

"Wanting them to be happy isn't selfish, darling," agreed George peaceably, "but you have to let them be happy in the way that *they* want to be happy, whether it satisfies any goals of your own or not."

Anna blushed a little, but accepted his words with good grace. "I will, Georgie. Watch them tonight. You can watch all of them, in fact, and tell me what you think when they go home."

George nodded his understanding, put the soup spoon in the china spoon rest, and went to let Jewel in at the front door as Anna carried his coat and briefcase down the hall and found a pair of shoes to wriggle into.

Recalling Timothy's comment about everyone being uncomfortable, she kicked the shoes off again and stepped into a pair of moccasins. Then she returned to the kitchen to greet her hesitant guest.

"Hi, Jewel," she said smiling. "Give me your coat, and George will show you where the salad bowl lives." Anna took the dripping jacket and directed a speaking glance at her husband, who shook hands with Jewel and then looked helplessly around the kitchen. From the closet, Anna heard him whisper, "The truth is, Jewel, that I don't know where the salad bowl lives. Where would you look, if you were me?"

His conspiratorial tone surprised a giggle from Jewel, and she relaxed a little. "He doesn't know where it is," said Jewel, basely betraying him to Anna as she returned.

"The man is helpless," Anna replied, giving him a knowing glance as she took a large, hand-made wooden bowl from a cupboard by the stove. "Here, let's just put in some of everything. George, bring me whatever vegetables you can find in the fridge."

George peered into the refrigerator and began rattling drawers and pushing jars. "Radishes," said George. "Carrots, snap peas, three kinds of lettuce...at least, I think this is lettuce, but what if it's really spinach?"

"I want it all," said Anna, "You get it from him as he finds it, Jewel." Jewel stepped nearer to George, receiving whatever he found until her arms were full.

"There's no more," said George. "Unless you want nuts or bacon or something like that?"

"No, just vegetables," Anna decided. "Come over here, Jewel. I've got knives for both of us, and here's another cutting board. There's no right way to do it, just slice whatever you can lay hands on."

"Would you like tea, either of you?" asked George. "I'm going to make a pot of jasmine, I think."

Jewel nodded, and then said, "Thank you, that sounds pretty."

"It is pretty," agreed George, "It's like drinking flowers. Anna likes it." He smiled at her. "I'm good at tea. No salad bowl involved."

"He *is* good at tea," said Anna, "It's one of his many endearing qualities." She caught Jewel's eye and smiled encouragingly. "So, other than a jewelry-making publications manager, who are you?"

Jewel cut a few slices of a cucumber and placed them neatly in the bowl. "I'm not anybody, really. I live about fifteen minutes from the church. I read as many books as I can, about cooking and jewelry and things." She paused, glancing at Anna uncertainly.

"Is that why you started coming to church? From reading?" asked Anna, handing her another cucumber as she finished with the first.

Jewel shook her head. "No, I didn't know anything about it until Fr. Nicholas invited me. I just came because he asked me to."

"So what do you think of it?" Anna gave her a frank look. "You can tell us, you know. We won't mind what you say."

"We're converts, too," added George helpfully.

Jewel gave him a little smile. "I'm not exactly a convert. I mean, I haven't joined. But I like to go there. I like—" she paused, looking from one interested face to the other, "I like to just be still there and take everything in. I try to sit near the aisle so I can smell the incense as the priest passes. I don't know all the words yet, but I follow in the book. Or sometimes not."

"'Be still and know that I am God'," quoted George sympathetically.

Jewel's face darkened a little. Anna offered her a carrot and the peeler.

"Did you grow up around here, Jewel?" asked Anna, after a pause during which Jewel moved to the sink to peel the carrot.

Jewel nodded. "More or less. I did college and a year of grad school at the U. But with a couple years in between," she added, being accurate.

"Are your folks still here?" asked George.

"I don't have any family now," said Jewel in an expressionless voice.

George glanced at Anna for help. Anna considered a tactful change of subject, but something kept her from letting the moment pass. "What happened to them, honey?"

Jewel stopped peeling and looked out the window. "My mother died when I was ten. I left home at seventeen to go to college and never came back. My dad had a girlfriend anyway. Several actually, but mostly one at a time, I think." She handed Anna the carrot and found some radishes. "Did you two grow up here?"

"I did, but George didn't," said Anna, covertly peeling the other side of the carrot before cutting it into pennies. "George is a farm boy from South Dakota. He came here for school and never went home again, except for holidays, when he took me with him. We met in college, and we married on the day after graduation."

Jewel sighed, coming back to the counter with the radishes. "Really? That sounds so nice."

"It has been," said George. "We've been lucky."

"Do you have children?" asked Jewel, making conversation.

George and Anna looked at each other across the kitchen. "We always wished we had," they said, almost in unison. George lifted the whistling kettle from the stove and poured hot water into a blue china pot. He measured loose tea into a tea ball and let it sink into the pot. In a few moments, a delicate sweetness rose to mingle with the aroma of meat and herbs. There was a lull in conversation. Anna checked the soup and washed the lettuce. George watched the tea pot and poured out three cups, with honey and a little milk, when it was ready. He handed a cup to Anna, who set it next to her on the counter, and to Jewel, who held it up to her face, breathing the scent of jasmine with apparent delight.

The doorbell rang. Jewel started.

"I'll get that," said Anna.

Looking around her dining-room table half an hour later, Anna felt hope and curiosity stirring inside her. The room looked bright, the table inviting. Hot soup steamed fragrantly in blue stoneware bowls, the salad added color to the meal, and a basket of crusty rolls was being passed around the table. In the center of the table stood a blue vase full of red leaves collected from the tree outside her kitchen window. George, bless him, had started a conversation with Xenia and Elizabeth, who sat next to each other on his right at the long oval table. Jewel sat on his left, with Anna on her other side. Dorothy sat between Anna and Timothy, who had Elizabeth on his other side.

"Now that we're all served," said Xenia, breaking suddenly into the murmur of talk around the table as the basket of rolls came to rest in front of her, "I'll tell you that today, I sold the entire collection of jewelry that Jewel has made for me. All that hadn't sold already."

Friendly applause broke out spontaneously around the table, and Jewel blushed to the roots of her hair. Her eyes, fixed on Xenia's face, were shining.

"Who bought it?" asked Dorothy, eager for the story.

"A fifty-five-year-old bride," said Xenia, with an odd little smile. "She's one of my regular customers, and I've been selling her clothes to wear on dates with this man for two or three years at least."

"It took him three years to propose?" asked Timothy, raising his eyebrows.

Xenia shook her head. "No, I think it took her three years to say yes. She told me she thought she was too old for love, but that can't be all true if she bought a new outfit for almost every date."

"Maybe that was hope," said Anna. "Sometimes one half of your brain says one thing and the other says something else."

"Fifty-five is older than most people are when they marry," pointed out Dorothy. "I wonder if she has a story."

"Everyone has a story," said George, dipping his spoon into his soup. "Can you pass me the butter, Dorothy?"

Dorothy passed it. "I meant that maybe she had been married before, or had doubts about him, or something like that."

Xenia snorted. "The woman who doesn't have doubts about a man hasn't spent enough time thinking about him."

"Xenia, you are dreadful," said Anna, with loving frankness.

"I am," agreed Xenia. "But whatever her reasons, she thought Jewel's work was beautiful. Just her style.

She bought one of everything, cleaned me out. You'll have to bring me more as soon as you have it made."

"I have several sets," said Jewel, her hands smoothing the napkin in her lap. "I was planning to bring them over to you later this week, if that will suit you."

"The sooner the better, and the more the better," said Xenia. "She'll be showing her trousseau to her friends and then it'll be the honeymoon pictures and 'oh darling, where *did* you get that necklace, I *must* have one'." A burst of laughter escaped her, half derisive, half triumphant, and she began to eat her soup.

"I wonder if she knew," Dorothy began, gazing dreamily at the red leaves in the blue vase. "I wonder if she knew how her life would be, that she would find love at fifty-five, after three years of courting, and buy all those clothes and all that jewelry. How much fun that must have been!"

"Love and shopping, two of the highest high points in a woman's life!" laughed Elizabeth. "Maybe she knew, maybe she didn't. Most of us are pretty surprised at the way our life turns out, don't you think?"

George nodded, swallowing a mouthful of soup. "You know, I was destined for part ownership of my uncle's beef cattle concern, and here I am, several states away, teaching law, with not even a cow to my name." He paused, his head on one side, gazing at his wife. "But that's not to say that I didn't live out any of my plans. As soon as I met Anna, I planned to marry her, and I did that. I always wanted to own my own home, and in two more years, I'll have done that, too."

"What did you plan for your life, Anna?" asked Dorothy, turning to her hostess.

"Well, I'm with George on the marrying; that was certainly part of the plan. And I do love our home." Anna smiled a little ruefully. "I think I'm still making the rest of my plans. I'm a work in progress."

"Aren't we all!" Elizabeth chimed in. "I was going to be an army nurse and go to Vietnam, but I fell down a flight of stairs and broke my leg before I finished the first month of nursing school. It didn't heal properly, so the army wouldn't take me. So I went to library school instead because I could do that sitting down." She chuckled. "That broken leg was a blessing in disguise. I loved being a librarian, and I met some of the best friends I have to this day during my training."

"What about you, Timothy?" asked Dorothy, her face alight with interest. "What are your plans?"

Xenia choked on her soup. Anna studiously avoided her sharp gaze.

Timothy put down his spoon. "I don't make plans, in a large sense. I plan what I might do in a day, in my work, but I don't try to plan my whole life. I don't want to limit myself to the findings of my own imagination."

"But there must be things you hope will happen," suggested Dorothy.

"What God wills," Timothy said simply. "What about you? You're the youngest one here. You've got the most time left for planning." He gave her a friendly smile, and Dorothy smiled back at him.

"I'm planning to finish college and get my teaching certificate," she replied, "and I want to have a home of my own. I want to be married and have children." She blushed faintly, and Anna wondered if she had suddenly felt conscious of saying these things to an eligible man who was the object of her girlish fancies.

"What about you, Jewel?" Xenia's dry voice broke the little silence, drawing attention away from Dorothy and from Timothy, who had gone back to eating his soup. "What are your plans?"

"My plans are to make you all the jewelry you can sell and to be the best publications manager I can. Those are the only plans I have," said Jewel in a clear voice, with a quick glance at Timothy, whose eyes were on her as she spoke.

"You don't want to make limits for yourself either," said Timothy, watching her.

"It depends on the limits," said Jewel coolly. "I like limits, and I like people who abide by them."

"It does depend on the limits," replied Timothy intently. "A boundary is not the same thing as a limitation."

Jewel looked down at her soup.

"I remember the first plan I ever made for myself," said Anna, coming to her rescue. "I was four years old, and my big sister was going to kindergarten on the bus. I wanted to go, too, but my mother said I couldn't go until next year. So I decided I would stow away. I found my sister's backpack and tried to climb into it, and I zipped my little dress right into the zipper and had to be rescued."

Elizabeth laughed heartily. "I got further than you did, Anna, but I took my dog and ran along behind the bus until the big kids inside told on me to the bus driver and he stopped the bus and sent me home. I was so mad, hopping up and down in the muddy road, watching that bus drive away."

"They left you all by yourself in the road?" asked Dorothy, shocked.

"Oh, bless you, honey, we ran all over the neighborhood by ourselves in those days. I'm old! When I was a little girl, we didn't have computers at all and there weren't many televisions. We just had no way of knowing how scary the world was out there where we couldn't see it."

"When I was a kid, we were allowed to play anywhere on our own street," said Timothy, rejoining the conversation. "All the moms on the street had their own signal to call their kids in to dinner. One mom had a cowbell, and one had a whistle, and there was even a mom with a trumpet." He grinned. "Her kids always ran home the fastest."

George chuckled. "What was your call sign?"

"A Chinese gong. I always wondered where it came from. Nothing else in the house looked anything like it." Timothy reached for another roll. "That gong always made me think about archeology. I'd imagine some archeologist digging up our house one day a hundred years from now and drawing all kinds of wrong conclusions about us based on that gong."

Xenia stared at him, oddly intrigued. "Such as what?"

"I don't know for sure. The gong just wasn't like anything else. It would be bound to catch the archeologist's attention. Would he think we were travelers? Or maybe that my dad had been in the service and brought it home from Asia? It was a really nice gong. Not some fake garden gong from a mail-order company."

"Where did it come from?" asked Anna curiously.

Timothy shook his head. "I don't know. For some reason, I never asked."

Xenia snorted. "Well, then how do you know the gong doesn't have a story? Your parents may have been to China or India or anywhere else before you were born. How do you know?"

Timothy looked surprised. "I don't."

"Maybe they were missionaries," suggested Dorothy.

"Timothy would know if they had been," said Xenia.

Dorothy's eyes grew soft. "Maybe it was a memento from their honeymoon."

Xenia snorted.

Timothy laughed. "I don't think so, Dorothy. They honeymooned on Orcas Island."

"I love the San Juans," said George. "It's a short journey, but you feel far away from everything when you get there."

Anna glanced around the table. Xenia's eyebrows were arched disdainfully. Dorothy was gazing earnestly from Timothy to George and back again. Elizabeth was nodding agreeably, between bites of buttered roll. Jewel was keeping her eyes on her soup.

"What's your favorite place to vacation, Elizabeth?" asked Anna, nudging the conversation away from Timothy's gong.

"Louisiana," said Elizabeth promptly. "I love all my cousins, and I love to see them all at once. We sit on the porch talking until dawn, and when we aren't talking, we're cooking and eating."

Jewel looked up from her soup. "That sounds fun, Elizabeth."

Elizabeth smiled kindly at her. "It is fun. I come home with good memories every time I go."

"My uncle's ranch was like that," George recalled. "The end of the day was the best, when the chores were done and we could talk him into telling stories about the old days. He was an expert on the old west. He read every book about it he could find. He loved the rodeo, too. He took us every time it came to town."

"My cousins have a house near Seaside, in Oregon," said Dorothy. "We go every summer. The beach is beautiful, but I think the tourist area is a bit crass."

"It probably is," said George, smiling at her. "Anna, is there more soup?"

"Yes, dear," said Anna, "and you can all save room for dessert because Elizabeth brought us a pie."

"I'd made it before you phoned to tell me not to," Elizabeth said apologetically, and was instantly drowned out with assurances that her pie would be a welcome end to a delicious meal.

"Are we going to knit tonight?" asked Dorothy, as George rose and went into the kitchen.

Anna looked around the table and glanced at the flat brass clock hanging behind Xenia. "Not tonight, Dorothy. Let's just enjoy each other's company and linger over dessert."

"Good," said Xenia, "I forgot my knitting."

Anna could feel Jewel stirring beside her. She watched Jewel take a long drink of water, set down her glass, straighten her napkin, and begin to crumble the remainder of a roll on her plate. Leaning closer, she whispered, "Do you need to leave?"

Jewel turned to her quickly, relief washing over her face.

"Come with me," Anna whispered, turning back to the table to say easily, "Jewel's got an early start ahead of her in the morning, so I'll just walk her out. Elizabeth, you get the pie going."

Anna could feel Xenia's gaze, and Timothy's, on her back as she led Jewel to the door, but Elizabeth and Dorothy were chatting about making flaky pie crust and hardly noticed Jewel's departure.

At the door, Anna gave Jewel an impulsive hug. Jewel's shoulders felt stiff and unaccustomed in her embrace. "Come again whenever you like, Jewel. You're always welcome, even when it's not a knitting night."

Jewel's head rested suddenly, briefly, on her shoulder. With a whisper of thanks, she went quickly down the walk, almost running to her car.

Chapter 20

"This morning," said Fr. Nicholas, stepping down in front of the iconostasis, "we are blessed to remember our friend and Xenia's husband, Andrew Gregory, who died on this date, twenty-one years ago." He paused in front of a tall, narrow table, covered with a red and gold brocade cloth, on which rested a glass dish of koliva[3], white with powdered sugar, decorated with candied almonds in the shape of a cross.

Jewel started, almost dropping her prayer book. It upset her to hear the name of someone she knew mentioned in a service commemorating the dead. Suddenly, Xenia could no longer be a simple player on the present stage. She had something in common with Jewel's old life, a death and a life constrained by grief.

Jewel looked around. She could not see Xenia. Her grip on the prayer book tightened. *What's going to happen now? This can't be like a funeral, can it? We already had the whole liturgy. I remember my mom's funeral. It was a service all by itself, and everybody cried.* Her attention shifted momentarily to Fr. Nicholas as the chanting began around her.

"Among the spirits of the righteous brought to perfection, give rest, O Savior, to the soul of your

---

[3] Boiled wheat traditionally brought to church for services commemorating the dead.

servant. Keep him in blessed life with you, O lover of mankind."

I wonder what he was like. I wonder what Xenia was like, when she was married to him. Why isn't she here? Does it still make her too sad, after twenty-one years? Why did he die? Xenia isn't old enough to have been a widow for that long. He must have died very young.

"Within your peace, O Lord, where all your Saints repose, give rest also to the soul of your servant, for you alone are immortal."

Maybe I can think about something else until this is over. I can think about the necklace I'm going to make this afternoon. I can think about the Summer Market. I can think about playing Parcheesi with my mother on rainy Saturdays. No, no, something else, think about something else. There's Timothy chanting. He knows the words by heart. I guess people die a lot. Or else they get remembered a lot. Is Anna here? Yes, there she is. At least I came too late to get caught by Mrs. Edon today. What a relief to sit by myself.

"You are our God who descended into Hades and delivered from suffering those who were bound there. Grant rest also to the soul of your servant."

God went into Hades? He did? To do what, I wonder? Did He really go into hell and deliver people? I don't think I ever heard anything like that before.

"Most pure and spotless Virgin, who ineffably gave birth to God, intercede with Him for the salvation of the soul of your servant."

Pure and spotless. Well, she would have to be, if she was going to take care of God when He was a baby. You wouldn't want just anybody doing that, if you were God. He must be a very careful parent. What would it be like if God was your parent? What if He could say, "No, you can't come near Jewel. I want someone pure and spotless to take care of her." But I would have to be pure and spotless for that to happen. Which I'm not. Who would think someone like me could be protected by someone like Her?

Jewel closed her prayer book. Around her, the congregation had begun to sing.

"Memory eternal, memory eternal, may his memory be eternal." They were all singing from memory now, the prayer books closed, and there were tears in many eyes. Perhaps they always sang this song at memorials. Perhaps they were all remembering their own dead, in company with Xenia's husband. Jewel flinched as a paper cut stung the finger she was rubbing compulsively around the edges of the prayer book. A chill shook her, and an old memory surrounded her, a memory of her mother. Her mother's hair had been long and black, as soft and slippery as silk. As a little girl, whenever she was tired or sad, Jewel would climb into her mother's lap and pull her mother's hair around her like a blanket. Her mother's hair smelled like flowers.

Unconsciously, Jewel fingered the skin at the back of her neck, feeling the cropped ends of her hair. Her long hair had been a bond once, the last physical link between herself and her mother. But men had changed that. They had touched her hair and tangled their fingers in it. Jewel would not let her hair grow long again.

The congregation moved around her. Anna appeared beside her and touched her arm. Jewel blinked, recovering herself.

"Hi, Anna," she said, feeling oddly shy.

"Hi, Jewel," Anna smiled and tucked Jewel's hand under her arm. "Come and talk to Fr. Nicholas. He knows you're running off every Sunday without saying hello to him, and he wants to see you."

Jewel swallowed nervously. "Is he mad at me?"

"No, no! He likes you. He's never forgotten how kind you were to him at the market, and he's hoping to be friends with you. Don't worry." Anna patted her hand. "He's a very nice man."

Jewel let Anna lead her. She watched Fr. Nicholas greeting the people ahead of them in line. Many of them kissed his hand, and once or twice, he laid his hand on someone's head and seemed to be giving a blessing. He was handing out pieces of antidoron, the blessed bread, to each person from a basket held by an altar boy who stood beside him.

"I caught her, Fr. Nicholas," said Anna laughing, "and here she is!"

Fr. Nicholas gazed at Jewel for a moment before a smile broke over his face like light. "My friend from the Summer Market! You came back!" He grasped her hand, pressing a piece of antidoron into it, resting his other hand on her forehead, blessing her. "I have prayed to see you again, and here you are."

"I come here most weeks," Jewel said shyly. "I'm sorry I didn't find a way to say hello to you sooner."

"No, no, do not be sorry," he smiled again, in sympathy. "There is such a crowd here, sometimes, after liturgy. It can be hard, when you are not accustomed to it."

Jewel smiled back at him. "I'm glad you got better."

Fr. Nicholas laughed. "I appeared to be at death's door, no doubt! You were so kind to me, and I was a complete stranger to you. This warms my heart whenever I think of it."

"I thought you might faint," said Jewel, uncertain how to respond to his gratitude.

Fr. Nicholas smiled. "Bless you," he said.

Anna walked with her to the door of the sanctuary and paused, plainly debating whether to ask Jewel to stay for coffee hour.

"It was nice to see you and to meet Fr. Nicholas again," said Jewel, settling the strap of her purse over her shoulder. "I have to go now."

"Are you sure? George and I would love to have you come eat with us."

Jewel hesitated, then leaned closer to Anna. "I like to go home afterwards. Sometimes, like today, I have a lot I want to think about."

Anna nodded understandingly. "Then we'll see you next week." She put her arm around Jewel's shoulders. "Take care of yourself."

"Thank you," said Jewel, feeling shy again. "I'll try."

Chapter 21

"Among the spirits of the righteous brought to perfection, give rest O Savior to the soul of your servant. Keep him in blessed life with you, Oh lover of mankind."

Xenia heard nothing after these words. Hunched on a bench on the church's front porch, the sounds of the service drifted out to her, but she could get no further than the terrible uncertainty the chanted prayer could not surmount. Was he among the righteous? Had he been brought to perfection? Did Christ love him and keep him in blessed life there, beyond the reach of his wrathful wife?

What if he was? What if Christ loved him and kept him in blessed life even now, even in this very moment, in every moment since the moment of his death? Perhaps even in the flawed and misspent moments of his life? What if her good-natured, ineffectual, fatally generous husband really had been a fool for Christ? What did that make her, the grieving woman who could not relinquish her right to sit in judgment over him?

Unwillingly, Xenia's thoughts turned to Fr. Nicholas's words at her last attempted confession. *...it sounds as if you were the standard of rightness in the marriage. You, instead of Christ. You saw your own way as orderly and your husband's way as foolish.*

"My way was right," murmured Xenia. "I know it was. I followed the teachings of the church and of plain common sense. How can it be right to condone what he did when what he did was so obviously wrong? He killed three people and himself. And it was preventable. The choice I urged him to make *would* have prevented it. Why isn't that the answer to everything?"

For a few minutes, she sat still while her mind ran the sickening, familiar course of arguments and justifications. It made her tired, after so many years. A wave of revulsion shook her. For a few seconds, she was so tired of her anger that she wanted to be rid of it simply for the sake of regaining normal life. If she could not have the comfort she chose, she would take any comfort available to her, even that of oblivion.

A little breeze brought a sudden scent of incense, and Xenia sighed deeply, relaxing against the back of the bench.

Just try, whispered a small voice deep within her. *Try thinking of him in a new way.*

"But I can't," said Xenia to the voice, so lost in her meditation that she spoke aloud, hardly noticing the sound. "If I let go of this anger, I will have to love him again, and he's dead. What if I can't love him anymore? What if I can? He's still dead."

Try, whispered the voice again. *Just try.*

Xenia opened her eyes very wide and then slowly closed them. Unbidden, a memory rose before her, escaping from long suppression. It was a memory of her wedding night. They had spent it in a small mountain cabin, one of several small cabins arranged around the rim of a meadow. Andrew had built a fire in the fireplace, and they had sat on a blanket together, watching the flames. He had held her hands, both of them, his fingers intertwined with hers, murmuring scraps of poetry, dreaming in the firelight. She could see his face, every detail, illumined by the soft light and by love. She remembered the smoky scent of the room, the texture of the blanket, the warmth of her bare feet basking on the hearth.

In joy and grief, Xenia lifted up her voice and wept.

Chapter 22

When Jewel came out of church, she saw Timothy waiting beside her car. He wasn't leaning on it. He was just standing beside it, with his keys in one hand, watching her cross the parking lot toward him. Jewel lowered her head a little, refusing to make eye contact. He stepped back as she came up to the car and waited politely while she opened the door on the driver's side and got into the car. But before she could close the door, he said, "Come and have coffee with me, Jewel."

"No, thank you," said Jewel.

Timothy bent his head, bringing himself down to the level of Jewel's face, where she sat in the car holding her keys and staring fixedly at the windshield.

"You aren't very comfortable around me, are you." It was a statement, not a question, and his voice was a little humorous, but gentle.

"No," said Jewel, before she could stop herself.

"Why not?" he asked.

Jewel sat still, plainly hoping he would go away.

"Be fair, Jewel. Have I offended you in some way?"

"No," she said again.

"Then why?"

"I've got nothing to offer you, Timothy. I'm not— available."

"Are you married?"

Jewel shook her head.

"Engaged?"

She shook her head again.

"You just don't want to play, is that it?"

"Yes," she said, faintly relieved.

"Fair enough. But I still want to have coffee with you." She could hear the smile in his voice, but decided it would be better to go on looking at the windshield.

"I don't date, Timothy," she said, trying to be clear.

"Why not?" he asked.

"Why are you so persistent?" she cried.

"I like you, Jewel."

"You don't like me, Timothy. You don't even know me. There's nothing here for you."

"What do you mean by that?"

"I'm not who you must think I am," said Jewel, in a lower voice, painfully conscious of the church parking lot full of other parishioners coming out to their cars.

"Who do I think you are?" persisted Timothy, impervious to his surroundings.

"I'm not a church girl, Timothy. I just visit here. I don't belong. You're a chanter. You never miss a Sunday."

"Why does that mean we can't have coffee?"

Jewel put the key in the ignition, feeling close to tears. "Because, Timothy. Just because." Timothy closed the door for her, then tapped politely on the glass. With a sigh, she rolled down the window. He crouched beside the car, bringing his face once again on a level with hers.

"You must have a story, Jewel," he said, quietly. "You must have something you think can't be told, something that would drive me off. I'll take that risk on myself. I'm not asking you to tell me anything. Not yet. I'm just asking you to join me for coffee."

He wasn't getting the message. She turned, looking into his face, so close to hers, right there in the window. She felt the enchantment of that deep, gentle voice. Her head sank until her forehead rested on the wheel.

"Just as friends?" she heard herself asking. "Just once, just as friends?"

"Just once," agreed Timothy, "Just as friends. That's my truck over there. Follow me."

"I will," said Jewel, without raising her head, "but I'm only coming this time to tell you that I can't ever come again."

Timothy grinned at her and strode away.

She almost drove off and left him, but her sense of fairness told her that it was now her fault he was going out to coffee with her, and it would be rude to stand him up after agreeing to go with him.

But just once. This is my chance to drive him off. I need to make this final. I can't have another man in my life. I can't ever do that again. It makes no difference that he's a church guy. A man is a man, and even if it did make a difference, I wouldn't be any different. I would still be me, and there's nothing that can make me right again, not like that. There's nothing that's going to make me like Dorothy. I wonder if he's ever even kissed a girl. Her mind fumbled, trying to sort the disparate images, the deep beautiful voice chanting the sacred prayers, the stalwart, active body, the dark, watchful eyes, the warm fingers slipping away from hers on the frosty glass.

"Holy God, Holy Mighty, Holy Immortal, have mercy on us," chanted Jewel, the words rising spontaneously to her lips, showing her the first small imprint upon herself of the days she had lingered in Orthodoxy. The prayer repeated itself in her mind all the way to the coffee house.

Timothy led her to a small round table by the window and held a chair for her to be seated. He asked her preferences and went to stand in line for their coffee. Jewel sat where he put her and stared unseeingly out the window. After a minute, she turned her head and stared at Timothy standing in line instead.

When he returned, he held two cups of coffee, each with a cookie balancing on top. He set down the cups, placed a napkin for each cookie, and took a seat.

"I got cookies, too," he said, breaking the ice. "I like cookies."

Jewel took a sip of coffee, set down her cup, and looked him squarely in the eye.

"I lived with six different men, one right after another, from the time I left home at seventeen until I moved out on the last one a few years ago."

Timothy set his cup down, too. "I'm sorry, Jewel," he said simply, and his eyes, clear and full of sympathy, filled her with grief.

"So now you know why I can't date." She started to lift her cup, but her palms were sweaty and she couldn't grasp it securely. She set it down and began to shred the paper napkin under her cookie.

"No, I don't," he said, after a moment of silence. "I don't know why you can't date. Do you want to tell me?"

Jewel's lips began to form the word "no," but she could not say it. No one had ever asked her. No one had ever cared or even wondered what had happened to her. Even Sara, who loved her, had always been more interested in solving her problems for her than in understanding them. She looked at him carefully, trying to read his face, his body language, his aura, something, trying to gauge the danger, trembling on the brink.

"You can tell me," he said gently. "I won't make you sorry you did."

"Please," she whispered. "Please don't make me sorry." She drew a deep breath, flattening her hands on the table, and she told him.

"My mom died when I was ten, and my dad went to pieces. He had more women in and out of the house than I could count. I never knew who was going to be there when I got home from school, or what they would be doing. I left as soon as I could. I did nothing in high school but study. I almost lived at the library, and when I was home, I kept my door closed always. I knew if I got into college, it would be somewhere else to live. And it was, but by the end of my first year, I had already moved in with the first one, the first man I lived with."

She began to smooth the surface of the table with her fingers, pressing the shreds of napkin aside. "That first time, I was in love, and I thought he was in love, and I thought it was forever. It was going to mean a home of my own, a place where someone cared about me, and I would never have to go back to where I came from again. But he broke up with me at the end of the year, when he went home for the summer, and I was broken-hearted and desperate not to go home, so I moved in with his best friend, who had a basement apartment in the house where we had been living."

She noticed, in an abstracted way, that Timothy, without taking his eyes from her face, was moving her coffee cup and cookie out of the way of her restless hands. "It was one of those old houses, you know, the kind someone rents out to college students. You get a bunch of roommates and move in. Except in my case, I was sharing more than the room with my 'roommate'. There were four more after him, and mostly, they got worse and worse. I finished college somehow and even got a job, but my life was such a tangle. I was all broken up inside, and I couldn't seem to solve the problem. I kept looking for love. I was sure love would save me, but eventually, I had to admit that I couldn't find it and the search was destroying me. When I moved out for the sixth time, I promised myself I would never do it again. My friend helped me find a place of my own, and here I am. I haven't even gone out for coffee with a man, until now. I got away from where I was, but I can't get away from what happened and how it made me feel. I can't be the person I would want to be, to fall in love."

Timothy did not fill the silence when she stopped speaking. He sat quietly for a while, absorbing her story. He spoke again just before the tension became unbearable, just as she was beginning to curse herself for speaking. "You still want to be that person," he said slowly, making the discovery as he spoke the words. "You gave up because you thought you had to, not because you wanted to."

Jewel felt her fingers tightening, grasping at the surface of the table as if she were actually physically slipping over the fortress wall, seconds away from plummeting to her death. To admit this, to say to him that she still longed for love, would bring the sum of her efforts to nothing. It would make her vulnerable to him, and to the weakness of her former self. She gazed at him helplessly but could not speak.

"You can trust me, Jewel," he said, answering her need as if she had spoken it. "I understand that you don't know that yet. I won't hurt you, and I won't rush you. I'm not scared away by your past life, and it doesn't make you lesser in my eyes. I make mistakes myself."

He paused to bring her coffee cup back within reach of her hands and waited for her to pick it up. It was still warm. She took a sip and found it oddly comforting.

"What I want is a chance with you," he said. "Maybe we have something to offer each other. I want to find out."

Still grasping her cup, Jewel let her eyes move freely over his face, studying, exploring. He sat still, his hands relaxed, giving her time. His eyes followed hers, noticing what she was noticing, showing her that he withheld nothing from her.

Her eyes returned to his. "Are you sure?" she asked.

"I am," he said.

Chapter 23

Anna settled back in her chair and looked expectantly across the table at George. They were seated by the window at the Seattle Tennis Club, enjoying a late lunch together on a cold November afternoon. Beyond the empty lawn, she could see the gray swells of Lake Washington wearing white crests under the wind's touch. A single sail showed where a lone enthusiast had brought out his boat, more enchanted, perhaps, with the brisk air currents than depressed by the chill.

George winked at her and lifted his menu. "This seafood salad thing looks good. With soup on the side."

"You always want soup," murmured Anna, glancing at the list of lunch specials.

"I like soup," said George firmly, "and when I'm buying, I have what I like."

"You have what you like regardless," retorted Anna, with affectionate derision.

"That's because people like me," replied George smugly.

Anna kissed her fingers to him and turned unblushingly to greet the waiter by name. "Edward, he wants soup, of course," she said, "and seafood salad. I want an enormous slice of chocolate cake with a side of icing to eat with a spoon, but I'll have what he's having, and a plate of fresh fruit for us to share."

By long-established custom, they saved the most interesting conversation until the end, with two cups of coffee and the rest of the fruit between them.

"So," began Anna, eagerly, "you've seen my knitters now, several times. I want to know everything you think about Jewel, and then I'll tell you why I want to know."

"I wonder if I can guess," mused George, turning his coffee mug idly on the table.

"Don't try to guess. Tell me what you think instead," prompted Anna.

"How old is she, do you think?" asked George. "She's a little hard to place, age-wise."

"Do you think so?" Anna was a little surprised. "I'd imagine she's about thirty, or a little less. Why?"

"Well, it's all part of the impression I have of her. Sometimes she seems a little awkward, and that makes her seem younger, but on the other hand, she's usually the most self-contained person I ever met, and that makes her seem older. I gather from the little she said about herself that her family life was a disaster. Maybe that accounts for it, partly."

"Maybe. What else do you think?"

George was silent, sipping his coffee. Anna let the silence lengthen, aware after years of marriage of all the rhythms of his conversation and his mental processes. "She must have been lonely," he said finally.

"What do you mean?" asked Anna.

"I mean, that must be why she came to the knitting group, the first time," George explained, "and maybe that's why she keeps coming. She doesn't seem to have connected with the group, except maybe with you."

"I hope she has connected with me," Anna admitted. "Did you notice—what did you think of her and Timothy, the night they all came to dinner?"

"I thought she was warning him off," said George frankly. "But on the other hand, he doesn't look like the man to be easily discouraged."

"I don't think he would pursue her if she told him plainly that she wasn't interested," said Anna, with a small sigh. "I wonder if she's really not interested, or if she's just worried about something."

"Who knows?" replied George, unhelpfully.

Anna folded her hands on the table and waited till his gaze returned from the window. "George, I have a feeling about Jewel. She needs me to do something or be something for her. Nobody else can do it, or will do it. I don't know what it is, but every time she's come to the house, the feeling has gotten stronger. What should I do?"

"Pray," said George, with the sweet, intimate smile that could still shake her and bless her after two decades of married life.

Anna reached across the table and felt the strong, encouraging clasp of his hands on hers. "I want to do something that matters, so much. For months now, I've been feeling...barren. Like nothing I do has any life or really matters. I'm just filling my days, keeping up a routine that has become an end in itself. I don't mean to be ungrateful, and in most senses, I'm not dissatisfied. I love you so much, and I'm happy to be of service to you in any way I can. There's just this void—" her throat tightened, but she swallowed the tightness, determined to tell him everything. "There's a void, where my child should have been. I'm always standing on the side, supporting something instead of being something or doing something myself. I host a knitting group, and I don't even know how to knit. I'm like a frame with no picture, George. I need to make something human. I need to give life to something. I feel like I just make work for myself, to fill the emptiness." She stopped speaking, and George handed her a napkin, to wipe her eyes. She took it, with a little laugh, turning away from the room to hide her private grief.

"I don't feel like that about you, Anna," said George, lowering his voice. "I don't feel like that about you at all. You make my life for me, every day. I would be homeless and helpless without you." His hands tightened on hers, and she had to reach for the napkin again, grieved that such honest devotion could thrive on her imperfect self. "But if you feel like there's something more you're meant to do in life, let's find it. Tell me how to help you, and I will."

"I wish I knew, for sure," said Anna wistfully. "I'm always wishing and wondering, reading about things and trying to plan what to do, but I never hit on something that really fits. That's why I want to follow this feeling I have about Jewel. It's so persistent. And it's not just because I hope she falls in love. It's really not. It's for her own self, whoever she is inside. I think she needs me. I hope she does. And I hope I can really be of service, not just try to fill my own need to be needed. Do you see what I mean?"

George nodded encouragingly. "I do see. How are you going to do this?"

Anna shook her head a little. "I'm not sure. I need to think it through."

"Ask her out for coffee or something," suggested George. "Get to know her on a more personal basis, without all the knitters around. Probably something will present itself to you. Something will just come up naturally, and you'll know what to do."

"Alright, I will," Anna decided. "There, I made a plan. I'll call her when we get home and invite her."

"Good," said George, smiling. He lifted their clasped hands and kissed her fingers. "Here's to you!"

Chapter 24

Anna took Jewel to the Tennis Club. She wanted the emotional continuity between her conversation with George and her first attempt at making friends with Jewel as he had suggested. They sat at the same table by the window, her usual table, and she wanted that, too, in case this would be the first of many memories that she and Jewel would share.

Jewel slipped into the chair across from Anna and laid her purse carefully under her seat. "Hi, Anna. Thank you for inviting me." She folded her hands in her lap. "I told them at work that I would be gone for two hours. I haven't had a lunch break all week."

Anna smiled at her. "Good for you! It's nice to get away every now and again. Let's order," she suggested. She opened her menu. "It's all good. You can't go wrong."

Jewel obediently opened the menu and studied it intently. "It does look good," she said, reading the descriptions.

"I like menus to have pictures," said Anna, trying to escape the air of formality that seemed to be hanging over them like starched drapes. "Cookbooks, too. I want to know how it's going to come out before I decide to make it."

Jewel's eyes came up quickly from the menu. "I like pictures, too. It helps me understand the directions if I can see what it should look like. But I'm sure you have been cooking longer than I have."

"Are you saying I'm old?" asked Anna, deliberately teasing her.

Jewel was shocked. "Oh, no! I didn't mean to be rude. I'm sorry. It's just that food is so good at your house it's hard to imagine that you would still need the pictures."

Anxious, and not much sense of humor, thought Anna. *I'll have to be more careful.* Aloud, she said reassuringly, "It wasn't rude. And I use the pictures all the time." She lifted the menu. "I'm going to have the salmon Caesar salad and a cup of soup, in honor of George. George always has soup."

"That sounds good. I'll have the same thing," said Jewel, playing it safe.

Anna signaled the waiter, gave him their orders, and asked for a pot of tea and two cups. When it arrived, she poured a cup of tea for each of them and pushed one across the table to Jewel.

"There," said Anna. "Now we can visit in comfort while we wait for our lunch."

Jewel glanced around the room and out the window. "This is a very nice place," she said, diffidently.

"It is," agreed Anna. "I like to look out at Lake Washington while I eat. There's something about water. I never get tired of looking at it."

"I think it's because it doesn't have edges," said Jewel, unexpectedly. "Especially when it's big enough to have waves, like that. It feels like it goes all the way to the sea, or to the edge of the earth, or something. You can't feel shut in, when you look at it."

Anna's eyes lit with understanding. "Yes, exactly! That's just how I feel. How perceptive of you!"

A flash of sympathy passed between them. Jewel's face flushed with pleasure. There was a moment of silence as lunch arrived and they started eating. Anna searched for something to say that would keep the conversation on a personal level. She was hoping to inspire an exchange of confidences.

"I don't like to feel shut in," she said. "I like to feel that every option is still open to me. But it's not always true, unfortunately. Maybe that's why staring at the water is so appealing. It keeps the feeling alive, even when reality doesn't bear it out."

Jewel was gazing at her, her fork dangling in the air halfway to her mouth. Anna smiled at her. "Do you know what I mean?" she asked, encouragingly.

Jewel dropped her fork. "Yes!" she exclaimed. "I just can't believe *you* do!"

Anna laughed. "My life is very nice, Jewel, but it's not perfect. I don't think anybody's life is perfect."

Jewel took a few bites of her salad, gathering her thoughts. Then, "Do you mind if I ask you about it? I mean, about why you feel shut in? I feel like that sometimes." She stopped speaking, watching Anna's face.

"I don't mind at all," said Anna, secretly rejoicing. "I've just been feeling frustrated recently. I feel like I do the same things over and over again, and they're very nice, but they don't have any lasting meaning to anyone. I wish I could think of something more important to do."

Jewel nodded, and her expressive eyes showed Anna sympathy and incredulity. "Maybe what you do has more meaning than you realize. Maybe people like what you do. It might make them happy."

"I think I often do make people happy, but I still feel like there's something more I could be doing."

"Being happy is more important than some people think," said Jewel, frowning. "People who aren't happy do stupid things, trying to make themselves feel better. If you make people happy, you might save them from doing something stupid."

Anna looked at her thoughtfully. Here was a statement that had more personal meaning than the wording might suggest. "Do you think so? I hadn't thought of it like that."

Jewel returned her attention to her salad.

"What about you?" asked Anna, reclaiming Jewel's attention. "What makes you feel shut in?" She held her breath. It was an enormous question to ask of someone who kept so much to herself.

Jewel's eyes flitted to Anna's face, then returned to her salad. She prodded it with her fork. "Things do, sometimes," she said obscurely. "Remembering does, more than anything."

Silence fell, and Anna did not attempt to break it. For several minutes, they devoted themselves to eating, each following her own train of thought.

Jewel finished her salad and pushed the plate neatly to the end of the table. She folded her hands in her lap, studying Anna's face across the table. Anna pushed her own plate over next to Jewel's and smiled at her. "There. We've cleared the table. Now tell me what's on your mind, Jewel. I can feel the brain waves all the way over here."

Jewel bent her head. "I was thinking about my mother. There are things she might have taught me, don't you think?"

"Lots of things," said Anna promptly. "She would have loved that."

"There are things I want to know," Jewel's voice was almost a whisper, and she leaned closer, as if she worried about being overheard. "I think about it at your house. I don't know how to have a nice party, like that. I don't know how to greet everyone at the door or what I should serve, and I need to look in a book to know how to make anything. You talk to all the people, and you keep things together. Even with Dorothy. I don't know what to do with her when she wants to sit with me at church. I can't stop her from doing it. I can't stop anyone from doing anything, even when I really want to.”

Anna’s heart cramped in her chest.

“I think my mother would have taught me,” continued Jewel, her fingers coming up from her lap and beginning to smooth the surface of the small steel teapot. “It must be why I don’t know. Other people know. I try things out. I try to make dinner for Clay and Sara, my friends. But Sara always brings something. I can’t stop her. It’s always a potluck, so I can never do everything myself, to see if I can.” Her eyes, returning to Anna’s eyes, were black with frustration.

“Your mother would have taught you everything she knew, love,” said Anna, struggling to communicate around a welter of emotion. “I’m sure she started when you were a little girl. She just didn’t have time to finish.” She hesitated a moment, watching Jewel’s nervous fingers on the teapot. “I’m not an expert on anything, Jewel, but I would be happy to show you all my tricks. I learned to entertain because of George’s job. I made lots of mistakes in the beginning. I’ve spilled wine on a university president, and I’ve invited a professor and both his ex-wives to the same party, but it didn’t kill me or them.” She laughed, a little shakily. “It’s not as hard now. You could learn easily, Jewel. I can see that you are someone who watches the people around her and notices things about them. That’s the real secret to being with people. If you’re paying attention, you can often figure out how to keep them happy."

"Would you really teach me?" asked Jewel, awed.

"Of course!" cried Anna. "Jewel, it would be so much fun. Come over this week. No, I know what. The knitting group is meeting again next week. Come over a few hours early, and we can set it all up together. You can help me host. I would love the help and the company!"

"Would everyone else think it was strange?" Jewel frowned, hesitating.

"Not at all," said Anna. "I've often hosted parties together with various friends. It makes the job more fun."

"It will be amazing," said Jewel, seizing her chance to be like Anna's friends. "I can't wait, Anna." She stopped, her face suddenly alert. "Do you have a signature dish, Anna? The one that people always ask you to bring?"

"I do! Well, several actually. If it's dessert, I bring homemade cream puffs. If it's a main dish, I bring beef burgundy. And I have a nice Asian coleslaw that I bring if someone wants a side dish."

"*Three* signature dishes," breathed Jewel. "I can make red carrot salad with my own dressing," she confided, as an afterthought.

"That sounds delicious. You'll have to make it for me," said Anna, closing the deal. "Come around five o'clock, if you can. That will give us plenty of time."

"I will." Jewel clasped her hands in her lap. "I wish it was already next week!"

Chapter 25

A merciful God kept Jewel late at work every night in the week before Saturday, the day Timothy had promised to call. Returning home, she would plunge wearily through the door, shedding the remnants of her day, eat canned soup in a fog, and tumble into bed, asleep almost before she could pull the quilt over herself for warmth. She had no time or energy for introspection, using all her mental powers to focus on her work, refusing even to glance in the direction of her personal being.

On Friday, she sent the last document to press and escaped for a few hours to have lunch at the Tennis Club with Anna. That evening, she went to bed at six thirty and slept fourteen hours without dreaming, almost without moving. When her eyes drifted open, she knew a moment's confusion at her own waking. A soft gray day filtered through the window blinds. She began to reach for her alarm clock, instinctively, before she realized she had not set it and it had not wakened her. She was warm and comfortable, and there was no need to move. For several seconds, she savored the luxury of waking naturally at the end of deep sleep.

Then her life began to return to her, in fragments. It was Saturday morning. Timothy would be calling. Timothy, a man, would be calling her. Timothy, an attractive single man hoping to spend time with her, would be calling her, expecting her to answer her phone. Jewel sank deeper into the bed, pressing urgently back toward sleep, or any other available shelter. She pulled the pillow over her head, then sat upright, alarmingly awake. A surge of nervous energy, laced with nausea, drove her from the bed into the cold, unforgiving air. Two steps brought her out of the bedroom into the living room. Her eyes fell on the rocking chair, her mother's chair, crushed in a cab on the day she escaped from Trevor. It was mended now, but she could see marks on each dowel, under the paint, at the point where each had broken. Jewel closed her eyes and pressed her forehead against the wall.

She was still standing there, fending off memories, when the telephone rang. She jumped, and her heart pounded suddenly in her ears. She stared at the phone for a minute as if it were a vivid hallucination that might vanish in a puff of highly colored smoke if she touched it. It continued ringing, loudly, realistically, as if it were an actual phone, activated by a real call from a real person. Timothy, for example. Jewel raced across the floor and snatched up the receiver.

"Hello?" she gasped.

"Good morning, Jewel. Did I wake you?" It was Timothy, calling her as planned.

"No, I'm awake." What else should she say? Her mind remained blank.

"Good. I'm going running around Green Lake today, and I'd like to take you with me. Will you come?"

"Yes." This was the right answer. If she was going to say no, she should have said so last Sunday when he told her he would call her today.

"Eat breakfast first. It's raining, but it should be a good run. Do you have rain gear? I've got some you can borrow, if you like." He paused, letting her get a word in, if she had a word.

Jewel tried to think. Running. Rain. Green Lake. Oh. "Where should I meet you?" she asked.

"On your doorstep, if you like. Or you can meet me in the parking lot by the community center. You know where they rent out paddleboats in the summer?"

"I'll meet you there," said Jewel. She wanted to arrive in her own car. She wasn't ready to be picked up on her doorstep. It would feel too much like a date.

"I'll be there at ten. Let me give you my cell number, in case you can't find me." Jewel found a pencil to write down the number and then, a little abruptly, she said goodbye and hung up.

Should I shower? That would be silly. I'm about to go running. No shower. No makeup. I'm not even going to wear earrings. It's going to be cold out there. Where is my hat? If it's not okay to have hat-head, I don't want to go at all.

An hour later, resisting the urge to look in a mirror, Jewel pulled a red stocking cap firmly over her ears, and ran out to her car, clutching a water bottle and her keys in one hand, a fanny pack with her phone, her wallet, and Timothy's number securely inside in the other.

Rain sparkled on her windshield as she pulled out of the driveway, and she turned on her headlights and wipers. It was a classic November day, Seattle style, gray and wet, cold and quiet. The rain seemed little more than wind-blown mist, billowing moisture that somehow drenched the world as completely as a monsoon.

She drove down the interstate for fifteen minutes, then made the quick right-then-left-hand turn from the exit ramp into a neighborhood of well-kept houses built in an era when three stories were common and no two homes were alike. Ordinarily, she relished the sight of these sturdy structures, noting their freshly painted trim, the gardens flourishing in the small front yards, the ornamental stained glass set in the occasional window, the solid brass knocker on a solid oak door. Green Lake was a wonderland of artistic living, the right house, the right clothes, the right food, the right interests, the right music. It was the perfect marriage of affluence and earnestness, of iPhones and organic home-made cookies. Jewel loved Green Lake. It was like a movie she couldn't stop watching. She couldn't see any way to enter it, as a world, but neither could she resist its lure. Coming down a short, steep side street, she waited for the light, then crossed Green Lake Drive into the parking lot by the community center, her eyes fastening immediately on Timothy's truck.

Climbing out of her car, she fought against a rising feeling of dread. Her stomach growled anxiously. She hadn't been able to swallow more than a muffin. Now, when it was too late, she was hungry. She glanced hopelessly into the vacuumed interior of her car. Not even a stale cookie crumb there, nothing to rescue her but a well-filled water bottle. Could she run on empty?

"You look a little green around the gills," said Timothy, at her elbow. "Did you forget to eat breakfast?" He looked different without his glasses, with raindrops on his face and a ball cap on his head. His black rain gear whispered as he moved to hold out his arm to her, elbow crooked. "I've got the rest of my breakfast in the truck. Let's finish it before we run." He smiled reassuringly, and the feeling of dread receded before a flash of gratitude. She took his arm, as if he were an usher at a wedding, and let him escort her to his truck. He opened the door, and she climbed into the seat, clutching his elbow to balance on the wet running board. When she was safely in, he closed the door behind her and came around the front of the truck to climb in the other side.

Jewel looked curiously around the cab. This truck was the first thing she had ever seen that belonged to him, other than his knitting. It was clean, but not spotlessly so. An icon of St. George and a hand-carved wooden cross hung by a leather strap from the rearview mirror. She tucked her feet carefully against the base of her seat, avoiding a box full of CDs. On the console between the front seats stood a brown paper bag, tipping a little toward the gear shift, and there was an insulated metal coffee mug in the beverage holder. The bag smelled good.

Timothy opened the other door and climbed in, closing it behind himself. He put the key in the ignition and turned it on. Byzantine chant immediately filled the cab, and his hand leaped to the volume knob, turning it down to a quiet murmur. His fingers traveled to the heat control, turning it up a little, and came to rest on the bag of food. Reaching inside, he produced a small sausage biscuit, still wrapped. With a grin, he held it out to her. "Breakfast? No bites taken from it, I promise. Not even sniffed yet."

"Thank you," Jewel felt a little answering smile beginning to bud on her face. She unwrapped the biscuit and bit into it. It tasted good. She glanced at him, to see if she should be making conversation, but he was leaning back in his seat, relaxed, keeping time with one finger to the murmuring chant. She wanted to ask him to sing along with it, but the allusion to Dorothy seemed too clear. Instead she finished her biscuit, folded the paper, and peeped into the bag before dropping it in. Timothy watched her.

"You're a very tidy person, Jewel."

"I like to be," she replied seriously. She drank thirstily from her water bottle, closed the top, and folded her hands around it in her lap. "Do you want to run now?"

"Relax. You need to digest a little first."

"I'm sorry," she said automatically, feeling that she had been unprepared.

"Don't be," he said easily. "It's warm in here, and we aren't on a schedule, are we?"

She sat back carefully. After a moment, "You don't have anything against schedules, do you?" she inquired.

"Nothing at all. I live by a schedule almost every day. But I also make a point of resting from my schedule, when I can. Today, I'm resting." He put his head on one side, a quizzical look on his face. "What else do you want to know, Jewel? You can ask."

Jewel blushed. Her mind buzzed with questions, but she could think of none that would not sound horribly gauche, even impertinent, if spoken aloud.

He straightened in his seat. "You should ask me things," he said earnestly. "You hardly know me."

Should she? She wondered, suddenly, whether it actually mattered if she was gauche, or in any other way unacceptable. What could she lose? She felt herself to be so far outside the bounds of ordinary experience, so unlikely to exist in such a circumstance at all, that it seemed safe to say whatever came into her head. At some level, she was certain that a sharp steel pin would burst this shining bubble any second now, and she would sink back into the mundane, regretful passage of her own life, tantalized by this brief escape, but not materially altered by it. She drew a breath.

"It's just—I don't—I'm not sure how to do this, Timothy," she blurted. "I've never been on this kind of date, if this is a date. Is this a date? I don't even know how to be attractive to your kind of man." She felt her hot cheeks grow hotter.

Timothy laughed. It was a distinctly masculine sound, confident and bracing. He leaned toward her, meeting her eyes. "It is a date, Jewel, and believe me, you're doing fine." He laughed again, leaning back in his seat. "If you don't know how, it must just come naturally."

Jewel pressed her hands against her cheeks, willing the blush back down into her veins. She felt the flatness of her hair under the wool hat and the absence of makeup or perfume on her unshowered body. She looked down at her rain gear, which enveloped her from her chin to her shoes. She wanted to laugh with him, but the only sound she could make was like air escaping from a balloon.

"Don't let it make you nervous," said Timothy kindly. "I don't want you to 'think of me as a brother', that's all. But you're perfectly safe with me."

Jewel hoped that a ready flow of intelligent conversation was going to spring into her head, if not now, then as soon as they began to run around the lake. She wished for some kind of manual, a handy pocket-size book entitled How To Be With Nice Men. Chapter 1: What to say when they ask you what you want to know... "Do you have a family, Timothy?"

"I'm an orphan," he said, in a quiet voice that robbed the statement of humor. "But I had two good parents until my early twenties. Walter and Hannah. I was their only child, and they loved me every day of my life."

"Oh no!" exclaimed Jewel involuntarily. "How did you...if you don't mind my asking, how did you live through it, when they died?"

"I went to church, and I stayed there until I could manage life in the world again. I just sat in there, next to Saint Timothy, and sometimes Fr. Nicholas would sit with me, when he could. His wife was still alive then, and she sat with us, too. They would sit on each side of me, holding my hands, just as if they had been my father and mother. It was like they were filling those places for me, until I could learn to manage with them empty. I can't remember how long it took. It felt like a month of Sundays, but finally, I was okay again. Or at least," he shook his head, "I couldn't regain the life I lost, the one where I had a family, but I started making a new life, and after a while, the new life got bearable, and I started to feel something like normal again."

Jewel pondered this, staring blindly through the windshield. "Maybe that's what it was," she said, almost to herself, her eyes slowly refocusing.

"That's what what was?" asked Timothy curiously.

"I never thought about it the way you put it, what you said about making a new life. When my mom died, there wasn't any…there was no Fr. Nicholas, for us. We didn't make a new life. We fell apart."

"But you made one, by yourself. It just took you more time. You didn't have help, like I did."

Jewel frowned, doubtful. "I don't know if I did. I made a new life, but it didn't work as well. I mean, I never felt normal again. I just added another layer of broken things, on top of the life that was broken by her death. And now, I've distanced myself from all of that, from the men and all of it, but I still don't feel right. I don't mean that I'm still mourning her. I miss her, but she's been dead for twenty years. It's just that I miss having a mom to tell me things. I wish I knew what she would tell me."

"It's not your grief for her that feels unnatural to you," suggested Timothy. "It's what came after it. Why do you feel like that hasn't gone away? You said it had been years now…"

"It has." She straightened, suddenly uncomfortable. "Can we run now?"

"In a minute," said Timothy, persistent. "Why do you feel like it hasn't gone away?"

Jewel moved restlessly in her seat. "I don't feel right. It's like—" she stared at him, waiting for the words to come to her— "it's like there are marks left on me that I can't wash off. I feel like damaged goods…I'll have to be returned, for a refund." Tears welled unexpectedly, stinging her eyes, closing her throat. Her hands slipped across her lap, seeking a paper napkin from the paper bag. She heard a quick movement beside her and felt the warmth of Timothy's fingers, holding her hand. Instinctively, her hand turned toward his, palm to palm, clinging together on the crumpled paper. He touched her face lightly, gently, with his free hand.

"God doesn't take you back till you've run the whole race, Jewel. Don't give up on yourself. Take a big breath and get up. Get back in the race."

Jewel tried to stop crying. It took several minutes. "Tissue?" she asked in a squeaky whisper, wholly unwilling to let go of his hand to search for one.

Timothy reached his free hand into his coat pocket and brought out a fistful of paper napkins. "I take lots," he said, grinning, "I like to have enough so I can spill on everything. Here—" he shook out a napkin and began to pat her face with it, clumsily, until her inherent tidiness surged up within her and she reached for the napkin and finished the job herself.

"Now come on," said Timothy, opening the door. "Let's go running."

Chapter 26

Jewel sat quietly on the edge of her chair at church, watching the flood of hungry people surging out of the sanctuary doors, headed for the fellowship hall. She drew a deep breath and let it out slowly, enjoying a sense of peace and well-being laced with a triumph out of all proportion to the event that caused it. Jewel had turned down an invitation to sit with Dorothy and Mrs. Edon. She had worshiped alone, letting her eyes and her mind roam where she willed.

It had been shockingly easy. Mrs. Edon hailed her across the parking lot, waving as Dorothy stepped out of their car. Dorothy waved, too, and they caught up with her as she arrived at the church door. Jewel held the door for them, giving herself a moment to plan her escape.

They lit candles by the icons, crossing themselves, and waited for her to light a candle also, as if she were one of the family. "It reminds us that Christ is the light of the world," whispered Dorothy.

"Oh," said Jewel. "That's a nice thought." Mrs. Edon began to move toward the sanctuary door and Dorothy turned to follow her, smiling over her shoulder at Jewel. It was now or never.

"If you don't mind," began Jewel, "I think I'll sit by myself today." Mrs. Edon's eyebrows went up and Dorothy looked startled. Jewel rushed into the explanation she had thought up, hoping it would appease them. "I get distracted when I sit with people I know. I want to focus on the service more, so I thought I would sit by myself at the back." She stopped, bracing herself for disapproval and persuasion. It didn't come.

"That's wonderful," said Mrs. Edon, her face lighting. "I know just what you mean. You want to just lose yourself in the liturgy."

"I'm glad you like it so much," exclaimed Dorothy.

"We won't disturb you," said Mrs. Edon, reaching to pat Jewel on the shoulder. "We'll see you after the service."

"Yes, you can come in to coffee hour with us and tell us what you think," added Dorothy, and she linked arms with her mother. A smiled passed between them as they entered the sanctuary.

"Phew," said Jewel to the empty air. "I did it." She waited till she could see that they had joined Mr. Edon and Dorothy's brother near the front. Then she slipped through the glass door and found the empty chair she had sat in on her first visit to the church. No one was sitting in it. It was her chair, waiting for her to return to it. Jewel sat down, tucked her purse under the chair, and stood with the rest of the congregation. In the front of the church, just to the right of the iconostasis, she saw Timothy in his black chanter's robe. She smiled. He looked very serious and sweet.

Jewel spent the service in blessed solitude, listening to Timothy's voice chanting the ancient hymns and prayers, lost to her surroundings, divorced from memory, adrift on the fathomless depths of possibility. Normal life seemed to hover on the horizon, not yet attained perhaps, but finally visible. As the service came to a close, she sighed, reluctant to return to the world. She sat down, reaching under her chair for her purse.

"So," said Dorothy, appearing in front of her, "did you like it?"

Jewel jumped. She tipped back her head, looking up into Dorothy's expectant face, seeing Mrs. Edon listening over Dorothy's shoulder. "Oh. Hello. Yes, it was very nice." They nodded eagerly, waiting for more. Jewel could see people coming up behind them, looking for a way around. Mrs. Edon and Dorothy were blocking the rear aisle in front of Jewel's chair, which was set with its back against the glass wall.

"I liked it," said Jewel. "It's nice here."

Mrs. Edon suddenly sat down on an empty chair beside Jewel's. Dorothy looked at her mother and stepped closer, as if she had been expecting this. Jewel's head turned awkwardly, looking from Mrs. Edon beside her to Dorothy in front of her. She felt a prick of alarm in the pit of her stomach.

Mrs. Edon leaned closer and laid a hand on her arm. "Jewel, Dorothy and I were talking just now about how special it is that you are so interested in coming to church and learning about our precious faith. We want to support you in any way we can." Dorothy nodded emphatically, her bright blue eyes staring down into Jewel's face.

"Thank you," Jewel began, hesitantly, but Mrs. Edon cut her off.

"We thought it would help you to know a little about our customs, so you can be as comfortable as possible here. It's always better to hear these things from someone who knows you, rather than from a stranger."

Jewel was startled. She did not think of Mrs. Edon as someone who knew her.

Mrs. Edon glanced at Dorothy, and Dorothy dropped down beside her mother, kneeling to bring herself on a level with them, to be part of the conversation. "She means your clothes," she said to Jewel. "We wear longer dresses to church, and most people don't wear dresses without sleeves, or with lower necklines."

"Or they wear a little shawl," said Mrs. Edon. "Something to cover the shoulders.

Dorothy giggled. "One rule of thumb I've heard is 'up to the neck and down to the knees'."

Jewel blinked at her. Two women she did not know had stopped behind Dorothy and appeared to be listening to the conversation.

"You look very nice," said Mrs. Edon. "We just thought you'd like to know, for next time." She stood up and held out her hand to Dorothy, who grasped it and rose from her knees without tangling herself in her long blue skirt. "Let's go see if Daddy and Basil have found us a table, shall we?"

Jewel made a little sound in her throat. Her voice came, a second late. "Thank you. Thank you for telling me and everything. I have to go now." Her eyes plunged toward the door. There was no Anna to help her through, but many of the people had already left the sanctuary. Her glance bounced to Fr. Nicholas and veered away. "I have to go now," she repeated breathlessly. She brushed past Mrs. Edon and Dorothy, pushed her way through the door, and ran past the alcove, where a deacon was putting out the candles. The front door swung open ponderously under her shaking hand, and she ran into the cold morning air.

"Jewel!" It was Timothy's voice, calling to her from the side entrance to the church.

Jewel swerved toward his voice and bumped into the top rail of a fence that ran along the walkway in front of the church. She grasped the rail with both hands and felt her knees, not covered by the hem of her dress, graze the splintery wood of the lower rail. "I have to go home," she said.

Timothy was walking around the garden, his eyes on her hands. It didn't take him long to reach her. "Why do you have to go home?" he asked, resting his hand on the fence rail and bending his head to look into her face. "You're coming out for pancakes with me, remember?"

"I don't feel good," she repeated. "I want to go home."

"Did something upset you, Jewel?"

"It's about my clothes," she explained in a strangled whisper. "I didn't know about them, and I want to go home because other people will see."

Timothy frowned. "What's wrong with your clothes?"

"Too short, and not up to my neck." Jewel swallowed against the lump in her throat. "Mrs. Edon explained, since I'm not Orthodox." She swallowed again. "I think some other people heard her telling me."

"Mrs. Edon is a—" he broke off. "Come sit in my truck, Jewel. No, just come," he said firmly as she began to protest. He put his hand on her shoulder and started walking. There was nothing to do but walk with him.

He started the engine, as he had done at Green Lake, turning down the music, turning up the heat, and he shifted in his seat so he could face her. Jewel sat in the passenger seat where he had put her, staring at the hem of her coat, which was just as short as her dress.

"Tell me everything she said," Timothy commanded.

Jewel told him, and he listened in silence, frowning. When she had finished, he reached for her hand. Jewel winced and curled her fingers protectively into her palm. Timothy's fingers closed on her wrist, turning her hand in his. Jewel saw that her palm was full of splinters from the fence.

"You were rubbing your hands along the fence rail," said Timothy. "That was how I knew you were upset." He let go of her wrist and shrugged himself out of his coat. From the small black case on his belt, he took a Swiss army knife. He glanced up. "It has tweezers," he said, slipping them out of a slot in the back of the knife. "I can fix this for you."

Jewel held out her hand.

"Now listen very carefully," he said, catching the end of a splinter with the tiny steel tweezers and carefully extracting it. "You can throw out everything Mrs. Edon said to you. Look around the church next time you're here. People wear everything. You wouldn't come dressed to go clubbing, but anything else you might want to wear is fine."

"If it was fine, she wouldn't have said anything," said Jewel, unconvinced. "She doesn't think my clothes are right, and if she doesn't, other people don't either."

"There's a whole range of how people dress," Timothy responded, extracting another splinter. "Really conservative Orthodox women come to church with their heads covered and don't sit on the same side as the men. There's nothing wrong with that, but our church isn't like that. You can see for yourself that everyone sits together and almost nobody's head is covered. Not even Mrs. Edon's. The point is that she was way out of line. Your clothes are good."

"I don't fit in here. That's why I don't look right."

"That's in your head," said Timothy bluntly, tilting her hand to get a better angle. "Brace yourself, this one is pretty deep."

"You could be saying she was wrong to make me feel better."

"I could," agreed Timothy. "I want you to feel better. But I'm saying it because it's true. Your problem is that you just took her word for it. You didn't look around. If you had looked around, you would have noticed that nobody else in church dresses like Mrs. Edon either. Except Dorothy."

Jewel felt a small surge of shock. It had never occurred to her to question the word of the apparent expert.

Timothy grinned at her. "That's a very funny face you're making, Jewel. You never looked around at all, did you? You were a deer in the headlights. Next Sunday, take a look. Here's my bet. Mrs. Edon is hoping to drum up recruits, so she and Dorothy want to convince you to be like them before you figure out that no one else is."

"But, I thought—" Jewel's voice trailed away.

"You bought into it, that's all," said Timothy, not unkindly. "There isn't a dress code in the kingdom of heaven, Jewel. Of course we all try to be respectful, but that's all. God isn't in there measuring hemlines or whatever she said. There's nothing wrong with how

Dorothy dresses if it helps her lead a good life. But there's nothing wrong with how you dress either."

"There used to be," said Jewel, suddenly confiding. "These are my new clothes. I burned all the old ones."

The tweezers sprang from Timothy's grasp and bounced off the dashboard. "You burned all your clothes?"

Jewel nodded. "They were all from men. Sara helped me. We just made a pile in her fire pit and poured starter fluid on it, but we did it in the middle of the night so her housing association wouldn't see it, in case it was against the rules."

"That's awesome!" Timothy lunged under the steering wheel to retrieve the tweezers and came up shaking with laughter. "You are a crazy woman, Jewel. Crazy scared and crazy brave. I wish I had been there to see you chucking their stuff into the blaze." He lifted her hand again, looking for splinters he might have missed. "Tell me more. What else did you do, when you started over?"

"I threw my cell phone in Puget Sound," said Jewel, sitting straighter. "This man Trevor knew—Trevor was the last one, the one I left—well, first Trevor left seventeen messages on my phone, after I had already found his new girlfriend on Facebook, and then when I got away and was staying with Sara, this friend of Trevor's called and wanted me to come to dinner on his yacht and talk about how Trevor didn't know how good he had it. They all had my number. So I just threw away the phone. It felt good," she remembered, "but I wished the splash would have been bigger."

"For the satisfaction," agreed Timothy, understandingly. "Yeah, something like that should make a splash like a boulder falling off a cliff."

Jewel's face crinkled into a smile.

Timothy set the tweezers in the cup holder and ran his thumb gently over the palm of Jewel's hand. "That's all the splinters that I can see. Can you feel any that I missed?"

"No, it doesn't feel like there are any left. It just feels a little raw."

"Keep it clean and don't rub it on anything for a day or two," he advised. He slid the tweezers back into the knife and returned it to its case.

"Thank you, Timothy."

"You're welcome, Jewel." He grinned at her. "Now can we go have pancakes?"

Jewel looked at her hands, avoiding his eyes. "Can I ask you one more thing?"

"You can ask me anything you want." He settled back in his seat, giving her his full attention.

"Do you think she could tell about me, from my clothes?"

"No," said Timothy emphatically. "The only thing she knows is that you don't look just like her."

Jewel was silent.

"Do you want to look like her?" asked Timothy incredulously.

"I just wish I looked normal," said Jewel wistfully. "I want to feel like other people."

"You do look normal. How you look isn't the same as how you feel. That's the problem. You look great. What you feel is on the inside." He grinned suddenly. "Too bad you can't have a bonfire for that!"

Jewel pulled at the hem of her dress, straightening it across her knees. "Well, at least people can't see it."

"People who care about you can see it," he said softly. "But that's nothing to be afraid of."

Jewel closed her lips, unwilling to reveal what she knew about fear and love.

"Pancakes," said Timothy. "I'll bring you back to your car when we can't eat another bite."

"Okay," said Jewel. "I'll come."

Chapter 27

Xenia sat on the blue-cushioned barstool behind the glass counter in her shop, clearing away the receipts collected during a profitable afternoon. The Christmas shopping season was upon her. Clients poured through the shop, jostling each other, rattling the merchandise off the racks. Words streamed around her, requesting, describing, reminding. Clothing and jewelry flowed through her fingers. Yet Xenia felt detached from everything in the world except what moved inside her, in the quiet center of her mind. She had dealt with her clients with brisk competence. No one looking at her could have guessed she was decades away in a fire-lit room on the rim of a mountain meadow.

Momentarily empty of customers, the shop seemed still as a deep pool hidden in the forest, its smooth surface undisturbed by breeze or current. A faint fragrance of spices tinted the air. Beautiful colors and textures met her eyes wherever they wandered. Quiet music filtered from the expensive sound system. Xenia sat still, drifting toward meaning.

A flicker of motion outside the shop-front window caught her eye. Mrs. Edon and Dorothy were crossing the street toward her shop, tugged along by the wind filling their matching blue umbrellas, laughing as they clutched ineffectually at their billowing skirts. Xenia's reverie blurred and vanished. She pursed her lips, irritated by the interruption of her thoughts, irritated still more that the Edons were such good customers.

"Well, won't this be fun," said Xenia acidly to the blue Gzhel cat perched on a decorative ledge behind the sales counter. "Goodie and Two-shoes have come to buy Christmas dresses from the Lonely Widow!" The cat's un-winking porcelain stare reminded her of Dorothy.

"Xenia!" Mrs. Edon burst through the door, shaking her umbrella indiscriminately in front of her. Xenia stepped quickly from behind the counter and took it from her as graciously as possible, hanging it on the hook behind the door. Dorothy entered more slowly, closing her wet umbrella neatly and handing it to Xenia with a little smile.

"It's the office Christmas party this time, Xenia," began Mrs. Edon, removing her long wool coat and handing it to Xenia with the ease of long habit. "My husband's office, you know. I'm still a homemaker." Mrs. Edon smiled kindly, meeting Xenia's eyes for the first time since entering the shop. "Will you be doing something festive for the holiday this year?"

Xenia's nostrils flared slightly. "Yes, I will, Mrs. Edon. And is this a formal party, in the evening? I have a new designer this season who I think you will appreciate. Evening gowns, you know. Come back this way—"

A discrete chime of bells heralded the opening of the shop door. Xenia and Mrs. Edon paused, turning instinctively toward the sound. A woman in a cranberry wool coat and matching cloche stepped into the shop, rubbing the soles of her patent-leather pumps on the first few feet of carpet as if it were a doormat. Black hair, gone white around her face, escaped in wisps from an elaborate French twist under the cloche. She paused to pull off suede driving gloves and drop them into a discretely expensive black handbag. Then, lifting her head, she came toward Xenia with her hands out and a smile of recognition on her carefully made-up face. It was Eugenia, the fifty-five-year-old bride.

"Xenia! I'm back. The honeymoon's over, and the Christmas party approaches. What do you have for me today?" She clasped Xenia's hands briefly and half turned to begin scanning the contents of the shop. Her eyes fell on Mrs. Edon and Dorothy, who were gazing at her appreciatively over Xenia's shoulder. Eugenia's lips curved slightly. "I'm sorry, did I interrupt you? I can wait a moment if you're busy." She nodded at Mrs. Edon.

Mrs. Edon spoke quickly, cutting Xenia off. "I'd imagine we're here for a similar reason, so perhaps Xenia can help us both. I'm shopping for evening wear for my husband's office Christmas party."

Eugenia laughed politely. "I'm here for the same reason, and I want something extra special because this is my first office Christmas party as his wife."

Mrs. Edon clasped her hands together joyfully. "Congratulations! What a special way to enter into this blessed season!"

"Yes," said Eugenia, lightly. "And I know Xenia will have just what I need. Mine was an autumn wedding, and I find I've left a few things out of my trousseau."

Xenia heard a rapturous sigh escape from Dorothy's parted lips. She glanced at her and saw that her cheeks were flushed and her eyes shining. So were Mrs. Edon's. Xenia stepped back toward the counter, foreseeing that her services would not be required for several minutes.

"It must be so enjoyable for you," Mrs. Edon was saying. "I remember how much I loved my own wedding year, and you know it's never so much fun to shop for yourself as it is when you have a husband waiting at home to see what you'll buy."

"Yes, he's very attentive," replied Eugenia.

"I love weddings," pursued Mrs. Edon. "They're such an affirmation of love and hope! And so romantic!" Her gaze rested on Dorothy, plainly lost in daydreams beside her, then returned to Eugenia. "You know," Mrs. Edon said confidentially, "I'll have another wedding to plan for one day soon."

"Oh?" Eugenia's eyes rested on Dorothy speculatively. "May I offer you congratulations?"

Dorothy blushed. Xenia coughed loudly and dropped a paperweight on the floor behind the counter.

Mrs. Edon laughed. "These things take time, you know. But someday soon! Come along now, Dorothy, let's get started or we'll have your future wedding planned before I'm ready for Daddy's party."

Xenia stepped out from behind the counter. Eugenia caught her eye.

"I'll just browse through the jewelry here for a moment," Eugenia said. "I'll let you know when I'm ready to look at gowns."

"I always like to look at the gowns first," said Mrs. Edon comfortably, "so that works out very nicely."

"This way," said Xenia, withdrawing her affronted gaze from Dorothy's face and commanding herself to stick to the task at hand. "As I was saying, I have a new designer I think you will like. Traditional style, of course, but the lines are outstanding, and the quality of the fabrics is, of course, exceptional."

Mrs. Edon nodded intelligently, then glanced back over her shoulder, looking for Dorothy. "Did she find something she wanted, I wonder?"

"Possibly," said Xenia tersely. "I'll see if I can assist her as soon as I get you started. Here." Xenia came to a halt in front of a rack of evening gowns hanging along the wall. She lifted out a floor-length green velvet and hooked it on the end of the rack where Mrs. Edon could see it better. "This perhaps? Or I have the same style in midnight blue and also in burgundy."

Mrs. Edon fingered the velvet gently. "This is lovely, Xenia. Let me have a moment to look through them. I think this will be just what I want."

"Take your time. Let me know if you need something or want to try some of these. I'll see how Dorothy is getting on before I talk to Eugenia."

Mrs. Edon looked up briefly. "Oh, is that her name? Such a lovely person."

Xenia left her without replying. A swift step behind a collection of silk blouses hid her momentarily from the three women in her shop. Mrs. Edon would be occupied for some time, savoring the experience of selection. Judging by her facial expressions earlier, Xenia suspected Eugenia would linger in the shop, waiting to request Xenia's attention until Mrs. Edon was gone. Xenia knew both women well. They were, at best, an unlikely combination. And where was Dorothy? A quick glance found Dorothy beside a display of chiffon scarves a few feet away. *May I offer you congratulations? These things take time, you know. But someday soon!* Xenia shuddered. It was a depth of fantasy she could not tolerate. The fire-lit room glimmered within her suddenly. When her eyes fell on Dorothy again, she strove with an unexpected surge of pity.

"Can I help you, Dorothy?" asked Xenia. Dorothy turned at the sound of her voice, and as their eyes met, Xenia felt the meaning of the question change within her. She stepped closer. "It's not you he loves,

Dorothy." She kept her voice low, electrically conscious of Dorothy's mother at the back of the store.

Dorothy made no sound. Her eyes, staring, were the blank blue eyes of the porcelain cat, a hard surface incapable of absorption.

Xenia tried again. "It's Jewel he loves. Jewel. Not you. Timothy will never see you as a woman. Not like her. You're a child to him. You must not go on like this, if you want to keep your self-respect."

Dorothy flinched. Her lips moved. Her voice came in a small, tight whisper. "Why are you saying this to me?"

"Because," answered Xenia, shocking herself, "because I hope it will help."

Seconds passed. Xenia heard her pulse throbbing in her ears. Dorothy seemed frozen, her fingers tangled spasmodically in a pink chiffon scarf.

Xenia walked away. Her ears caught the scuffling sound of Dorothy's flight, the crash of the chime as the door slammed behind her.

Xenia sighed. Shaking her head, she returned to the rear of the store.

"Mrs. Edon?"

Mrs. Edon smiled at her. "I've decided on the green velvet, Xenia."

"Perhaps I'd better hold it for you," said Xenia, in an expressionless voice. "Dorothy left the shop just a moment ago, and she seemed upset."

Mrs. Edon's eyebrows jumped toward her hairline. "Dorothy left? But I haven't finished here. How could she be upset?"

Xenia kept her mouth shut. Dorothy could decide whether this was Mrs. Edon's business.

"Well, I'd better see if she needs anything," Mrs. Edon decided. "Thank you, Xenia. I would like you to hold it. I'll be back for it in a few minutes, I'm sure."

Xenia followed Mrs. Edon to the door, being careful to give her Dorothy's abandoned umbrella as well as her own.

"I'll be open till seven o'clock tonight," said Xenia.

Mrs. Edon nodded and hurried out.

Xenia moved quickly to where Eugenia waited for her by the jewelry, noting that her client still wore her coat and hat. Like Dorothy had been, Eugenia seemed lost in thought, but her face in abstraction had none of Dorothy's bright, oblivious sparkle.

"You didn't buy that here, Eugenia," Xenia said, nodding at her cranberry wool coat.

Eugenia laughed ruefully. "No, but I should have. You don't carry much outerwear, do you, and you know I would buy it from you if you did. Your taste is excellent."

"Meaning it's just like yours," replied Xenia dryly.

"But of course!" Eugenia laughed again.

Xenia looked into her face, detecting a false note in the laughter, but made no comment. She began to walk toward the display of evening dresses on the far wall.

"Everyone's shopping for Christmas parties today. I bought from two new designers this year. One is there in the back, where Mrs. Edon was making her selection." Xenia paused, directing a frank look at Eugenia. "You met her earlier."

Eugenia lifted an expressive eyebrow.

"But I think," continued Xenia, "that you may prefer the other." Reaching the collection she sought, Xenia fingered the sleeves of several dresses. "This designer takes his themes from medieval tapestries, so you get a lot of the aura of wassail and smoke-filled halls and God rest ye merry gentlemen, but the colors and fabrics are good, and the style of these two might become you. Or," she turned a little toward an adjoining rack, "I have this line, all in layered silk chiffon with this metallic scrollwork embroidery at the neck and sleeves. These necklines are all cut to set off jewelry, so I'd advise you to try them if you are planning to wear a really good piece, maybe a well-set gem pendant or one of the more intricate filigree necklaces I have on display over there."

Eugenia's eyes followed the wave of Xenia's hand and drifted back to the dresses in front of them. She touched a few, making a pretense of considering them, but Xenia sensed that her attention was only intermittently engaged. After a few moments of something that looked very like dithering, Eugenia clasped her hands together and gave another light laugh. "Advise me, Xenia. Pick three for me to try, and

I'll try them. Otherwise, I'm going to close my eyes and drop my finger on a dress, and that will be it."

Xenia snorted. "Since when have you needed help choosing your clothing?"

"Please?"

Xenia selected three dresses without hesitation and started toward the fitting rooms. Eugenia fluttered after her, pausing for a moment to examine an extravagant paisley shawl.

At the door of the fitting room, Xenia stopped abruptly. "Eugenia, what is the matter with you today?"

Eugenia's head jerked around, her eyes widening. "Well, really!"

Xenia could see that she had offended her client, but this was a client of long-standing who knew no one else would pamper her like Xenia did. *Besides, this is my day for giving advice to the lovelorn, isn't it? I bet her marriage is off to a rocky start and she's planning to patch it up with a gorgeous dress. Fool.*

"Really what, Eugenia? I've known you for years. I can see that you are not yourself today. If someone had told me you, of all people, would ask me to choose your dress, I'd have said the building would fall down first."

Eugenia eyed her warily.

"You can tell me, if you like," said Xenia, with surprising gentleness, "but I can probably guess."

Eugenia took a step toward her and bent her head to whisper in Xenia's ear. "It's Frederick. He's happy, of course, but I'm not used to it. To marriage, I mean. It annoys me to have things out of place around the house. I know it shouldn't. And I can't sleep, at least, not very well. I promised myself I'd be as beautiful as possible for his office party, to give him pleasure, so he'll feel I don't mind about things. I don't want to hurt his feelings, but maybe I have, already." She was silent for a moment, peering earnestly into Xenia's face. "You were married once, weren't you? Was it like this for you, too?"

"Worse," said Xenia, in a low voice. A full minute passed slowly as the two women stood together by the fitting room, the heavy curtain still held open in Xenia's hand. Xenia let the minute pass, choosing what to speak about, feeling the awkward newness of her ability to speak about any of it, to anyone. At last, she met Eugenia's anxious gaze. Like Eugenia, she chose to whisper her tale, from one woman to another.

"I wish I could tell you that the irritation will all pass. It may, for you. For me, it never did, and when I look back, I see that it consumed me. My husband—" she breathed in and out once, assuring herself that she was not going to panic— "did more than leave things out of place around the house. Still, he was a good man. If you let Frederick see your irritation, you can't expect to escape the consequences. And this—"she clutched at the slippery chiffon already hanging on the hook in the fitting room— "won't help you for much longer."

"What consequences?" whispered Eugenia, bringing her face even closer. Xenia thought abstractly of adolescent girls huddled in locker-room corners, relaying stolen information their mothers were too embarrassed to provide.

"You'll hurt him. He'll see he's irritating you, and it will shame him, and he'll grow angry with you. He wants to perform well. You'll make him feel foolish and clumsy, and he won't find you quite as desirable as he once did." Xenia sucked in another deep breath. "You must decide now which you want: your former life or your husband. You can't have both."

Eugenia gasped, but her eyes were fixed on Xenia's face as if she could not draw them away. "I want my husband, of course." Her whisper was firm, almost strident.

"Do you?" Xenia regarded her with lifted brows. "How much?"

"What do you mean?" Eugenia looked startled.

"I mean that there is probably a part of you that secretly wants your former life more. You'll have to kill that part of yourself if you want to be content in your new life." It sounded brutal, but as the minutes passed, Xenia was conscious of a growing compulsion to save Eugenia from herself, to save all impatient women everywhere from alienating their imperfect husbands.

There was an awkward silence. They seemed frozen in place, the two whispering women. Xenia broke the spell. "Don't tell me anything more," she whispered, "you'll only regret it. But you may trust me with your confidence. I understand where you are coming from."

Eugenia reached impulsively to clasp Xenia's hand, still folded around the tapestry door curtain. "Thank you, Xenia," she whispered. "You may trust me also." She stepped past Xenia into the fitting room and lifted the first chiffon dress from its hook. "This is lovely," she said in her normal voice. "If this fits me, I won't need to try the others. And if you have any more pieces by Jewel, something to go with it, you may bring me those as well."

Just as Xenia was turning away, Eugenia spoke again. "How did he die, Xenia?"

The kind words struck her like hurled stones, but she remained erect.

"He died helping a friend," she said.

Chapter 28

Jewel came two hours early on the evening of the knitting meeting at which she would help Anna host. Still laboring under the shadow of Mrs. Edon's criticism, Jewel spent half an hour staring at her closet, wondering what she had that would be appropriate to wear. One part of her mind told her that Timothy's judgment could be trusted. The other part told her that Dorothy would be looking at her clothes tonight, as she always did. The fact that they wouldn't be in church would make no difference to Dorothy.

She finally chose a red angora sweater and black wool slacks, covering her body from her neck to her ankles. None of it seemed especially tight. She added a black jasper bead necklace and earrings, and her black flats.

"I look like I'm going to the office," she said. "I wish I could ask Anna what to wear." She considered calling Anna. No, it would be too humiliating. She pulled on a black wool coat and walked out to her car, solving the problem by making it too late to do anything about it.

Anna met her at the door with a hug. Jewel wasn't prepared for it. Her purse got caught between them and her head twitched back instinctively. But Anna just smiled and drew her into the house.

"I'm so glad you're here," exclaimed Anna, leading her into the kitchen. "The weather's just awful enough to make me worry, but everyone has called to let me know they're coming, so we'll have a full house. In fact, Dorothy is bringing her mother and Xenia is bringing a friend." Anna's voice dropped to a conspiratorial whisper. "It's the fifty-five-year-old bride. I hope Xenia tells me what her name is."

"Mrs. Edon is coming?" Jewel tried to make the question sound like small talk.

"Yes, she said she and Dorothy are having dinner out tonight and would just come straight here." Anna took Jewel's coat and hung it in the coat closet. "Why don't you put your case here with your coat? I'm not sure whether we'll actually get around to working tonight."

Jewel drove Mrs. Edon from her mind and followed Anna into the kitchen. Anna had set out two bowls of soup and some muffins, and they perched on the tall bar stools by the counter to eat.

"George spent the afternoon shoveling and threw his back out," said Anna, putting a muffin on a small plate for Jewel and pushing the butter dish toward her. "I tucked him in with pillows and a heating pad, and I'm going to bring him something to eat before people start coming. I think he just wants to sleep."

"That's too bad," said Jewel. "It would have been fun to have him with us tonight."

"I'll tell him you said so." Anna smiled. "He'll be pleased. Now let's think about what we need to get done."

Jewel set down her spoon and fixed her eyes attentively on Anna's face, ready for wisdom to be imparted.

"I promised to teach you all my tricks, didn't I?" Anna propped her elbows on the counter and rested her chin on her hands. "Let's see…well, for a little gathering like we'll be having tonight, I start by looking over what I know people are bringing and see what I can provide that will fit in well. So, for example, tonight, I know that Xenia is bringing her ginger cookies. Those are her signature dish," she added, with a touch of humor. "Elizabeth is bringing a pie, probably Boston cream or her homemade pecan pie. Her sister in New Orleans has a tree and sends her an enormous box of nuts every year." She paused, tilting her head so she could look directly at Jewel beside her. "Dorothy said she was bringing lemon squares. I thought that was a little odd."

Jewel's face darkened. "Well, at least I didn't bring any this time." She started guiltily. "Oh, Anna, I forgot to bring anything at all. I didn't even think about it until this minute. There have been so many things in my mind that it fell right out." She wrung her hands.

"Jewel, honey, it doesn't matter. You're going to be making things with me."

"The lemon squares I made came out of a box," said Jewel forlornly. "I made up that red carrot salad I told you about, but it's not a dessert, and anyhow, there aren't any red carrots around at this time of year."

Anna patted her back. "You need to have a second signature dish so you have something to bring to parties in the winter. Let's think of something, and we can make it tonight."

Jewel was silent. Suddenly her face cleared. "Oh! I know what I want it to be! Anna, can you teach me to make brownies from scratch? I can do it from the mix, but I want to make real ones. There was a girl in my fifth grade class who made them with her mother and brought them to school on her birthday, enough for everyone in the class. Hers had a pink candle in it, in a plastic flower holder so it would come out easily when she was ready to eat the brownie. And she brought pink napkins and pink plates to serve the brownies on. But they weren't from a mix. She told us all that she made them with her mother from scratch." Jewel sighed. "Her mother was the girl scout troop leader, too."

Anna got up quickly and went to a tall cupboard above the stove top. "I don't know if I have the ingredients on hand for brownies from scratch, but I have something that's almost as good. A few weeks ago, one of the university wives gave me a Ghirardelli brownie kit as a hostess gift." She reached into the cupboard and brought out a square brown tin bearing the famous blue emblem. She looked at Jewel hopefully. "It's not quite the same as making brownies from scratch with your mother, but we could serve them on my crystal plates with pink linen napkins."

"I would like that," said Jewel happily. She slid off her stool and held out her hands for the box. Anna gave it to her and found her a black apron with white polka-dots and a ruffle around the hem.

An hour later, the house smelled deliciously of warm brownies, and Jewel was putting the final touches on a dessert table she had arranged entirely by herself. Anna had thrown open all her cupboards and let Jewel choose dishes and glasses and silver, reminding her to think of what her guests would need as she made her choices. Now Jewel was piling red and green apples into a gold-rimmed crystal bowl to make a centerpiece. It was hard to make the apples sit gracefully in the bowl. One side of the arrangement seemed lumpier than the other. Jewel's tongue slipped out between her teeth as she prodded a green apple away from the rim.

The doorbell rang. Anna stopped filling the tea kettle and looked up. "You can answer the door, Jewel. Just tell them I'll be right out, and help them put their coats away and get settled in the living room."

Jewel rubbed her palms nervously on her apron. "Will they think it's funny for me to answer the door at your house?"

"No, they'll think you are helping. Go ahead now. You don't want to leave them standing on the porch on such a cold night." Anna turned back to the sink.

Jewel went straight to the door and opened it quickly. "Come right in. Anna's just in the kitchen and

I'm helping her." She stopped. Dorothy stood on the front porch, and beside her was Mrs. Edon.

"Hi, Jewel," said Dorothy lightly, stepping past her into the house. She turned, holding out a plate of lemon squares. They were covered in plastic wrap, but there were toothpicks in some to hold the plastic away from the perfect dusting of powdered sugar. "I'll just put these on the table. Mama, the coat closet is right down the hall by the kitchen." She walked away into the dining room, leaving Jewel still holding the doorknob in one hand, gazing stupidly at Mrs. Edon.

"Hello, Jewel," said Mrs. Edon with a friendly smile. "You look very nice." She leaned closer and added in a whisper, "There's a little smudge of something on your cheek. Oh, and on your other cheek, too." She leaned back and said in a normal voice, "Now where did she say the coat closet was?"

"Down the hall," said Jewel. She turned away, preparing to shut the door, and saw Elizabeth coming slowly up the walk, holding a pie with both hands and looking down at her feet.

"I'm just making sure I don't hit any black ice," Elizabeth called out, sensing that the door was open above her but not looking up. "I'll be right there."

Jewel came out on the porch and held out her hands, taking the pie as Elizabeth reached the steps and offering her arm to give the older woman support. "George shoveled everything," Jewel said, "but it's always good to be careful."

Jewel helped Elizabeth into the house and closed the door. Elizabeth took her pie into the dining room. Keeping her back to the hall, Jewel lifted the hem of her apron and scrubbed her cheeks vigorously. The doorbell rang again.

It was Timothy. Relief surged through her at the sight of him. He was standing on the edge of the porch, banging the snow off his boots, his paper bag of knitting rattling and swinging in one hand. He looked up when she opened the door.

"Hi," he said, with a slow smile. "Aren't you a sight for sore eyes." He came across the porch, stopping just inches in front of her, looking down into her upturned face. "Nice apron."

"You're a sight for sore eyes, too," said Jewel blissfully.

"I smell brownies," said Timothy, lingering. "Tell me you made brownies."

"I made brownies." Jewel's eyes sparkled. "I made them with Anna. They're Ghirardelli brownies, and even the batter looked tasty."

"Make sure I get one," commanded Timothy.

"We have crystal plates for them," said Jewel eagerly. "Wait till you see." She stepped back, letting him come through the door. She heard something moving behind her and saw Timothy's expression change to one of studied courtesy.

"Hello, Mrs. Edon," he said, over Jewel's head. His free hand came up and rested on Jewel's arm, turning her but keeping her close. "Did you hear we're having brownies?"

"How nice," laughed Mrs. Edon. "Dorothy made lemon squares. I think Elizabeth brought pie." She added, "I'm just on my way to the kitchen to see if Anna needs any help."

Jewel felt Timothy's hand tighten on her arm. "I've been helping Anna tonight," she said. "I think she has everything ready."

"I'll just check," Mrs. Edon said brightly.

They watched her go.

"Good girl," whispered Timothy. "Don't let her get you down." He reached into his knitting bag, bringing out a box covered in gold foil. "Here, these are truffles."

"She told me I had smudges on my face when she came in," whispered Jewel, holding out her hands for the truffles. "Chocolate or something. I was just scrubbing them off when you got here."

"Too bad," murmured Timothy. "I'd have been happy to help you with that."

Jewel blushed. Timothy followed her into the dining room, where she set the box of truffles on a crystal plate.

Anna came through the dining room, bringing Mrs. Edon with her. The doorbell rang.

"I'll get that," said Anna quickly. "Jewel, why don't you and Timothy go in and sit down? I put your case on the table by your usual spot."

"Good idea," said Timothy cheerfully, propelling Jewel toward the living room door. "No don't take off the apron. I like it."

Mrs. Edon's hand fluttered to her lips. She stepped back quickly to let them pass.

Once through the living room door, Jewel realized that another problem awaited her. Mrs. Edon's workbag sat in the middle of the sofa, between Jewel's seat and Dorothy's. There would be room for her to sit down, but it would be crowded with three women on the sofa. Jewel glanced at Timothy, who was seating himself in his chosen place, the chair he had set on the other side of Jewel's end table. If she sat on the other side of him, she would be next to Elizabeth, where Barbara used to sit. Then she remembered that Xenia would be bringing a friend. It wouldn't be fair to ask her friend to squeeze in with the Edons while Jewel took a better seat. Xenia's friend would sit in Barbara's old place next to Elizabeth, and Jewel would sit next to Mrs. Edon. *That's what a good hostess would do,* thought Jewel, encouraging herself. *I'll just focus on my jewelry and try to face Timothy more than her.*

She sat down and made herself turn and greet Dorothy. Dorothy nodded and went back to her knitting. She seemed out of spirits. Jewel decided not to think about why that might be. Not yet, anyhow. She needed to focus on what was happening around her.

Anna came in, bringing Xenia and the fifty-five-year-old bride. "Everyone," began Anna in her gracious, hostess voice, "I'd like you to know Eugenia. She's a friend of Xenia's, and I'm very happy to have a new face to add to our group." She smiled at Eugenia. Eugenia smiled back and nodded toward the circle of faces looking up at her from around the room. "And also Mrs. Edon," continued Anna, gesturing toward the sofa. "She's Dorothy's mother, and she was fortunately able to join us tonight." Mrs. Edon acknowledged the introduction with a nod and cast a smiling glance at Elizabeth and then Xenia.

Jewel's stomach fluttered. She felt a sensation midway between terror and delight. Eugenia was wearing a necklace and bracelet that Jewel had made for Xenia's store. *Will she know it's mine when she sees me working tonight? Will she say something? Will it be awkward?* Her gaze twitched toward Mrs. Edon, who was settling herself between Jewel and Dorothy on the sofa. Jewel saw her put her arm around Dorothy and give her a little squeeze. Dorothy looked into her mother's face. Jewel opened her case and fiddled with something in the top tray. It was hard to cope with the mixture of aggravation and envy that Dorothy aroused in her.

Instinctively, Jewel turned her face toward Anna. Anna caught her eye and smiled.

"Now, are we all in?" Anna's glance ran around the room, bringing their attention to herself. "Let's start with a prayer, and then we can get right to work." Everyone rose and there was a little silence as they waited to see whom Anna would ask to pray. "Jewel, I think it's your turn to pray tonight. Everyone else has had a turn, except our two newest members, and I don't want to put them on the spot."

Jewel jumped, clutching at her case as it slid to one side. Her eyes flew to Anna's face. Anna gave a little nod, her brows raised, her eyes opened wide. She was sending Jewel a message. Jewel could see that she was. *Why does she want me to do this? She knows I'll be bad at it. I don't know any prayers, do I?* She gazed beseechingly at Anna. Anna nodded again and her hand moved slightly, urging Jewel to begin.

Jewel drew a deep breath and rose to her feet, folding her hands tightly against her apron. She heard Timothy's chair creak as he stood up. Her mind cleared suddenly. "I only know one prayer, and I didn't remember it till just now. It's a prayer my mother taught me when I was a little girl." She closed her eyes, and her memory conjured a clean kitchen table and her mother's voice, prompting her to put down her spoon and fold her hands. Jewel's lips parted. The little prayer came welling up and she spoke each phrase almost before she had fully remembered it. "Be present at our table, Lord. Be here and everywhere adored. Thy creatures bless and grant that we may feast in fellowship with thee. Amen." Jewel opened her eyes and smoothed her apron with her hands.

"Thank you, Jewel," said Anna warmly. "I'm sure your mother would be happy that you still remember that."

"Amen," said Timothy. "May her memory be eternal."

There was a murmur of assent, the small sounds of work bags opening and furniture creaking as each woman settled back into her seat. Jewel realized she was still standing and sat down, pulling her jewelry case onto her lap and re-opening it.

"Do you know the Orthodox table prayer yet?" asked Mrs. Edon, opening her work bag.

"I remember my mom teaching me that," said Timothy, before Jewel could answer her. "I remember resting my chin on the back of my chair, staring at my food while she said the words."

"We tried to start the little ones saying it with us as soon as they could understand." Mrs. Edon patted Dorothy's knee. "I loved hearing their little voices blessing dinner before we ate it."

Silence fell for a moment.

Eugenia leaned forward suddenly, setting down her needlepoint. "Would you mind telling me all of your names?" she asked. "I'll start, if you like. I'm Eugenia, and I know Xenia because I've been coming to her shop since it opened. In fact, I think I was her first customer."

"You were the first customer who bought something," said Xenia drily. "You bought a navy blue dress and a silk scarf to wear at the neck."

Eugenia nodded. "I remember that. It was for a trip to New York. What a long time ago that was."

"I bet I was your second customer," remarked Elizabeth. "I have no idea what I bought, but someone at church told me you had opened the shop and my curiosity brought me over on the double." She chuckled. "You know, Eugenia, we've probably been in that shop together any number of times and never noticed each other. It's funny what you don't see when you aren't looking."

Eugenia laughed. "You wouldn't be looking for someone you didn't know you would ever know, is that what you mean?"

"Something like that! I'm Elizabeth, by the way. I was a librarian at the university for years, and I go to Xenia's church. We all do, and just about all of us go to her shop, too. Except him, of course!" Elizabeth jerked a humorous thumb at Timothy, who grinned responsively.

"I'm Timothy," he said to Eugenia. "I like to knit, so they let me come here."

"Why do you knit, Timothy?" inquired Anna. "I've always wanted to know."

"Family tradition," Timothy answered promptly. "My great grandfather was an infantryman in World War I, and he learned to knit in the trenches in France.

A lot of them did. It gave them something to put their minds on, and probably they needed the socks. When he came home, he taught my grandfather. I guess he was trying to share something from his wartime experience with his son. My grandfather taught my dad, and my dad taught me. It was our trademark. It was like a secret password, or some kind of family high sign. Nobody expects a man to knit."

"That's for sure!" Elizabeth chuckled.

Jewel secured a second bead on the silver wire in her hand and decided she should join the conversation. "I'm Jewel," she said, adding bravely, "I make jewelry for Xenia's shop."

Eugenia exclaimed delightedly. "You're Jewel! You made nearly all the jewelry in my trousseau! Your pieces are so original, but always in a tasteful way, and they go so well with what I choose from Xenia's collection. I always feel as if they were made especially for me!"

Jewel glanced quickly at Anna. Anna was beaming at her. Jewel's eyes returned to Eugenia.

"I'm very happy that you like them," Jewel said shyly.

"Do you take requests, Jewel?" asked Xenia pointedly, giving her a sharp, directive nod.

"Oh," said Jewel, realizing that Xenia was making an opportunity for her. "Oh, yes, I do, if you like. Is there something special that you want?"

Eugenia gazed thoughtfully at the open case in Jewel's lap. "You know, there are several things, when I think of it. For example, I have a tunic, a dress almost, that my sister knit for me. She knits so well, like Xenia. Her pieces are of professional quality. This one is made from a yarn that changes colors—amber, rose, something almost turquoise." She turned to Xenia. "I was going to bring it in next weekend and look for a skirt or leggings, something to go with it. Jewel, if you could meet us at the shop? Also, I might want a brooch for a winter coat. And I will definitely want new things in the spring." She set down her needlepoint again and rummaged in her purse. "Here, this is my card." She held it out, and Jewel got up quickly, crossing the room to receive it. "You should make this a regular thing, Jewel. I'm sure many of Xenia's clients would order custom jewelry if you were available to discuss it with them in the shop while they were making their purchases."

Xenia snorted. "Jewel has a full-time job and a life, Eugenia." Her eyes narrowed. "But you have a point. I could feature her on specific dates. The first Saturday of the month, perhaps, or during the big annual sales."

Jewel stood rooted to the floor, clutching Eugenia's card, staring at Xenia's lips as they spoke these magical words.

"Well?" said Xenia brusquely. "Would you do it?"

"W-w-yes!" stuttered Jewel. "It would be such an opportunity."

"Here, here!" cried Timothy, waving his knitting in the air. "I'll bring all the guys from work."

Xenia looked down her nose at him. "My shop does not cater to the 'guys from work', Timothy. This is no help to her."

"They have wives," explained Timothy.

"Oh, yes, I suppose they must." Xenia sounded vaguely surprised. "In that case, go ahead."

"I'll round up the church ladies," offered Elizabeth. "I'm good with church ladies."

"I could pass the word among my friends," said Mrs. Edon, in a cool voice. "Many of them already shop with you, Xenia, and I often receive compliments on the things I buy from you."

"That's because they look so nice on you, Mama," said Dorothy, taking her eyes off her knitting for a few seconds to smile at her mother.

"Yes, they do," agreed Xenia, equably. "You're a wonderful advertisement for me, Mrs. Edon, and don't think I don't appreciate it." Her sudden burst of laughter startled almost everyone.

Jewel returned to her seat and laid Eugenia's card carefully in the top tray of her jewelry case. She felt light and warm, like a butterfly flitting over a flower in the sun. Across the end table, her eyes found Timothy, his face glowing with triumph and delight.

"Time for dessert, ladies and Timothy." Anna's voice recalled Jewel's thoughts to the carefully arranged dessert table. She closed her case and jumped up, eager to reach the dining room in time to serve her brownies personally.

Anna went straight through to the kitchen to bring in the hot water for tea. Seeing Jewel come into the dining room, she said, "That's right. If you could start serving things, I'll put this into a carafe."

Eugenia came first. Jewel lifted the square silver spatula by the brownie pan suggestively, and Eugenia moved toward her. Thrilled, Jewel scooped up a brownie and laid it carefully on a crystal plate. Then she set down her spatula and tucked a pink linen napkin under the plate, holding it out to Eugenia.

"Here," she said, proudly. "I made this myself."

"Thank you, Jewel. It smells heavenly. And I can't wait to see what you're going to design for me. I'll look forward to meeting with you."

"I'm looking forward to it also," replied Jewel, giving way to an irresistible urge to smile.

Elizabeth came into the room, with Xenia beside her. Behind them came Timothy, who walked around both ladies and started purposefully toward Jewel.

"This one is for you, Timothy," said Jewel, wielding her spatula. "It's the biggest one on the plate." She reached for the pink napkin and held out the crystal dessert dish. "Taste it," she added anxiously. "Is it good?"

Timothy bit into the brownie, keeping his eyes on her face. He chewed slowly, with the air of a man tasting a fine wine.

"Jewel," he said, "I never liked anything better than this." He laughed, full of joy. "Give me another!"

"Well!" Elizabeth chuckled. "So *that's* it! Give him another, honey. You can see he's ready to take the whole plate."

Jewel blushed, feeling the eyes of every woman in the room watching her. "Would you like anything else with it?" she asked, lifting another brownie onto the plate he held out to her.

"No, thank you," said Timothy. "I've got everything I want right here."

Chapter 29

"God bless that man!" exclaimed Anna, lapsing gracefully into her armchair with a sigh of ecstatic satisfaction.

Xenia stopped sipping her tea. "Who? Timothy? What's he done now?"

"I'm not sure, but I'm sure he's the one who did it. Do you know what just happened, just now, right in my front hall as I was saying goodnight to Jewel?"

"Surprise me," said Xenia.

"Jewel hugged me! It was a real hug! You don't understand what this means to me, Xenia." Anna sighed again, letting her gaze drift into the room, unaware of the tea Xenia had prepared for her, which was cooling on the round table between them.

"You're right. I don't." Xenia looked inquiringly at her friend.

Anna sat forward, eager to explain. "I have this feeling about her, Xen. It started sometime after the first knitting meeting, and it's gotten stronger and stronger. The night I had you all over for dinner, it was so strong that I invited her to come before the rest of you so I could get to know her better. I made some progress, but I didn't get far. Remember how she left early? As I was saying goodnight to her in the hall, I gave her a hug, trying to encourage her, and she was so stiff and awkward about it. It's like she had no idea how to be hugged, or couldn't remember. Or like she was so embarrassed she could hardly wait for it to end. But then suddenly, for just a second, her head dropped down on my shoulder, and it was the most natural, unconscious thing, as if she couldn't help it. It's like she remembers how to be loved, somewhere inside. Ever since, I have been praying and praying. I'm certain God means me to be part of her life in some way. I took her to lunch one day. And she came early tonight and we made brownies together. It was more fun than anything I've done in recent memory. She was so excited, baking and playing with all my nice dishes." Anna suddenly noticed her tea cup and picked it up gratefully. Her eyes met Xenia's over the rim.

"But what does this have to do with Timothy?" asked Xenia, interested but keeping to the question at hand.

"Well, tonight, as we were saying goodbye, I started tentatively to hug her, and she hugged me back, a real hug, and once she got started, she couldn't let go. I just held her and patted her head, and it was the most...Xen, it was *maternal*. It was the first moment of my life when I felt like that part of me had a chance at expression. I'm not her mother, but there was something universal about it. It's like I have mothering in me, even though it's never been called for, and she needs a mother, even though she doesn't have one anymore. It was like a gift and a need finding each other. It was beautiful." She stopped, out of breath. She wiped her eyes, but she was smiling. "Timothy did this, somehow. You can see he's part of her life now, in some capacity, and look at what it's doing for her! She's showing emotion. She's talking. She even prayed, although I could see she was terrified when I asked her to do it."

"You can take credit, too, Anna," remarked Xenia, unwilling to give all the glory to the man knitter, although she felt, being just, that he had exceeded her original low expectations. "I can see what you mean about the change in her, but you had a hand in that, or she wouldn't be hugging you. Maybe she has a feeling about you, too."

"Do you think she's falling in love with him?" asked Anna dreamily, not from any apparent doubt, but merely to relish the confirmation of her hopes.

"Of course she is," answered Xenia, lifting her tea cup.

"What was wrong with Dorothy tonight, do you think?" wondered Anna, following her own train of thought.

"Me," said Xenia cryptically.

"You?" Anna looked surprised. "Did you do something to her?"

Xenia put down her cup. "I pounced on her when she came to the shop with her mother, and told her that Timothy wasn't interested in her. Or words to that effect. She looked as blank as my blue china cat."

"Goodness!" Anna's eyebrows rose. "What made you do that?"

"Mercy," said Xenia tersely. She lifted her cup again, then placed it carefully on the table. "And fifteen minutes later, I was giving marriage advice to someone else. I hardly know myself." She paused, dropping all pretense of humor. Anna also put down her cup and leaned toward her friend.

A silent moment passed.

"I don't know if I will ever tell this to anyone else, Anna...It was at church, just recently, on the day of Andrew's memorial."

Anna started to speak, but a swift motion of Xenia's hands silenced her. "I was there. You didn't see me because I was outside, on the bench. But I could hear it, most of it. As I was sitting there, I felt a voice. I felt it. It didn't make a sound, and it was inside me, perhaps in my head or somewhere else in me. It told me to try thinking of my husband in a new way. I refused, of course, dragging out my good reasons as I always do. But I felt the voice again, and then—I remembered Andrew." Her hands moved again, commanding Anna's understanding. "I *remembered*, Anna. I thought it was all long gone, erased. This memory was like a survivor, like a person who runs through a wall of flame to escape. You can't believe he still lives, and yet he lives, his face, his voice, his essence all intact. It was a memory from the mountain cabin, on our wedding night. I saw every detail of his face, I heard his voice reading to me, and I felt the warmth of the fire on my feet. It was real, a tangible thing." Xenia rested her trembling hands on the round table between the tea cups, recovering her voice. "It was like...I can hardly describe it, it all happened so quickly and so...cohesively. It's hard to describe in separate intervals, as a process. I went back through the wall of flame myself, Anna. I don't mean that I went back in time or went up to heaven or that I went anywhere at all. I was still on the bench. But it changed what I know...what I am willing to know. It gave me back what I might have known once, in the beginning. I felt my own heart again, and yet I'm still alive. It didn't kill me, after all, to let go."

Xenia drew a breath, and then another, refilling her lungs with air, seeing her own tears mirrored on Anna's loving face. "The memory re-opened a door. Other memories have come through, now. I never know when it will happen. I was in the shop yesterday night, closing up, when suddenly I smelled him. I smelled his scent...his aftershave, his favorite soap...it was so strong I dropped what I was holding and whipped around before I realized I wouldn't see him, standing behind me. This morning, I bumped into the bookcase in the hall, and a book fell out of it. It fell face down, and when I turned it over, the page it had opened to had Andrew's handwriting on it. He loved poetry. He used to scribble in the margins, things the poem made him think of. I thought it was so untidy." Xenia's tears welled again, and Anna came around the table and threw her arms around Xenia.

"I'm so glad," Anna wept. "You're here. You're alive again!"

"So that's why I told Dorothy," finished Xenia, releasing herself to find a tissue in her pocket, "and then the other woman, about her marriage…You know my patron saint. She said awkward, truthful things to people. It was a way of loving, I think. This is my first chance to live up to her. In fact," she drew another deep breath, "I'm almost ready to see Fr. Nicholas again." She laughed, wiping her eyes. "I'll need to be in church for Jewel's wedding!"

"Would you go to her wedding?" asked Anna.

Xenia sighed. "I would try."

Chapter 30

"Are you finished here?" Sara came around the corner of a shelf of books and found Jewel standing in the aisle beside it, staring into the distance. "You look finished. You look like you need coffee as much as I do."

"What did you say?" asked Jewel, turning her head.

"Exactly my point," said Sara, taking her arm. "Let's go get coffee. We've been popping in and out of stores all afternoon. We're numb. Let's go to Starbucks. It's too cold to walk any farther."

"Coffee is a nice idea," said Jewel, allowing herself to be led out of the bookstore. Her cell phone rang as they reached the sidewalk.

"You answer that while I text Clay and tell him where to meet us," said Sara, pulling her own phone out of her purse.

"Hello?" said Jewel, holding the phone to her ear.

"Hi, there," said Timothy's voice.

Jewel's eyes sparkled. "I'm Christmas shopping with Sara, and I'm going to get you a present."

"I'm Christmas shopping all by myself, and I'm going to get you a present." Timothy sounded pleased.

"Is that Timothy?" hissed Sara, putting her ear close to Jewel's phone.

Jewel nodded, trying to focus on what Timothy was saying.

"Give me the phone!" shrieked Sara, reaching for it.

"Is that Sara?" asked Timothy in Jewel's other ear.

"Yes," said Jewel, sidling away from her.

"Come on!" said Sara, bouncing after her. "Where is he? Does he want to join us?"

"What does she want?" asked Timothy. "I can hear shrieking, but I can't make out words."

"She wants me to give her the phone," answered Jewel, embarrassed.

"She wants to talk to me?" Timothy sounded surprised. "Well, put her on then."

"Ha!" said Sara, who had been shamelessly eavesdropping. "Now you have to let me have it." She plucked the phone out of Jewel's hand. "Timothy? Hi, this is Sara, Jewel's life-long friend. Merry almost Christmas to you. Are you out shopping, too?"

Jewel stared at her phone in Sara's hand. Maybe the signal would die. Maybe the phone would spontaneously combust.

"Okay, that's perfect, because so are we," Sara was saying, gesturing and making faces at Jewel as if the moment were too entertaining for words. "We're about to go to coffee at Starbucks. It's the one right on the corner of Main Street and Fifth Avenue in Edmonds. Do you know where that is? Of course, you probably have GPS. Oh, you live near here. Good, then it will be easy. We'll be there in about five minutes, so just join us as soon as you can. My husband Clay is meeting us there, too, so you won't have to hang out with just women." Sara giggled excitedly. "Do you want Jewel back now? Dumb question, huh? Here she is." Sara thrust the phone into Jewel's hands. "He wants to talk to you again, sweetie."

Jewel held the phone to her ear. She could hear Timothy laughing. She tried to think of something to say to him that wouldn't hurt Sara's feelings. Nothing came to her.

"Jewel? Are you there?"

"Yes. I'm sorry, were you—were you busy?"

"Don't be sorry. I'll be glad to see you, and if Sara is your life-long friend, I certainly want to meet her."

"Well, if you're sure." Jewel was not feeling friendly toward her life-long friend.

"I'll be there in twenty minutes. Save me a seat next to you." Timothy hung up.

Sara grabbed her arm and hugged it. Jewel almost lost her balance.

"Hooray, I get to meet him!" crowed Sara. "Coffee with the handsome chanter! This is going to be way more fun than Christmas shopping."

"Sara, if you dare call him that or do anything else to embarrass me, I'll—I'll pour my coffee over your head. I can't believe you did this to me." Jewel yanked her arm free from Sara's grasp and stopped walking.

"Oh, come on, Jewel, don't you want to see him?"

"Not like this, I don't."

"Not like what? What's wrong? He's your friend, right? Well, I just asked your friend to join us for coffee."

Jewel frowned darkly.

"Well, okay, maybe I did just a little more than that," Sara admitted, "but how else am I going to get a chance to meet him? Besides, it will be fun, like a little double date. Don't worry about it. It's not like you haven't ever gone out with him. The man is showing interest."

"That isn't the point. You butted in on my conversation and forced him to come. He couldn't say no if he wanted to, without being rude."

"Trust me, babe, he didn't want to say no," Sara retorted, unabashed. "Come on, we'll be late."

Jewel walked in silence, her head bowed, her arms crossed on her chest. Beside her, Sara was happily texting her husband, warning him of the part he would be expected to play in the coming encounter.

Obedient to Sara's instructions, Clay had arrived before them and was holding a table for four. Sara dropped her purse into a chair and pulled off her jacket. "Now you sit down with Clay, grumpy girl, and I'll get in line and order us coffee. What do you think Timothy would like?"

Jewel had no idea. She wanted to call and ask him, but she was afraid to take her phone out of her purse.

"Get him plain old coffee and cream," suggested Clay, leaping into the breach.

Sara bustled off.

Jewel sat down across from Clay and began to take off her coat, watching her fingers unbutton it.

"So I'm guessing you got ambushed," said Clay humorously.

Jewel looked up. "She took the phone away from me and made him agree to come."

"Well, at least it's only coffee. Seems like a pretty neutral thing, right?"

"It was embarrassing," said Jewel. "What if he didn't want to come?"

"I wouldn't worry about that," said Clay easily. "He's a guy. He likes you. He's probably high-fiving himself."

Jewel turned to look out the window. She saw Timothy's truck pulling into a parking space across the street. Leaning forward, she watched intently as he climbed out and stood waiting for a car to pass so he could cross. She searched his face for signs of his true feelings, wanting to know how he looked before he came into Starbucks and put on his company manners. She saw that he was swinging his arms and whistling.

"Is that him?" asked Clay, as Timothy came into the shop and approached the counter. "Maybe you better go tell him he doesn't need to stand in line."

Jewel pushed back her chair and darted past a group of women carrying their steaming cups to a table by the window. Reaching Timothy, she tugged on his sleeve.

"Hi, Jewel," he turned his head and smiled down at her. "Did you already order?"

"Yes, and we ordered plain coffee with cream, for you. Do you want it, or would you rather have something else? Sara is just giving the order now." She pointed to Sara, who had reached the front of the line and was learing on the counter, talking to the barista.

Timothy tucked her hand under his arm. "Plain coffee is fine. Show me where we're sitting."

Jewel led him to their table. "Clay, this is Timothy," she said, staring intently at a point just past Clay's right shoulder.

Timothy held out his hand and Clay stood up to shake it. "Nice to meet you, Clay. You're Sara's husband, is that right?"

Clay grinned. "That's right. It's a man-sized job, but I like it."

Timothy laughed and sat down across from Clay. Jewel slipped into the chair next to Timothy. She heard their voices, exchanging pleasantries, but her attention was centered on calming herself, preparing for what might happen when Sara returned.

"It's him!" cried Sara, arriving at the table clutching four tall, lidded cups in her over-stretched fingers. "These are really hot, you guys. Can you help me set them down?"

Timothy and Clay leaped to help her, and Sara stood between them, grinning like the Cheshire cat.

"Thank you, gentlemen. Thank you very much." She ruffled Clay's hair affectionately as she passed behind his chair to reach her own place, across from Jewel.

Sitting down, she reached across the table to shake hands with Timothy. "Hi, Timothy. I'm Sara, your overbearing hostess. I'm sorry, but I just had to meet you."

Jewel clutched the edge of the table.

Timothy laughed. "Hi, Sara. I'm glad to meet you."

"Wonderful," exclaimed Sara. "So, who are you and what do you do?"

"I'm the director of the financial aid office at the community college during business hours. The rest of the time, I'm outside playing or in church chanting. What about you?"

"I'm a Catholic school gym teacher, and I'm Jewel's best friend. I've known her since kindergarten. She was so cute back then. Big eyes, big pony tail, skinny little legs. Oh, and this is my husband, Clay. But you must have already met him."

Clay nodded at Timothy across the table and leaned back in his seat. Clay had plainly decided to let events take their course. Sara had taken the bit in her teeth and bolted. As far as Clay was concerned, it was every man for himself.

"Are you from around here?" Sara inquired, staring at Timothy with her round, bright eyes. "I wonder if you went to our school. Wouldn't that be funny if we grew up right next to you and never knew you were there?"

"I didn't grow up right in this area. We lived further north when I was a kid, up near Bellingham. My parents had some land there, and we didn't move down here until I was in my teens," said Timothy, giving Jewel's cup a little nudge, as if to remind her it was there.

Jewel wrapped her hands around the warm cup and pulled herself together. "Your cousins live in Bellingham, don't they, Sara?" she asked, attempting distraction.

Sara gave her a mischievous look. "Yes, they do, Jewel. Have you told Timothy about the time we went up to visit them, when we were fifteen?"

"No, I haven't," said Jewel stiffly. Her hands tightened around the coffee cup.

"Oh, goodie!" Sara laughed. "Then I will."

Timothy laughed with her, then leaned forward. "Now, come on, Sara, you can't go telling all her secrets in front of Clay and me. I thought there was some big rule against that, among you women."

"Someone has trained you well," returned Sara, "Alright, I won't embarrass her."

Clay set down his cup. "I want a cookie. Does anyone else?"

No one else did. Clay got up and went to the counter. Sara watched him go, then turned her eyes to Timothy.

"Clay and I met in a coffee shop," Sara said dreamily. "It was in college, right down there at the U. Jewel and I both went there. So did Clay. He was in electrical engineering, and he's actually a lot smarter than I am. I just talk more than he does." She smiled mirthfully. "But as I was saying, we met in a coffee shop. I had just ordered my drink, and I was chatting with the barista. I picked up my drink and swung around, not looking where I was going, and crash! I slammed right into Clay. Coffee everywhere. Whipped cream, caramel, everything. All over him! You would think he would hate me, right? But he laughed. We both did. We laughed our heads off, and he asked for my number because we could see that we were just like each other."

"You are just like each other," agreed Jewel, relieved that the conversation had shifted to a topic that could only be awkward by implication. "You laugh at the same things, and you get mad at the same things. But mostly, you just float along, being happy in your life."

"We fight sometimes," said Sara, watching her husband approach the table with his cookie, "but it doesn't seem to matter much."

"I think people who never fight at all don't know each other well enough," remarked Timothy, laying a casual arm along the back of Jewel's chair. "If two grown adults are agreeing on every subject, somebody's hiding something."

"That's a little cynical, don't you think?" asked Sara.

"It's not cynical." Clay slid into his chair. "It's realistic. People don't always agree. Not in real life.

Just like you don't wear high heels and pearls when you vacuum the house," he added, grinning at her.

"Oh!" exclaimed Sara, rising to the bait. "Do you ever watch those old shows? They make me nuts. Look at Mrs. Cleaver! Just look at her! I have three brothers, and I'm here to tell you that no woman can live in the same house with even two boys and keep all her hair in place and her blouse tucked in. I just wonder why they made the show that way. I can't believe people were ever like that, even back then."

"I don't think Mrs. Cleaver's meant to be historically accurate," Timothy remarked, turning his empty cup with one hand. "I think people used to entertain themselves by making up stories about how they wished their lives could be."

Jewel thought this sounded like a very good idea, but she could see that this opinion would not be welcomed by her companions, so she remained silent.

"That's all very well and good," said Sara, pushing her empty cup to the end of the table. "But the problem is, people watched the shows and believed them! You can't go through life thinking it's actually possible to *be* Mrs. Cleaver. Not if you want to stay sane, you can't."

"Do you think anyone really did?" asked Clay.

"I think some people did," replied Timothy, glancing briefly at Jewel. "Some people still do, or at least, some people still watch TV to find out how to behave in real life. The older generation doesn't seem to do it as much anymore. Maybe they all learned the truth after trying to be Mrs. Cleaver." He grinned humorously at Sara. "But I see it all the time with kids at the community college."

"Me too, at school," agreed Sara. "Even with the little ones." She laughed suddenly. "Listen to us! We sound like we're already parents! Any minute now, we'll be talking about 'young people today'!" She pushed back her chair. "We should get going. We're having people to dinner, and I don't even know what I'm serving yet."

They all rose, pulling on their coats, clearing away the cups. Then Sara took Clay's arm and started for the door. Timothy stood by the table while Jewel buttoned her coat and tucked her purse under her arm. Then they followed Sara and Clay out to the sidewalk.

"Good bye, sweetie." Sara threw her arms around Jewel and kissed her. "See?" she whispered in Jewel's ear, "I told you everything would be fine. And yes, I like him."

Jewel nodded and stepped back. She knew Sara meant well, but she wondered what Timothy had thought.

He shook hands with Clay and Sara, saying goodbye, and he waited until they were out of earshot before he turned back to Jewel.

"Relax," he said, smiling at her. "What are you afraid of?"

"I was afraid she was going to embarrass me," Jewel admitted. "I didn't want her to grab the phone and put you on the spot like that. She means well. She's just—"

"Nosey," Timothy laughed. "But there's no harm done. She obviously cares about you, and she's trying to look out for you."

Jewel was silent.

"It was pretty awkward for you," observed Timothy. "You didn't have much to say."

"I didn't want to say the wrong thing." Jewel looked away. Even now, it was possible to say the wrong thing, to make it look like she shared Sara's assumptions about Timothy's place in her life. They were not wholly unfounded, but they might be premature.

Timothy took his keys out of his pocket. "This is unfamiliar ground for you, is that it?"

Jewel's eyes flew to his face. He smiled. "I'm getting pretty good at reading your mind," he said.

"Sometimes." She felt breathless.

"Do you need a ride home?"

Jewel shook her head.

"I'll call you," he said, turning toward his truck. "I have to attend an event at the college tonight, but I'll call you tomorrow."

She watched him cross the street and climb into his truck. As he pulled into traffic, he waved. Jewel waved back, and her eyes followed his truck until it disappeared around a corner.

Chapter 31

The telephone rang while Jewel was making breakfast for herself on Monday morning. Surprised, she set down the butter knife, wiped her fingertips on the dishrag, and answered it.

"Hello?"

"Don't worry, it's only me," said Timothy's voice. Jewel smiled and cradled the phone against her cheek.

"Oh. Hello, Timothy."

"Sorry to call you so early. I want you to meet me for dinner tonight. There's something I want to say. It's important. Can you come?"

Jewel's smile faded. "Where do you want me to be?"

"Chanterelle, on Main Street in Edmonds. Be there at seven. I'll meet you at the door."

"Okay."

"Very good. I'll see you tonight."

Jewel stood looking at the silent phone in her hand. Breakfast no longer seemed like a good idea. She zipped the phone neatly into her purse and went into her bedroom to put on her shoes. Coming back to the kitchen, she pulled the phone out of her purse and tried to call Sara, but there was no answer.

"It's something bad," she said, and her voice sounded strange in the empty room. "He's being a gentleman about it, and that will make it even worse. It must be because of yesterday. Or maybe he's decided I'm not his type. I better be careful. Maybe he thinks we're only friends and he thinks I've been acting like it's more than that. I don't know. We haven't kissed or anything. See? This is why I said I don't know how to be with nice men."

She felt the palms of her hands begin to sweat and raced into the bathroom to run them under cold water. It helped a little. She put on her coat and went to work, grateful that she would be absorbed all day in proofreading a large document. Everyone knew the deadline was imminent. They would not disturb her.

At six forty-five, Jewel parked her car at the curb a block away from Chanterelle. She stood on the sidewalk for a few moments, pretending to look at the holiday lights on the shops that lined the street. The cold air stung her cheeks. She could have waited in her car, but after so many hours of struggling to focus on her work, the idea of watching minutes tick past on the dashboard clock was nauseating. She began to walk up the hill, passing under the old-fashioned black street lamp that stood outside the restaurant. Timothy was not there yet. She kept on, bowing her head into the wind, until she came to the corner. In front of her, a fountain stood at the center of the intersection. There was no water at this time of year, but lights were strung on the gazebo that arced gracefully over the empty space where the water would have been. Jewel stood on the sidewalk for several minutes, watching the stream of cars circle the fountain, some going on up Main

Street toward the library, some bearing right along Fifth Avenue.

"Lost?" enquired Timothy, beside her.

Jewel started. Her eyes sought his face anxiously.

Without waiting for an answer, Timothy drew her arm through his and walked her back to the restaurant. Jewel's first impression was of the clean golden color of the hardwood floor under her feet as they came in out of the cold. She heard Timothy telling the waitress he had a reservation. When he pulled out her chair, she sat down, resting her purse against the wall by the condiments. She unbuttoned her coat and opened the menu.

"You look hungry." Timothy's deep voice drew her eyes to his face. It was time to pay attention and get it over with.

"I am hungry. I didn't eat much today." Jewel bit her lip. That sounded pathetic. She straightened her spine. "What's good here?"

"Everything," said Timothy. "Steak, salmon, soup, all of it. Dessert is good, too."

Jewel was pretty sure that dessert would be beyond her. "Salmon sounds good," she said politely.

Timothy gave their order to the waitress, then watched her until she reached the kitchen. Then he turned back to Jewel, folded his large hands on the table, and took a deep breath.

Jewel pressed the soles of her feet against the floor, bracing herself. *Can I actually live through this again?*

Is there any chance I might just drop over dead right here on the restaurant floor?

"Jewel." He stopped, then said in a completely different voice, "Do you need some water or something? You don't look very good. Are you alright?"

Jewel grasped her water glass and took a long, cold drink. It was difficult to swallow so much water without choking. She set down the glass carefully.

Timothy took another breath, starting again. Then he let it out suddenly, leaned across the table, and took both her hands in his. "I want to tell you something, Jewel. I thought all day about how to say this the right way."

Jewel closed her eyes tight and then opened them wide, to keep from blinking. Timothy looked anxious.

"I know you have every reason to want nothing more to do with men, and I've tried to be a friend to you, to show that I'm not like the other men you knew. But friendship isn't enough for me, with you." She heard him take another deep breath. "I'm asking permission to court you, Jewel."

"To c-court me?"

"Yes." Timothy laughed nervously. "To court you. You know, where a man goes out with a woman on purpose to win her hand in marriage." His face sobered and he lifted her hands, his grasp tightening. "Will you do me the honor?"

Jewel's lips parted, but no sound came. She nodded her head vigorously and the words tumbled out. "Yes!

Yes, I will. I thought I did something wrong. I was sure you were bringing me here to break it to me. I couldn't eat anything all day. I'm starving now." She laughed and felt tears running down her cheeks.

"I'll feed you," said Timothy eagerly. "We'll have one of everything and two desserts. I'll get us some bread right now, so you don't have to wait. Excuse me! Waitress!" He let go with one hand to signal their waitress, who was serving a nearby table. She came quickly.

"We need bread, please," Timothy told the waitress, whose eyes strayed to their hands clasped on the table. "She thought I was going to dump her, so she didn't eat all day. But actually, I'm going to marry her, so we'll need champagne also. Can you bring it right now, with the bread?"

"Coming right up," said the waitress, laughing. "And congratulations!" She hurried away.

"But you don't know that," whispered Jewel. "After you court me for a while, you might decide not to ask me to marry you."

"No, I won't." Timothy's eyes fell. "But I might ask you, and you might say no."

"No, I won't," said Jewel in her turn. Timothy's head came up. His eyes clung to her face, and she lost herself in their depths.

"Why do you want me, Timothy?" It was a question she could find no answer to.

"Because," he said simply.

"Because?"

He shook his head, almost impatient. "There are lots of reasons. You make me happy. I make you happy. You're beautiful. You want the things I want. But none of that's the reason. It's partly because you want things so much more than other women do. You know what you're missing. Well, I know what I'm missing, too. We both care just that much more about love because we know how it feels to live without it. But all of that doesn't add up to how I feel. I want you because I know you're the one."

"It's a miracle," whispered Jewel, almost to herself.

Timothy laughed and leaned toward her. Her eyes widened.

"Champagne and glasses," said the waitress, and Timothy leaned back, releasing Jewel's hands to make room on the table. Jewel watched the champagne tumbling into her glass. The waitress left them and Timothy lifted his glass.

"To life from now on," he said, smiling at her.

"From now on," echoed Jewel. They drank to it.

"Here," Timothy pushed the basket of bread in front of her.

Jewel buttered a piece of bread. "This is what I was doing when you called this morning."

"I wanted to catch you before you left for work." He helped himself to bread and she nudged the butter around the basket to his side.

"Well, you did." She bit into the bread. It was warm and fresh, smelling of yeast and melting butter.

"I'm trying to remember what I said," Timothy admitted. "I want to know how I scared you so bad that you couldn't eat all day."

Jewel shook her head. "It wasn't what you said, exactly. You just told me you had to tell me something important and asked me to meet you for dinner."

"And?"

Jewel unfolded her napkin and laid it on her lap. "I just know what that means, usually, in—in my life. I thought…" She smoothed the napkin a second time.

Timothy folded his arms on his chest. "I can guess," he said.

Jewel looked up from her napkin, sensing danger. "You can guess?"

Timothy let out a long breath. "Look, Jewel, this is what courting is for. It's for you to learn what it's like being with me, as opposed to being in hell, where you came from. And it's for me to learn how to talk to you without scaring you. Among other things."

Jewel turned thankfully to the waitress, who appeared by her side like an answer to prayer, with their dinner. She set a plate in front of each of them. "Will there be anything else? More champagne?"

"No, thank you," said Timothy and Jewel in unison.

The waitress left them.

Jewel ate her salmon and winter vegetables dressed with butter and herbs. She watched Timothy cutting his steak. She tried to imagine that she was sharing a dinner of her own making in a house where they lived as a married couple.

"What?" asked Timothy, spreading sauce on a bite of steak with the tip of his knife. "What's that look?"

"I have to learn to imagine this, all of this. It's hard to keep believing I'm here. At first," she confided, "I was sure you would like Dorothy best."

Timothy choked, swallowed, and roared with laughter. Jewel stared at him.

"It made lots of sense," she said, indignantly. "Much more sense than you liking me."

"Dorothy must be fifteen years younger than me, Jewel, and that's not even the half of it." Timothy shook his head. "How could that even seem possible to you?"

"She's got everything," Jewel said in a small voice. "Girls like me don't end up with guys like you."

"This one's going to," said Timothy. "You've got it all wrong, Jewel. Just because I go to church doesn't mean I walk around with a checklist, looking for the woman who matches up. I'm a man. I'm not looking for a role model. I want a wife." His eyes rested on her face, on her lips, parted in surprise. "Where's the dessert menu?"

"Do you want dessert?" asked Jewel in a calm voice that did not seem to belong to her.

"Do you?"

Jewel shook her head. Under the table, she rubbed her sweating palms on the crumpled napkin.

"Check, please," said Timothy, flagging down their waitress. Jewel buttoned her coat.

Gusts of cold air swept around them as they stepped onto the sidewalk. Jewel trembled inside her stiff wool coat. The moment seemed brittle. She glanced at the lighted restaurant behind her, at the quiet street passing her as they walked, hand in hand, to her car. She thought, oddly, of Sleeping Beauty. If only her own fairy tale could outlast the awakening kiss.

Timothy stopped walking, suddenly, caught in the pool of light under a street lamp. She saw the curve of his lashes, a shadow in the hollow of his cheek. His kiss came swiftly, insistent, sweet. She felt his lips smiling as his arms closed around her. It was a moment she could never afterward put into words.

Chapter 32

Jewel lay in a shimmering golden cloud, dreaming. She could feel the tweedy surface of her couch somewhere far below, but her eyes were drowsy and her heart was full of Timothy.

The persistent ringing of her cell phone penetrated the cloud. She picked it up slowly.

"It's Sara. You called this morning and my phone wasn't turned on. I'm sorry. How was your day?"

"Mmmmmm." Jewel roused herself. "My day was wonderful. How was yours?"

"My day was in no way interesting. Tell me right now why yours was wonderful!"

Jewel smiled at the phone. "Timothy asked permission to court me."

Sara shrieked. "I knew it! I knew it! I could feel it in my bones! Oooooo! Quick! Tell me everything."

Jewel settled comfortably into the sofa cushions. "I called you this morning because he called me really early and asked to meet for dinner so he could tell me something. Of course, I thought it would be something bad."

"Of course you did."

"But it wasn't. He wants to court me. He said that means when a man goes out with a woman on purpose to win her hand in marriage."

"Did he say that? Did he say 'Win her hand in marriage'?"

"Yes, he did."

"What else did he say? What did you do?"

"We had champagne and bread, and then our meal came. We talked, and he almost choked on his food when I told him I had thought he would fall in love with Dorothy."

"I told you. I told you! It was you all along."

"And then, what else? We were going to have dessert, but we didn't want any, so we went back to my car..." Jewel closed her eyes, returning for the hundredth time to linger in the perfect memory.

"He kissed you!" cried Sara. "He hasn't done that before, has he?"

"No," said Jewel. "It was my first kiss."

"Oh, Jewel, I wish I was there to hug you. It's almost worth coming out in my pajamas. Think what you just said. It *is* your first kiss, sweetie pie. The first one that matters."

They were quiet for a few minutes, absorbing the blessed fact.

"It's a miracle, really," said Jewel. "Don't you think? Was there ever anything in my life that turned out as well as this? Even tonight, I have to keep coaching myself to believe that it will actually happen. He says that's what courting is for, for me to get used to being with him instead of in hell where I used to be. And for him to learn to talk to me without scaring me."

"Awww....you're going to make me cry, Jewel. This is so perfect."

"Almost," said Jewel, wistfully. "Perfect would be if I didn't have to learn how to be normal for the man I love."

"No, that would be fantasy, honey. Perfect is a man who knows how to handle imperfection and doesn't mind doing it."

"He minds a little, I think. It hurt him, at first, when he realized I was expecting him to treat me like the other guys would have. I felt so bad about it. It was stupid, not to realize that being scared was a slap at him. I didn't mean it that way. I don't plan to be scared. It happens to me, and then I'm so busy drowning in it that I can't see anything else."

"I know, sweetie, I know," soothed Sara, "but it sounds like he knows, too. He knows what's wrong and why it's wrong, and he's still here. He's still 'courting you'."

"You like saying that word, don't you?" Jewel knew exactly how Sara would look, making her lips prim, her eyes shining with laughter and excitement.

"I love saying that word about you and your funny man. You've been out with the biggest meatheads I know. It's poetic justice that you end up with a man who wants to 'court' you." Sara sighed rapturously. "So, you're going to marry him, right? I don't even need to ask, right?"

"I think I need to be Orthodox to do that," Jewel realized suddenly. "That's how they do it, isn't it?"

"Probably. Well, that can be arranged, can't it? The question is, do you want to be Orthodox? That's probably a no-brainer. You'll do whatever you need to do, to marry him."

Jewel frowned. "I don't think he would let me, on those terms. I don't think I'd want him to."

"Well, then consider it as a separate question. Are you going to convert, for yourself?"

Jewel thought about it. "Do you know why I might? Because nothing turned out the way I expected. I thought they would all be like Dorothy, but they weren't. And I thought Dorothy would ruin everything for me, and she didn't. And I have Anna now, and Xenia sells my jewelry, and Timothy is courting me."

"So nothing turned out as you expected."

"Nothing. It makes me feel like I found the mother lode, or something like that. It's scary, though, because I don't know what I'm doing."

"Oh honey," cried Sara, "don't be scared of success. You'll sabotage yourself."

"That's what I mean," Jewel broke in. "I could sabotage myself just by accident now. I don't see things coming. The only things I know how to do are the things I decided never to do again. So now, I'm starting at zero."

"But with nice people, this time! They aren't going to make you feel bad, if you slip up."

Jewel was silent, unable either to explain her own argument or be reassured by Sara's.

"You two look so cute together," said Sara, returning to the subject that interested her most. "He's so big and you're so short."

"I'm not that short!"

"You're not that tall either!"

"I'm taller than you are, by at least an inch."

It was an old quarrel.

"Well, it means you can wear heels if you want to," remarked Sara, always practical.

"But I don't have to," said Jewel with relief.

"I don't have to with Clay either. It's a good thing. Real men don't care what you wear, for the most part." She laughed exultantly. "This is love on the other side of the bonfire, babe."

"I told him about that. He said he wished he had been there to see me do it."

"I'm glad he wasn't, though," said Sara. "That night was just for us."

"It's one of my best memories now, even though it was a hard day when it happened."

"Time heals, and all that," Sara agreed. She paused. "You know, Jewel, if this works out, you and him, you won't need me anymore. Not the way you used to. You don't need me now, like that, but I don't think you've realized it yet."

"I'll always need you!" cried Jewel. "You've been my friend for my whole life."

"I know, and you've been mine, but I was thinking about it when we all met at Starbucks. Your life is different now. You have other friends, not just me, and now you have Timothy. You have a good man, finally, who loves you. I was always the one who rescued you, and you don't need rescuing now. I don't think you will again."

"I don't want to be rescued. I just want to go on being friends, like we always have been," Jewel said urgently.

"We will, we will. I'm not walking out on you. I'm just being in the moment. It's okay for things to change. You should be happy. You worked hard to get here."

"As long as you know that I wasn't working hard to get away from you," Jewel insisted.

"I know, silly. Don't be upset. I'm not. I just want you to know that I know you can make it on your own. I think I had started to treat you like you couldn't, and I'm sorry about that."

"Don't ever be sorry, Sara. I wouldn't be here at all, without you."

Sara sighed. "It's better this way, you know. If you'd gone on needing me too long, eventually, you would have hated me."

"I can't imagine hating you," said Jewel seriously. "I always worried that it would be the other way around. I know you got tired of rescuing me sometimes."

"I did," said Sara frankly. "But maybe I needed to be the rescuer as much as you needed to be rescued. It will be interesting to see who we are now, in your new life. I wonder if Clay will be friends with Timothy like you are friends with me.”

“Everyone likes Timothy,” Jewel said positively. “Besides, he has a truck.”

“In that case,” Sara laughed, “we can look forward to many happy hours of girl time while they hang out in the garage.”

“What does Clay do out there?” wondered Jewel.

“Ask his truck,” Sara suggested. “Nobody else knows.”

“I love you, Sara,” Jewel said huskily.

“I love you, too,” Sara said.

Chapter 33

Christmas Eve. Jewel held herself motionless in the warm, scented air, her ears filled with the vesperal hymns and the censor bells, her nostrils with the streaming incense, her eyes with the crimson and gold embroidered festival robe of Fr. Nicholas and the bright poinsettias blooming at the feet of the saints on the iconostasis. Her mind drifted, a boat loosely moored, slipping forward and back on small waves of hope and sadness. Sometimes she pondered the miracle of Timothy, only a few feet away behind the chanter's stand, celebrating his Savior's birth. Sometimes she pondered herself, unaccountably present in a church, surrounded by people who were coming to know her better, now that Timothy kept her after liturgy for coffee hour. Her thoughts rested on the long, hand-made black robe he wore and the hours of willing service it represented, here in this sacred place. She tried momentarily to realize how she had come to be here, in the company, in the presence even, of a man like Timothy. He glanced toward her suddenly, still chanting, and his eyes lit, as if he knew her thoughts and could answer them. Jewel smiled at him, a little wistfully, and tried to fill her attention with the words of the hymn, blotting out the darker world, for this moment at least.

Your birth, O Christ our God, dawned the light of knowledge upon the earth. For by Your birth those who adored stars, were taught by a star, to worship You, the Sun of Justice and to know You, Orient from on High. O Lord, glory to You.

Jewel imagined the wise men, the familiar figures riding camels across a Christmas card. It struck her suddenly that they had been human beings, breathing in and out, making friends, dreaming dreams. What had convinced them, she wondered, to make the journey in search of the infant King? It must have been dangerous, inconvenient at least, to travel long distances in those far-off days. Were there wives and neighbors who were not convinced? Had they been teased and talked about when they announced their decision to make the journey? What makes some people able to see a star, and follow it, and leaves others clucking and bickering in well-intentioned obscurity? Which would she herself be, a traveler in the starlight or a nay-sayer, encamped in the familiar, resigned to imperfection? Her chance was upon her. She felt it. Here was the church. There was the man. She had expected neither, and she felt worthy of neither. Yet she could not turn her face from their brightness. She did not, she thought, have the willpower to give them up. It seemed a good sign, yet she could not trust her belief in it. She could see, so easily, how she might crumble under her own inexperience, how her failings might prove too great for such a miracle as this. Yet there were moments, flashes of inner light, in which she hoped that their inherent goodness would bless her yearning to belong in church and to belong to Timothy. If she could be here at all, in the presence of these possibilities, there must indeed be more wonders in heaven and on earth than were dreamt of in her hard-won philosophy.

Jewel reached for the little booklet on the chair behind her and began to follow the service more closely, murmuring along when she could pick out the melody, wanting to feel her own lips saying the words, as if she, too, were part of the praying multitude around her, welcoming this precious night.

Today the Virgin gives birth, to the Transcendent One, and the earth presents a cave, to the Unapproachable One. Angels, with shepherds, give Him glory. Wise men follow a star as they journey to Him Who is God for all ages, yet for our sake was born as a little child.

They were stunning words, to Jewel, beautiful, almost painfully laden with meaning. A virgin, giving birth. God reduced willingly to infancy, for love. For the first time, Jewel let her eyes rest on the gentle face of the Virgin Mother on the iconostasis. *Oh Holy Mother of God, you never lost what I can never regain. How can I be loved by a man who also loves you? How could we be contained, together, in his single heart?*

She felt a movement close by, a breath, the swish of fabric against a chair. She heard something whispered, but could not discern a word in the thread of sound.

"Jewel." The whisper came again, piercing the chant-filled air. Jewel turned her head.

Xenia stood behind her. She touched Jewel's shoulder. "Your life is not in what you have lost," whispered Xenia. "Your life is in what you have found. Take the gift." Xenia's eyes held hers. Her fingers tightened on Jewel's shoulder. "Take it," she whispered again. Then she stepped away, opening her prayer book. Her dark hair fell around her like silence.

Jewel's eyes snapped back to the face of the Virgin Mother, almost as if she expected to see a ripple across the icon's glowing surface, some evidence of movement quickly hidden. A candle flickered in the scented air. Around her, the tide of the service turned as the people filed past on their way to receive communion. Xenia was not among them. Jewel let her eyes wander to the row behind her. Xenia was no longer there.

Timothy came to her at the close of the service, putting his arm around her shoulders as if he shared the sharp pang of loneliness brought on by the cheerful crowd hurrying home around them.

"Come see Fr. Nicholas," he said, steering her into the line of people walking forward to greet the priest and receive blessed bread. He kept his arm around her as they moved slowly up the aisle.

When they reached Fr. Nicholas, Timothy pushed her gently forward. "This is Jewel, Fr. Nicholas."

"Yes, I know," replied Fr. Nicholas, smiling at her.

"I'm courting her," said Timothy proudly.

"This is wonderful news!" cried Fr. Nicholas. "You see, this is why we should always invite people to our church. I think I may take some credit for this match."

Jewel's face lighted. "I still have that postcard in my purse."

Fr. Nicholas lifted his hands, laying one on Timothy's head and one on Jewel's. "'A great mystery is being celebrated. How is it a mystery? They come together, and the two are made one. They have not become the image of anything earthly, but of God Himself'. God bless you both, as you make this journey." His hands moved to their shoulders, and his grip was surprisingly strong. His face shone with good will. "When you are ready to be married, come and talk to me. I will help you."

The crowd behind them pressed forward. Timothy took Jewel's hand, moving away. Looking back over her shoulder, Jewel saw Fr. Nicholas holding out his hand to Anna and pointing at Jewel. Anna smiled at her and turned back to Fr. Nicholas.

"Let's go home to my house," said Timothy, as they left the sanctuary. "You can help me cook dinner before George and Anna come. Anna says they're going to call their families first, so we have time to finish what I didn't get to before church."

Jewel nodded and made herself smile. Pressing through the crowd on their way to the door, she clutched the sleeve of his coat, unwilling even in the smallest sense to be parted from him.

Timothy had inherited his house when his parents died. It was a small house, neatly built of good materials, set in a square lawn on a quiet street. A wonderful old tree stood in front of it, casting dancing leaf shadows over the lawn in summer and stretching the gnarled lace of its branches to the heavens on moonlit winter nights. Timothy wore the key on a chain around his neck. He said it gave him a happy feeling of belonging to something.

In the tiny entrance hall, Jewel hung her coat in the tiny closet and reached for Timothy's coat, hanging it up too, clinging to the solace of this small act of homecoming. Then she walked down the short flagstone hall to the kitchen. Timothy was there before her, tying a large denim apron around himself.

"I need another apron," he discovered, "for you. You'll have to stay clear of the stove so you don't spill anything on your dress." He stood still, his hands on his hips, contemplating the miracle of a lovely woman in soft black velvet standing in his kitchen. Jewel stood still also, letting him look, drenched in the intangible miracle of his love-making which was, so often, no more than an inflection of his voice, a warmth in his eyes, the pure magnetism of his presence, the certain knowledge of desire held in check for her sake.

"Timothy," she whispered, just to feel the word crossing her lips.

"Jewel," he replied, as if her name were the only answer to his own.

"Dinner," said Jewel, breaking the spell.

"You're right," said Timothy, springing into action. "Could you set the dining room table? What you need is in the china cabinet in there. Except silverware, that's in here."

Jewel turned on the dining room light. It was a small room, furnished with his mother's things, much as it had been in his childhood. She spread a cherry-red cloth on the oval table and set two candles in cut-glass candlesticks at its center. There were napkins to match the table-cloth, and she opened the glass doors to take out gold-rimmed china plates, a little worn but still beautiful. Returning to the kitchen for silverware, she encountered a questioning expression on Timothy's face as he stood by the stove, stirring gravy.

"What were you thinking about tonight in church?" he asked, surprising her.

"What makes you ask?" she countered warily.

"Your face is expressive," he answered simply.

She opened the silverware drawer and began to select spoons and forks. "Do you want forks or spoons for dessert?"

"I want pie for dessert. It's a berry pie, so give us all an extra spoon. I also want to know what made your face that way in church. I could see you, while I was chanting."

"Made it what way?" she parried.

"It looked sad," he said. "Don't you like Christmas?"

Jewel sighed, accustomed by now to his persistence. She searched for something appropriate to say for a few seconds, then gave in to the chance to tell the truth. It was becoming habitual, in his presence, the instinctive reaction followed by the new opportunity. She was not sure yet which impulse would rule her, in the end.

"I was worrying, mostly. And thinking about things."

"What things?"

"About how I got here, in my life, and whether I can actually be here, with you, in church, so far away from anything I ever imagined would happen in my life."

Timothy stirred the gravy in silence. He never rushed into speech. He took time to think so he could say exactly what he meant. Jewel held her handful of silverware like a bouquet and waited to hear what it might be.

He looked up. "You said something like that before, at dinner the other night. About learning to imagine this. You don't need imagination, for this. I'm real. You're real." He tasted the gravy and reached for a salt cellar that was balanced precariously on the edge of the stove. "Tell me if I'm wrong, but I bet imagination was how you survived, in your old life. Somewhere to go, in your head, when you couldn't handle being where you were?"

"*Yes.*" Jewel almost dropped the silverware. It was deeply shocking to be so well understood. The spoons and forks clicked metallically as she adjusted her grip.

"It's understandable. But you can stop now. I want you to know the real me and be the real you. You won't worry so much, that way." He pushed the gravy off the burner and cleaned his hands on a towel.

The silverware clicked again. "I won't?" It seemed unlikely that focusing on her real self would end her worries.

"Think about it," he suggested, taking a basket from the top of the refrigerator and filling it with biscuits from a tray on the kitchen table. "What makes you worry?"

"I worry that I don't know what I'm doing, and that you'll get tired of all my mistakes."

"Where does that come from?" he asked, meeting her eyes. "Do I make you feel like that?"

"It comes from l-love," she said, in a strained voice. "I love you, and I don't want to lose you. It scares me, how many ways I could mess this up."

"That's not love, Jewel." He was standing very still. "That's fear."

"Are you saying I don't love you?" she asked painfully.

"No, I'm not. I'm saying your worries come from fear. Love doesn't make you fearful. Fear makes you fearful."

The bones in her hands throbbed. "I don't know what that means." The silverware clicked and shifted.

"Fear makes you think that love isn't enough." Timothy came around the table and took the silverware out of her hands. He laid it haphazardly on the counter.

"Your hands always give you away," he told her, smoothing the red marks on her palms with his fingers. "Don't be scared, Jewel. I'm on your side." He drew her closer, pressing her hands to his chest.

"What do you do when you're nervous?" asked Jewel, feeling his heart beat against her fingers.

"I don't get nervous much. When I do, it makes me silent. Clumsy, too. My mind goes blank."

"You were quiet that first night you came to Anna's." Jewel tilted her head so she could see his face. "Were you nervous then?"

"Yes. I think there were only two thoughts in my head the whole night."

"What were they?"

"I was thanking God that my Dad taught me to knit and asking God to get me your number." Timothy bent his head.

The oven timer chimed behind them.

"Dinner," murmured Jewel, nestling in his arms.

"It can wait," said Timothy.